The Development of Political Institutions

WEISER CENTER FOR EMERGING DEMOCRACIES

Series Editor
Dan Slater is Professor of Political Science,
Ronald and Eileen Weiser Professor of Emerging Democracies,
and Director of the Weiser Center for Emerging Democracies (WCED)
at the University of Michigan. dnsltr@umich.edu

The Weiser Center for Emerging Democracies (WCED) Series publishes cutting-edge research in the pivotal field of authoritarianism and democratization studies. We live in a historical moment when democracies seem increasingly fragile and authoritarian regimes seem stubbornly resilient across the globe, and these topics continue to be a central part of research in the social sciences. The WCED Series strives to collect a balance of titles on emerging democracies and enduring dictatorships, as one cannot understand the conditions under which democracies live and thrive without comprehending how they die and remain unborn.

The WCED Series is interested in the full range of research being conducted on authoritarianism and democratization, primarily in political science but at times from history, sociology, and anthropology as well. The series encompasses a global geographic reach. We invite works that are primarily qualitative as well as quantitative in approach and are interested in edited volumes as well as solo-authored manuscripts.

The series highlights the leading role of the University of Michigan Press, Weiser Center for Emerging Democracies, and International Institute as premier sites for the research and production of knowledge on the conditions that make democracies emerge and dictatorships endure.

The Development of Political Institutions: Power, Legitimacy, Democracy
Federico Ferrara

Aid Imperium: United States Foreign Policy and Human Rights in Post–Cold War Southeast Asia
Salvador Santino F. Regilme Jr.

Opposing Democracy in the Digital Age: The Yellow Shirts in Thailand
Aim Sinpeng

Normalizing Corruption: Failures of Accountability in Ukraine
Erik S. Herron

Economic Shocks and Authoritarian Stability: Duration, Financial Control, and Institutions
Victor C. Shih, Editor

Electoral Reform and the Fate of New Democracies: Lessons from the Indonesian Case
Sarah Shair-Rosenfield

Campaigns and Voters in Developing Democracies: Argentina in Comparative Perspective
Noam Lupu, Virginia Oliveros, and Luis Schiumerini, Editors

The Development of Political Institutions

Power, Legitimacy, Democracy

Federico Ferrara

University of Michigan Press
Ann Arbor

For questions or permissions, please contact um.press.perms@umich.edu

Published in the United States of America by the
University of Michigan Press
Manufactured in the United States of America
Printed on acid-free paper
First published January 2022

A CIP catalog record for this book is available from the British Library.

Library of Congress Cataloging-in-Publication data has been applied for.

Library of Congress Control Number: 2021038207 (print)
LC record available at https://lccn.loc.gov/2021038207
LC ebook record available at https://lccn.loc.gov/2021038208

ISBN 978-0-472-13283-6 (hardcover : alk. paper)
ISBN 978-0-472-03898-5 (paper : alk. paper)
ISBN 978-0-472-90278-1 (open access e-book)

DOI: https://doi.org/10.3998/mpub.12013333

Research for this book was funded in part by a General Research Fund grant from the Research
Grants Council of the Hong Kong S.A.R. (Project No. 11603915).

Cover image: *Barricade* (1931), José Clemente Orozco. © 2021 Artists Rights Society (ARS),
New York / SOMAAP, Mexico City.

For M.S.A.R.

CONTENTS

Digital materials related to this title can be found on
the Fulcrum platform via the following citable URL:
https://doi.org/10.3998/mpub.12013333

PREFACE

The Development of Political Institutions: Power, Legitimacy, Democracy sets out to improve upon existing explanations of the development of political institutions, taking a "historical institutionalist" approach to theorize dynamic processes of institutional reproduction, institutional decay, and institutional change. While the literature on "new institutionalism" has been most preoccupied with explaining the stability of institutional arrangements *within* countries and the divergence of paths of institutional development *between* countries, this book aims to specify an equally well-developed explanation for the temporal processes by which formal and informal rules and procedures, especially those constitutive of alternative political regimes, may, at different times, (i) acquire a measure of staying power and resistance to change, through their capacity effectively to structure the behavior of relevant actors (*institutional reproduction*); (ii) suffer major defections contributing to their destabilization and their declining capacity to structure the interactions between the individuals and organizations subject to their provisions (*institutional decay*); and (iii) experience major transformations in their form and functions, especially as a result of incremental processes (*institutional change*).

With regard to each of these outcomes, the book seeks to bridge the gap between "power-based" explanations and "ideas-based," "legitimation explanations" of political development. Major theoretical contributions to the historical institutionalist literature have explored the manner in which the "power-distributional" implications of political institutions—that is, their capacity to make "winners" and "losers" of individual and collective actors competing to secure "institutional equilibria" most favorable to their interests—fuel the intergroup conflicts that drive processes of institutional reproduction and institutional change. Meanwhile, though the tradition has long recognized the potential importance of ideas, the comparative branch of historical institutionalism has largely neglected the development of ideas-based, legitimation explanations, even as scholars in other disciplines have placed growing emphasis on the extra-rational process by which human beings form the preferences, beliefs, and identities that explain their behavior. In practice, bridging the gap between explanations grounded in the logics of "legitimation" and "power" involves the development of improved legitimation explanations as well as the formulation of an integrated explanation focused on the interactions between the "dynamics of power" and the "dynamics of legitimation."

Among its more significant contributions, the book theorizes the "microfoundations" of processes of institutional development, practicing a form of "methodological individualism" that is not coterminous with the assumptions of the rational choice research program. Indeed, to the extent that the social sciences are made more "scientific" by the development of explanations that are consistent with, if not entirely reducible to, the body of knowledge accumulated in disciplines operating at lower levels of aggregation and analysis, the book's grounding of the theory's microfoundations in the findings of experimental psychology demonstrates that the effort benefits greatly from the adoption of models of human motivation, cognition, and behavior in which nonmaterialist considerations are front and center. The book's main substantive chapters also examine the conditions, "structural" as well as contingent, accounting for whether, for how strongly, and for how rapidly sequences of institutional reproduction, institutional decay, and institutional change are set in motion, as well as some of the factors affecting the course of such processes downstream. A final chapter draws out the theory's implications for the viability of efforts to "engineer" desired real-world outcomes through the purposeful design of political institutions.

Though I must take sole responsibility for the fact that this book has been over five years in the making, as well as for any errors still left in its pages, I welcome the opportunity to acknowledge the kindness and generosity of several people who have been instrumental to its publication. At the University of Michigan Press, Dr. Elizabeth Demers believed in the project just as I was beginning to second-guess the wisdom of writing an entire book's worth of theory, while the anonymous referees offered plenty of excellent advice. I am also grateful for the trust placed in me by Professor Dan Slater, to whom I owe the honor of having my work featured in the Weiser Center for Emerging Democracies Series. Along the way, I was fortunate to work under a boss, Professor Mark R. Thompson, who continued to advocate for me when others may have begun to lose patience. Going further back in time, I will never forget the mentorship provided to me as a student by Professors Ronald A. Francisco, Erik S. Herron, and Peter A. Hall. I owe the biggest debt of gratitude, however, to my wife, to whom this book is dedicated. The time it took to write it was punctuated by some of the most trying experiences I have ever lived through. It is thanks to her that, through it all, I never lost sight of what I was working for.

Hong Kong S.A.R., 9 January 2021

CHAPTER ONE

Institutional Development

The Dynamics of Power and (De)legitimation

The origins of the modern debate over the legitimation of power and the moral foundations of political order are conventionally traced back to the writings of Niccolò Machiavelli ([1517] 1971; [1532] 1971). These themes, to be sure, have featured as a core concern of Western political thought since classical times. Machiavelli, however, is credited with formulating the first "full-fledged," explanatory theory in which a political order's (il)legitimacy ranks as a major cause of its (in)stability (Zelditch 2001: 42). Substantively, what most differentiates Machiavelli's treatment from the largely normative theories of classical philosophers is that whereas Plato and Aristotle assumed that a ruler acts in his own interests when he acts for the good of the ruled, with whom he shares a basic set of norms and values, what mattered to Machiavelli about the ideas through which a ruler secures his legitimacy is their capacity to conceal the extent to which his interests are necessarily at variance with those of his subjects. Indeed, having pioneered the notion that the stability of a system of rule hinges on the "voluntary acceptance" of the governed (Zelditch 2001: 42), Machiavelli had little to say about the values, norms, and beliefs in which a ruler's legitimacy may be grounded, save for highlighting the imperative that one must never dispense with the *appearance* of "mercy, good faith, integrity, humanity, and religious piety" (Machiavelli [1532] 1971: 284). Instead, Machiavelli (265) drew attention to the ruinous fate said invariably to befall so-called unarmed prophets—rulers who choose to rely on their capacity for persuasion alone in order to maintain their positions of power, in defiance of the fact that "the nature of peoples is changeable; and it is easy to persuade them of something, but it is difficult to fix them in that persuasion." Men in positions of authority must rather see to it that the force of their persuasion is always backed by the force of arms, so as to ensure that their subjects, "when they believe no longer," can be "made to believe by force" (265).

Five hundred years on, the importance of physical coercion as the fundamental "determinant" of power (Anderson 1976: 44) is seldom called into question. The role of ideas in the exercise of political power has proven decidedly more controversial in the centuries since. Machiavelli's "conflict theory" of legitimacy (Zelditch 2001: 42) has exerted a great deal of influence on Marxists and the proponents of other philosophies steeped in materialist worldviews. Meanwhile, contemporary versions of the "consensus theory" of legitimacy have been featured in the works of leading exponents of functionalism (Parsons 1951), modernization theory (Lipset 1959), and economic theories that "implicitly, if not explicitly, deny a role for power and conflict" (Tang 2011: 12), assuming that the choice of policies and institutions is motivated by concerns for efficiency or the general welfare. Thankfully, some of the twentieth century's most important writings on the subject have demonstrated that the central importance of power and conflict can be acknowledged without dismissing the ideas in which a political order's legitimacy is grounded as an instrument of mass deception or as a source of "false consciousness," in recognition of the influence such ideas can exert on the values, preferences, and beliefs of the powerful and the powerless alike. Antonio Gramsci frequently returned to the subject in his prison notebooks, in which he argued that "intellectual, moral, and political hegemony" is as crucial as physical force to the efficaciousness with which a class or group can assert, exert, and perpetuate its "domination" (*dominio*) (1977: 2010–11), the stability of which is boosted by the group's capacity to "make society truly advance" (2012). Most foundationally, Max Weber's ([1919] 1946: 78) definition of a modern "state" requires the successful assertion of claims to a "monopoly of the legitimate use of violence," which involves the formation of beliefs among all constituencies subject to its authority that its control of the means of coercion is rightful and proper.

Power, Legitimacy, and the Study of Institutions

For all its importance to the history of political *thought*, the study of legitimacy has largely faded from the research agenda of present-day political *science*, where its proponents still find it necessary to remind their audiences of the basic notion that "political power," insofar as it is based on "social cohesion," needs legitimating (Fukuyama 2011: 42–43). Certainly, the explanatory turn taken by the field of comparative politics in the last several decades (Hall

2003) has yet to produce a consensus over the role that legitimacy plays in the exercise and maintenance of political power, or for that matter the role it ought to play in explanatory theories of political (in)stability. For different reasons, two of the field's three major research traditions—as defined in Lichbach and Zuckerman (1997)—tend to dismiss its importance to whether individuals obey or disobey authority. Scholars in the "structuralist" camp tend to see obedience as a matter of the physical force and material resources that the more powerful bring to bear on the less powerful (e.g., Skocpol 1979: 31–32; Stinchcombe 1968: 150–51; Tilly 1985: 171–72). With notable exceptions (e.g., Levi 1988, 1997; North 1990; Przeworski 1991: 54–55), moreover, "rationalists" characteristically assume that compliance and noncompliance are the product of an instrumental calculus (Levi 1997: 30).

Left to carry the banner of legitimacy are scholars who share at least some of the assumptions of the "culturalist" tradition (Ross 1997, 2009), above all, the notion that institutions exert "normative force" by providing behavioral models or templates to which individuals often seek to conform, in accordance with a "logic of [social] appropriateness" (March and Olsen 1989; Hall and Taylor 1996: 939–40). It is from this perspective that a classic work on the *legitimation of power*, while not discounting the importance of either "prudence" or "advantage" as motivations for compliance and obedience, contends that human beings are "moral agents, who recognize the validity of rules, have some notion of the common interest, and acknowledge the binding force of promises they have made—all elements involved in legitimate power" (Beetham 1991: 27). Analogous considerations have more recently prompted Fukuyama (2011: 442) to reiterate that theories of "political development"—the study of which "necessarily centers around the process by which institutions emerge, evolve, and eventually decay" (Fukuyama 2014: 7; for similar views, see Huntington 1965: 393; North 1990: vii)—must treat "ideas" as "fundamental causes."

Notoriously "eclectic" and pluralistic in its approach to the workings of institutions (Hall and Taylor 1996: 939–40), "historical institutionalism" has from its inception been open to contributions focused on the role of ideas and the legitimation of power (e.g., Bell 2011: 893–94; Fioretos, Falleti, and Sheingate 2016: 8; Orren and Skowronek 2004: 79–83; Sanders 2006: 41–43; Thelen and Steinmo 1992: 22–26). Indeed, though ideas have not always featured among the tradition's "core analytical variables" over the past quarter century (Blyth, Helgadottir, and Kring 2016: 142), historical institutionalists have long contemplated explanations centered on the "dynamics of power" and the "dynamics of legitimation" as two alternatives for making sense of how institutional arrangements reproduce themselves over time (Mahoney 2000: 521–25; see also Orren 1991). Explanations based on the logic of *power* commonly take the following form:

> The institution initially empowers a certain group at the expense of other groups; the advantaged group uses its additional power to expand the institution further; the expansion of the institution increases the power of the advantaged group; and the advantaged group encourages additional institutional expansion. (Mahoney 2000: 521)

Explanations based on the logic of *legitimation*, instead, take the following form:

> The institution that is initially favored sets a standard for legitimacy; this institution is reproduced because it is seen as legitimate; and the reproduction of the institution reinforces its legitimacy. (Mahoney 2000: 524)

In other words, the survival and the entrenchment of institutions may be accounted for by positive feedback mechanisms driven by the logic of "increasing returns to power" (Pierson 2004: 36–37) as well as by the logic of what might be referred to as processes of "increasing legitimation." Processes driven by each of these mechanisms should exhibit the "relatively deterministic properties" that Mahoney (2000: 511) ascribes to self-reinforcing, path-dependent sequences of institutional reproduction—"relative," that is, to the contingency thought to characterize moments of institutional choice. Both mechanisms are also hypothesized to feature their own "dynamic of potential change," whose activation after a period of self-reinforcement threatens to disrupt the reproduction of the institution concerned, if not to set in motion processes of institutional change (523). More generally, Thelen (1999: 399) points out that "an understanding of political change is inseparable from—and indeed rests on—an analysis of the foundations of political stability."

In the time since Mahoney (2000) addressed the distinction between "power explanations" and "legitimation explanations" of institutional development, major *theoretical* contributions to the historical institutionalist literature have explored the manner in which the "power distributional" aspects of political institutions—that is, their capacity to make "winners" or "losers" out of individual or collective actors competing to secure "institutional equilibria" favorable to their interests (Thelen 2004: 32)—drive processes of institutional reproduction and institutional change (Mahoney and Thelen 2010). But while the literature on historical institutionalism did not participate in political science's ongoing "retreat from the study of power" (Pierson 2015: 124), the same cannot be said with reference to the discipline's "neglect" of the study of ideas (Berman 1998: chap. 2). Within historical institutionalism, ideas have on occasion continued to feature prominently in accounts of the development of institutions in a variety of settings (for a brief review, see Fioretos, Falleti, and Sheingate 2016: 8). Nonetheless, the tradition's growing engagement with rational choice institutionalism (Thelen 1999: 380; see also Katznelson and Weingast 2005) and its decisive shift toward a more materialist ontology (Blyth, Helgadottir, and Kring 2016: 146–47; Fioretos, Falleti, and Sheingate 2016: 8–9) are reflected in the fact that "ideas-based," "legitimation explanations"—as Mahoney (2000: 523) describes them, explanations grounded in "actors' subjective orientations and beliefs about what is appropriate or morally correct"—have not kept pace with the theory development that has benefited "power-based accounts" (Blyth, Helgadottir, and Kring 2016), even as scholars in other disciplines have placed growing emphasis on explaining behavior by concentrating on the extra-rational process by which human beings form preferences, beliefs, and social identities (e.g., Ariely 2008; Haidt 2012; Kahneman 2011; Sapolsky 2017; Tyler 2006). Especially within the tradition's comparative politics branch, it is only more recently that historical institutionalists have "increasingly turned to ideas" (Blyth, Helgadottir, and Kring 2016: 143) in their quest to improve upon explanatory theories of institutional development (see also Blyth 2016).

Once again, it is worth reiterating that the adoption of legitimation explanations requires no departure from historical institutionalism's signature emphasis on "big questions," macro-historical processes, and the importance of time (Pierson and Skocpol 2002). As Bell (2011: 890) has noted, "The notion of agency is actually well established within an important strand of HI thinking." Nor do legitimation explanations violate the tradition's foundational principles: namely, the notion that political institutions "structure power relations" between political actors, "privileging some and putting others at a disadvantage" (Thelen and Steinmo 1992: 2), as well as the idea that intergroup conflict drives processes of institutional development (Hall and Taylor 1996: 937–38). As Schmidt (2011: 53) herself has pointed out, a sizable portion of the scholarship on "constructivist" or (her word) "discursive" institutionalism has been the work of scholars "who might better be called discursive institutionalists within a historical institutionalist tradition because they see ideas as constitutive of institutions even if shaped by them." Hay (2011: 67), moreover, ascribes to "ideational," "discursive," or "constructivist" institutionalism a series of "analytical and ontological assumptions" that bear a striking similarity to the "distinctive social ontology" that Hay and Wincott (1998: 953) once attributed to historical institutionalism. Similar considerations have prompted Bell (2011: 884) to argue that "a suitably tailored version of historical institutionalism can accommodate a constructivist approach to produce a sophisticated and more rounded account of how interpretive agents interact dialectically with institutional and wider structural contexts and produce change."

More broadly, to the extent that the realization of historical institutionalism's full potential rests on the formulation of an improved account of "the relationship between structure and agency" (Hay and Wincott 1998: 951), especially as it pertains to the dynamics of intergroup conflict (Peters, Pierre, and King 2005: 1277–78), acknowledging that institutions are contested because of the distribution of resources they promote *as well as* the "animating ideas" (Goodin 1996: 26–27; Offe 2006: 12) that political actors want enshrined in a polity's institutional architecture, or for that matter the implications that alternative institutional equilibria have for the recognition of the status and dignity of different social groups, can only render accounts of intergroup competition more realistic. Indeed, it is not just the case that human conflict *can* center on competing ideologies, value systems, or claims for "inter-subjective recognition" (Fukuyama 1992) as much as it can be about scarce material resources; also, research on human motivation tends to support Fukuyama's (2011: 41) contention that material resources often feature in intergroup conflict as "markers of dignity rather than ends in themselves" (e.g., Kahneman 2011: 342; Baumeister 2005: 151–55).

This book, then, sets out to bridge the gap that currently separates legitimation explanations and power explanations of comparative institutional development by way of assembling an explanatory theory that accounts for the manner in which processes of legitimation and delegitimation—and their interaction with processes governed by the logic of power—contribute to the reproduction, the decay, and the gradual transformation of political institutions. In so doing, the book seeks to improve upon existing attempts by historical institutionalists to explain the development of political institutions over time—perhaps above all by addressing the issue of endogenous change, for which the "new institutionalist" literature as a whole has long struggled to produce a general explanation (Schmidt 2010). What is more, the explanatory theory assembled in these pages may inform efforts to "engineer" outcomes in the real world through the purposeful design and redesign of political institutions, the ineffectiveness of which has long been cited as an example of political science's own failure to live up to its promise (Sartori 1968).

Institutional Development: Reproduction, Decay, and Change

Before moving on to describe in greater detail the book's contribution to the field of comparative political development and the literature on historical institutionalism, a brief clarification of the study's explananda is in order. Consistent with much of the existing literature, this book defines "political institutions" as "humanly devised rules and procedures—both formal and informal" (Levitsky and Murillo 2009: 117), whose primary function is to "structure [political] behavior" (Mahoney and Thelen 2010: 4)—that is, to organize relations of power, govern intergroup competition, and regulate political behavior by way of prescribing certain courses of action, permitting or proscribing others, and imposing penalties on noncompliance (Ostrom 1986; North 1990: 3–6; Thelen and Steinmo 1992: 2–3; Hall and Taylor 1996: 938; Offe 2006). With regard to "institutional reproduction"—a concept whose usage is seldom accompanied by a clear definition—this study eschews conceptualizations overly preoccupied with an institutional arrangement's capacity formally to remain unchanged over a period of time. On the one hand, mechanisms of institutional reproduction popular in works of historical institutionalism are typically designed to explain *more* than the survival or persistence of institutions. The logic of "positive feedback" and "increasing returns," for instance, refers to temporal dynamics accounting for the growing *entrenchment* of institutions (Rixen and Viola 2014: 10). On the other hand, the literature on historical institutionalism has stressed the possibility that an institutional arrangement's reproduction may not even require strict continuity in its form and functions (Thelen 2004: 7–8). As Thelen (293) pointed out, "Formal institutions do not survive long stretches of time by standing still"—their stability being predicated on "their ongoing active adaptation to changes in the political and economic environment in which they are embedded" more than on "the faithful reproduction of those institutions as originally constituted."

Among the viable alternatives to defining "institutional reproduction" as an institutional arrangement's preservation in its exact original form, the solution adopted in this study consists of borrowing, with some modification, the definition Huntington (1965: 394) provided for "institutionalization" as the process by which institutions "acquire value and stability." While Huntington's definition of institutions is broader than the one adopted in this study, in that it encompasses organizations as well as procedures (on the need to distinguish the "players" from the "rules of the game," see North 1990: 5), there are at least two compelling reasons for conceptualizing institutional reproduction in this manner. First, it allows for a clearer conceptual distinction between processes of institutional reproduction and institutional decay—which Huntington (1965) himself described as the opposite of institutionalization—by allowing for the possibility that an institutional arrangement's survival might not signify its reproduction, in the event that it is accompanied by a decline in its value and stability. Second, equating institutional reproduction to the process by which institutions acquire value and stability renders an institutional arrangement's reproduction compatible with modifications to its form and functions, insofar as the adjustments in question render the institution less vulnerable to decay or displacement.

Indeed, just as Thelen (2004: 7–8) argued that an institution's reproduction often requires its "active political renegotiation," complete with "heavy doses of institutional adaptation," Huntington (1965: 394–401) believed the stability of institutions to hinge on their "adaptability"—their capacity to meet new challenges or to take on new functions in response to environmental changes. Based on these considerations, the study of institutional change featured in this book's penultimate chapter focuses on more fundamental forms of change. In this context, "fundamental change" describes an institution's displacement and/or replacement or, rather, a significant shift in its distributional and/or behavioral consequences, which can result from significant modifications to the rules in question as much as from the *failure* to modify the rules in response to significant changes in their interpretation and/or enforcement (Mahoney and Thelen 2010: 4).

Defining "institutional reproduction" and "institutional decay" as the processes by which institutions acquire or lose, respectively, value and stability also presents potential challenges, not the least of which are those arising from some of the possible meanings of the words "value" and "stability." Proceeding in reverse order, there has been a tendency in the literature from Huntington (1965) onward to equate an institution's stability with its resilience in the face of the passage of time. Levitsky and Murillo (2009: 117) put it rather succinctly: "By stability, we mean durability." This definition is appropriate when measuring the variation in the relative stability exhibited, over a period of time, by the sets of rules and procedures that have governed a particular field or domain of activity in a given country, relative to the same sets of institutions in other countries or to different sets of institutions in the same country. A country described as suffering from "regime instability," for instance, is generally understood to be one whose governmental institutions have frequently undergone cycles of breakdown and replacement, relative to other countries. In a study that seeks to explain how and why a particular institutional arrangement becomes more or less stable *over time*, however, it makes sense to distinguish "stability" from "durability," in the interest of contemplating the possibility that an institution's instability is neither an inescapable permanence nor a guarantee of its ultimate displacement. More suitable for a study of this kind, therefore, is *to define an institution's stability and instability based on its vulnerability to potential threats to its survival at a given point in time*. Of course, power explanations and legitimation explanations ascribe the instability of institutions to different causes: the former, to reversals of power or the breakdown of coalitions supporting the status quo; the latter, to the status quo's delegitimation.

Challenges of a different nature are presented by the word "value." For if, as Huntington (1965) implied (see also Fukuyama 2011: 452), an institution's reproduction (in his words, its "institutionalization") requires that the institution in question becomes increasingly "valued," subjectively, among the actors subject to its provisions, one would be right to object that legitimacy, instead of explaining or contributing causally to the processes of institutional reproduction and institutional decay, is more properly described as an aspect of this book's explananda. In turn, given this study's focus on improving legitimation explanations of institutional development, conceiving of institutional reproduction and institutional decay as defined, in part, by the extent to which an institution is subjectively "valued" violates a key requirement of social scientific explanations: namely, the specification of causes that are temporally antecedent to, and conceptually distinct from, their purported "effects." As Gerring (2012: 212) points out, a causal argument in which the purported cause is not "separable from the effect it purports to explain" is a tautological argument. Fortunately, the word "value" is amenable to definitions that enforce the requisite conceptual separation between this study's explananda and the dynamic processes hypothesized to explain their evolution over time. A possibility is to define an institution's value not on the basis of how positively or negatively political actors feel about its existence or performance (a component of legitimacy) but rather on the basis of whether an institution structures behavior in a reliable, predictable manner (i.e., its importance or value in shaping or guiding behavior). In other words, *an institution's value is determined by the extent to which it elicits behavior in compliance with its prescriptions and proscriptions.* Once again, power explanations and legitimacy explanations ascribe compliance to different causes: the former, to the presence of compelling enough incentives and disincentives; the latter, to the "normative power" of institutions, which helps to shape the motives and the beliefs accounting for the behavior of purposeful actors.

Putting it all together, the next three chapters theorize the development of political institutions along different dimensions. The chapters on institutional reproduction and institutional decay focus on what may be referred to as the *depth* of institutions. Rixen and Viola (2016) conceive of the depth of institutions as comprising two variables whose definition is rather consistent with the concepts of "value" and "stability" described in this chapter. The first component of an institution's depth—namely, its strength or weakness—is amenable to a similar conceptualization as the one provided above for an institution's value, which speaks to the extent to which the institution in question effectively and predictably shapes the behavior to which it is meant to apply. In this sense, "the degree to which an institution's attributes in t_1 have strengthened or weakened in t_2" (2016: 19) may be taken to mean the degree to which an institution has become more or less effective in generating compliance with its provisions. The second component of an institution's depth—namely, its "resistance to change" and its "robustness in the face of shocks" (19)—may likewise be said to match the definition offered above for the "stability" of institutions. By contrast, the chapter dedicated to institutional change deals with the scope or *breadth* of institutions. Variations in an institution's breadth, in particular, are understood to involve an increase or a decrease in an institution's attributes or features, as well as modifications made either to the content of an institution's provisions or to the range of activities and situations to which such provisions are meant to apply.

Throughout the book, special emphasis is placed on the development of political regimes, whether democratic or nondemocratic. Political regimes are more properly described as *configurations* of the "formal and informal institutions that structure political interaction" in a given polity (Snyder and Mahoney 1999: 103). Together, the institutions constitutive of different regimes "determine who has the power in society and to what ends that power can be used" (Acemoglu and Robinson 2012: 68), as well as regulate access to positions of authority and govern the political processes by which a society's laws and policies are drafted, deliberated, and enacted. Of course, the institutions making up a particular regime "often emerge at different times, often for different reasons," as opposed to "single moments of wholesale regime transition" (Capoccia and Ziblatt 2010: 240; see also Ziblatt 2006). Even so, it makes sense to address regimes as single institutions whose development is marked by the addition and subtraction of a varied set of attributes or features, as well as changes in their enforcement and stability, to the extent that it is possible to specify a set of criteria for whether the addition or subtraction of a given feature marks a change toward, or away from, a certain type of regime. Following Acemoglu and Robinson (2006, 2012), regimes are described as moving toward greater democracy when changes in their institutional features promote greater political equality and inclusion; likewise, regimes are described as moving toward greater *non*democracy when changes in their institutional features promote greater political inequality and exclusion.

A Synthesis of Power-Based and Ideas-Based Explanations

Practically speaking, bridging the gap between explanations grounded in the logics of legitimacy and power involves (i) the improved specification of legitimation explanations, working toward lessening the distance that separates them from power-based accounts in terms of their theoretical development; and (ii) the assemblage of an integrated theory with "corroborated excess empirical content" (Lakatos 1978: 32) relative to each of the explanations it weaves together—one capable of explaining aspects of institutional development for which explanations relying on the logics of "power" or "legitimacy" alone cannot fully account. With regard to the first of these tasks, the analysis benefits from the engagement of literature on the legitimation of power that has been largely overlooked by historical institutionalists. Each of the ensuing three chapters also examines the conditions, "structural" as well as "contingent," affecting the likelihood that processes of institutional reproduction, institutional decay, and institutional change, respectively, will be set in motion. What accounts for whether, for how strongly, or for how rapidly mechanisms of institutional reproduction based on the "dynamics of legitimation" are triggered? What circumstances are most commonly responsible for precipitating erosions of legitimacy leading to institutional decay? What does it take for the delegitimation of institutions actually to usher in institutional change? And what forms of institutional change will most likely follow, given the opportunities and constraints presented by the workings of different institutional arrangements in different contexts? More ambitiously, this book concentrates on processes of legitimation and delegitimation not only as the centerpiece of an alternative approach to making sense of the historical development of political institutions but also as the components of an integrated model centered on the interaction between the dynamics of "power" and the dynamics of "(de)legitimation."

Among the book's most significant contributions to the historical institutionalist literature is the effort made in the next three chapters to theorize the microfoundations of processes of institutional development. Theories of political development can be something of a black box, in the absence of causal mechanisms grounded in clear and realistic assumptions about individual motivation, cognition, and behavior. The fact that, "by reducing politics to the apparently fluid interactions of individuals" (Mahoney and Thelen 2015: 7), a great deal of work in political science "fundamentally misses the impact of power," among other macro-level variables or processes, in no way justifies neglecting the manner in which macro-level variables affect the decisions of *individuals* and vice versa (Levi 1988: 7; see also North 1990: 5). For if "structural features" often "play a key causal role" (Mahoney and Thelen 2015: 6), the macro-level outcomes to which they give rise ultimately hinge on what individuals actually *do* within the constraints set by the structural, institutional, and cultural features of their environment—the choices before them very likely including more than one *"historically* available" option (Capoccia 2015: 159). Accordingly, this study's basic premise is that the explanatory status of social scientific theories, including those that treat "ideas" as "fundamental causes," still turns on whether their workings are accounted for by causal mechanisms that refer to the actions of individuals, in keeping with the work of scholars whose "methodological individualism" does not exhaust itself in the assumptions of the rational choice research program (Elster 2007).

As noted, historical institutionalism differs from new institutionalisms of both the "sociological" and "rational choice" varieties in that it lacks a set of distinctive, "proprietary" assumptions about the precise manner in which institutions shape human behavior, having long contemplated the possibility that they might do so by influencing considerations of "appropriateness" as well as of "prudence" and "advantage" (Hall and Taylor 1996: 939–40). Indeed, while some scholars have taken issue with the notion that historical institutionalism lacks a "distinctive social ontology" (Hay and Wincott 1998), its "eclecticism" on this score potentially ranks among its most attractive features. On the one hand, historical institutionalism's social ontology stands out precisely because it can accommodate theories that tackle the complexity of phenomena such as the development of political institutions by studying the interplay of macro-level structures and macro-historical processes; "ideational factors" such as the identities, values, and beliefs shared by the members of certain groups; and the "intentionality" of human beings—a term that encompasses all behavior, whether or not it is attributable to "instrumental rationality," that is accounted for by an agent's desires and beliefs (Elster 2007). On the other hand, historical institutionalism's unprejudiced approach to human motivation, cognition, and behavior permits the development of theories that prioritize the realism of assumptions and mechanisms over their parsimony, predictive power, or doctrinal purity, thereby ensuring that explanations of macro-level phenomena are consistent with the manner in which human beings are known to think and act, as opposed to more or less fanciful, normative assumptions about the way they *ought* to behave.

Having said that, Hay and Wincott (1998: 951) were correct to point out that historical institutionalism's potential will not be fully realized until the tradition satisfactorily comes to terms with the relationship between structure and agency (see also Mahoney and Snyder 1999: 4; Peters, Pierre, and King 2005: 1284–85). In a similar vein, Berman (1998: 28) proposed that evaluating the role of ideas also requires that we "examine the *micro*foundations of politics and develop a theory of decision-making" capable of accounting for what "different actors want, and why" as well as for what "environmental factors influence the choices of political actors." Two decades later, the potential created by the eclecticism of historical institutionalism's social ontology may be said to have gone largely unfulfilled, as "the outline of a distinctive view of the relationship between structure and agency" (Hay and Wincott 1998: 953–54) that had emerged at the time never ushered in the development of a full-fledged explanation. Meanwhile, the attempts that have been made to theorize the microfoundations of processes of institutional development in accordance with the findings of cognitive psychology and behavioral economics (e.g., Weyland 2008; Fioretos 2011; Lenz and Viola 2017) have yet decisively to reorient the tradition. Indeed, a frequent criticism of historical institutionalism is that the approach "is still missing the 'micro-foundations' of macro-historical change" (Bell 2011: 886).

This book, then, contributes to a broader effort to reorient histori-cal institutionalism and steer it toward the realization of its full potential, through the specification of *a theory of institutional development equipped with microfoundations that operate in accordance with what is known about the workings of human psychology*. The resulting explanatory theory lever-ages the eclecticism of historical institutionalism while staying true to what makes its social ontology "distinctive," accomplishing a synthesis of ideas-based, legitimation explanations and power-based or "power distributional" explanations that improves upon the existing, "pure" versions of both. For their part, legitimation explanations can better account for the development of institutions when the dynamics of intergroup conflict are recognized as crucial to the manner in which ideas spread, new standards of legitimacy are established, and institutions come to exert their "normative force" (e.g., Lieb-erman 2002). Conversely, power-based theories of intergroup conflict and competition benefit from the support of an underlying psychology in which the affirmation of a person's dignity, morality, and convictions supplements considerations of material self-interest.

In view of the fact that the perceived interests and identities of relevant political actors do not perforce correspond to objective, structural condi-tions, a convincing explanation of intergroup conflict is necessarily one that acknowledges the significance of the ideas that bind mobilized social groups together. More generally, the theory assembled in these pages turns the tables on the common perception that nonmaterialist considerations are the stuff of the "soft" social sciences—in other words, the province of postmodern or interpretive approaches. Indeed, to the extent that the social sciences are rendered more "scientific" by ensuring that established explanations are con-sistent with, if not entirely reducible to, the body of knowledge accumulated in scientific fields working at lower levels of aggregation and analysis (Tooby and Cosmides 1992; Elster 2007; Hatemi and McDermott 2011), this book's grounding of the theory's microfoundations in the findings of experimental psychology demonstrates that the effort benefits greatly from the adoption of models of human motivation, cognition, and behavior in which nonmateri-alist considerations are front and center, notwithstanding the prejudice long held by a great many students of politics against treating ideas as anything other than a mask for "real" interests and motives.

Once again, the next three chapters theorize the manner in which the logics of power and legitimation drive sequences of institutional reproduc-tion (chap. 2), institutional decay (chap. 3), and institutional change (chap. 4).

Aside from assessing the significance of the contributions made to the literature on comparative political development, chapter 5 draws out the applied, normative implications of the theory assembled in this book, reflecting on the manner in which some of its key insights might help inform attempts to "engineer" desirable outcomes in the real world through the purposeful design and redesign of political institutions.

CHAPTER TWO

Institutional Reproduction

Path Dependence and the Dynamic Stability of Politics

Few research traditions in the social sciences are as closely identified with the study of a single explanandum as historical institutionalism is with the study of the stability of institutions. Over the past twenty-five years, however, the literature on historical institutionalism has witnessed a significant shift in the terms in which its leading lights describe processes of institutional reproduction. For the most part, the discursive shift reflects the tradition's changing approach to the issue of "path dependence"—or, more precisely, an increased reluctance to ascribe the stability of institutions to self-reinforcing temporal processes driven by "positive feedback" mechanisms. Initial efforts to "analyze the distinctive features" (Thelen and Steinmo 1992: 1) of what was then an emerging tradition drew attention to the effectiveness with which historical institutionalists had illuminated "the persistence of patterns or policies over time" through the deployment of causal mechanisms accounting for "the 'stickiness' of historically evolved institutional arrangements" (14–15). And though it was clear, even back then, that further progress would require moving beyond a model of institutional development in which "long periods of stability" are "periodically 'punctuated' by crises that bring about relatively abrupt institutional change, after which institutional stasis again sets in" (15), contemporaneous work seeking to differentiate historical institutionalism from other varieties of "new institutionalism" could not but list reliance on path dependence as one of its defining features (Hall and Taylor 1996: 938).

The rapidity with which path dependence went on to become one of the most frequently invoked and most commonly misused concepts in the social sciences (Beyer 2010: 1) attests to the transcendence of its appeal. A decade or so removed from some of the earliest attempts to extend its application beyond economics, Mahoney (2000: 512; see also Pierson 2000: 257) highlighted the growing popularity of the view that "increasing returns processes apply to the persistence of a broad range of social and political institutions." Predictably, however, the concept's usefulness suffered as its usage expanded and its meaning was correspondingly "stretched" (Sartori 1970; see also Rixen and Viola 2014). In response, Mahoney (2000: 508, 513–16) proposed that path-dependent, "self-reinforcing sequences characterized by the formation and long-term reproduction of a given institutional pattern" should be conceived of as the combination of "selection processes during a critical juncture," said to be "marked by contingency," and "relatively deterministic causal patterns" subsequently responsible for the reproduction of institutions. As mentioned in this book's introductory chapter, Mahoney (2000: 511, 523) qualified the emphasis placed on the "determinism" of the process with a discussion of the "specific sets of conditions . . . that cause the 'reversal' of path dependence" as well as the "dynamics of change" associated with each of the mechanisms potentially accounting for the self-reinforcement of institutions.

By then, Thelen (1999: 385) had already criticized conventional accounts of path-dependent processes as "both too contingent and too deterministic," raising important questions about the usefulness of models that failed to consider the likelihood that "stability—far from being automatic—may have to be sustained politically" (396). Practically speaking, Thelen's (2006: 154) contention that "institutional reproduction is a much more problematic concept than it is typically recognized" pointed the way toward further theoretical progress in two new directions. On the one hand, Thelen's (2004) own research approached the stability of institutions as an outcome predicated on the continuing capacity of the status quo's defenders to confront new challenges through "active political renegotiation and heavy doses of institutional adaptation" (7). On the other hand, in the face of the continuing popularity of "punctuated equilibrium models," Streeck and Thelen (2005) and Mahoney and Thelen (2010) have sought to develop a theory of "gradual institutional change" focused on the "change-permitting properties of institutions," as well as the myriad ways in which the status quo's opponents can go about exploiting an institutional arrangement's ambiguities, contradictions, and enforcement gaps in order to set in motion incremental processes capable of ushering in major institutional change. Remarkably, Mahoney and Thelen (2010: 8) came close to renouncing path dependence and increasing returns altogether, going so far as to argue that "there is nothing automatic, self-perpetuating, or self-reinforcing about institutional arrangements."

As significant and as constructive as the ongoing shift in emphasis from "path dependence" and "discontinuous change" to "dynamic stability" and "gradual transformation" no doubt has been, a case can be made that the sea change in the terms employed to characterize the stability of institutions overplays the shift's true substantive import. In Thelen's (1999: 385) phrasing, accounts of institutional reproduction relying on positive feedback mechanisms are not always as "contingent" or as "deterministic" as they are made out to be. As Pierson (2004: 51) originally pointed out, and as Capoccia (2015: 157) reiterated more recently, the emphasis placed on "contingency" was never meant to suggest that "critical junctures" are periods in which "anything goes." In fact, the recognition that there are moments in history when the temporary relaxation of structural constraints renders agents *relatively* freer to choose, or renders their decisions *relatively* more consequential, is not incompatible with the notion that the continuing presence of *some* constraints may cause the selection of institutions at critical junctures to yield outcomes marked by a (sometimes surprisingly) high degree of continuity with the past—a scenario addressed in North (1990: 89–91) and Thelen (2004: 34), among others. Most recently, Acemoglu and Robinson's (2012: 106–13) work, while still emphasizing the unpredictable, contingent nature of critical junctures, has shown that the divergent paths of institutional development observed in different societies can often be traced back to the consequences of "small institutional differences" that survived major disruptions or shocks to the system.

As noted, moreover, the emphasis placed on the *relatively* deterministic nature of the process of institutional reproduction did not prevent Mahoney (2000), among others, from recognizing that positive feedback mechanisms vary in both their intensity and their speed, nor did the formulation keep him from specifying the dynamics of change frequently responsible for disrupting or reversing such processes. More generally, the notion that institutions can be subject to self-reinforcement does not exclude the possibility that their persistence requires "the ongoing mobilization of resources" (Mahoney and Thelen 2010: 9). The logic of "increasing returns to power," that is, assumes that the actors advantaged by a particular institutional arrangement will find it in their interest to do what is necessary to ensure its reproduction, but the logic does not guarantee that they actually will do so, much less does it preclude the possibility that changes in the context in which institutions are embedded might complicate their efforts, weaken their capabilities, or threaten their position of advantage. In this sense, the forceful language recently employed by Mahoney and Thelen (2010: 8) on the subject of "self-reinforcement" is itself easily overinterpreted, potentially at the cost of losing sight of the reasons why institutions are frequently so resilient.

The approach taken in this book is founded on the premise that self-reinforcing sequences of institutional reproduction—temporal sequences in which an institution becomes increasingly stable over time as a result of endogenous, increasing returns processes (Rixen and Viola 2014: 8–9, 12)—*can* be set into motion as a result of an institution's establishment. This, however, is far from the inevitable consequence of a rule's entry into force, nor are self-reinforcing sequences of reproduction the only recognizable type of causal pattern or process conceivably triggered during moments of institutional choice. In addition, the activation of positive feedback mechanisms does not preclude the activation of countervailing dynamics, rooted in an institution's own "contradictions and challenges," that "complicate rather than contribute" to its "reliable reproduction" (Thelen 2006: 155). In Elster's (1998) words, that is, moments of institutional choice are marked by a degree of "indeterminacy" regarding both (i) which among multiple possible sequences of institutional development will be set in motion and (ii) the outcome that will eventually emerge when causal patterns pulling an institution's development in opposite directions are triggered more or less simultaneously. Aside from investigating the circumstances that render self-reinforcing sequences more or less likely to be triggered, therefore, this chapter reflects on the conditions that affect the intensity and speed with which they are set in motion. Crucially, such conditions also affect the likelihood that mechanisms of institutional reproduction will prevail over countervailing dynamics, as well as the amount of effort an institution's proponents will be forced to expend to jump-start the process, or defeat challenges to the institution's reproduction. A discussion of the dynamics of change whose activation later in the sequence threatens to compromise an institution's continued reproduction (Mahoney 2000) is featured in the next chapter's analysis of institutional decay.

With regard to the mechanisms that account for the potential self-reinforcement of institutions, the specification of which is taken up in the next section, this chapter's approach to the "dynamics of legitimation" and their interaction with the "dynamics of power" stands out for the departures it marks from prominent analyses of the importance of legitimacy to political stability, besides its aforementioned focus on the process's psychological microfoundations. Such departures primarily concern the issue of the public's compliance with formal rules and procedures, which often plays a decisive role—in concert with the cohesiveness and preferences of a society's elites—in upholding the stability of political institutions. Compliance, specifically, is treated as an "intentional" act explicable with reference to an actor's desires, beliefs, and capacities—in Levi's (1988: 52) words, compliance is "quasi-voluntary" in the sense that the choice to engage in it is not determined by but is still sensitive to the actor's knowledge of the penalties that sanction noncompliance.

In contrast with major works of "sociological institutionalism," the approach taken in this book envisions the cognitive process behind the decision to comply as one in which considerations of appropriateness often come up against other motivations (including material self-interest as well as matters of principle, dignity, and pride), as opposed to one marked by the automatic application of habitual, routine behavioral patterns or by the selection of the internalized "code of appropriateness" that best applies to the situation at hand (March and Olsen 1996: 251–53). In contrast with works on legitimacy authored by scholars in the "historical" and "rational choice" variants of new institutionalism, moreover, this book downplays the importance of ideology as the source of motivations for (non)compliance. While experimental psychology has in part rehabilitated the controversial "dominant ideology thesis" (Abercrombie and Turner 1978; see also Beetham 1991: 62; Scott 1990: 70–76)—having shown that human beings often do internalize the ideas that justify highly unequal social orders condemning them to a position of enduring inferiority—researchers have attributed the phenomenon not to "top-down" processes of indoctrination or brainwashing (but see Taylor 2006) but rather to the routine, "bottom-up" efforts made by average citizens to satisfy psychological needs arising from the workings of hierarchical societies (Thorisdottir, Jost, and Kay 2009). Accordingly, this chapter emphasizes the endogeneity of ideological preferences to the process of institutional development, up to and including the notion that an actor's perception of an institution's legitimacy can be a consequence as much as the cause of her compliance.

A Legitimation Explanation of Institutional Reproduction

Mechanisms of institutional reproduction propelled by the dynamics of power and legitimation account for an institution's *self-reinforcement*—in Rixen and Viola's (2014) sense of the term—to the extent that the institution's deepening entrenchment results from an endogenous process characterized by increasing returns. In this connection, Mahoney (2000: 523) explains that institutional reproduction "in a legitimation framework" is "grounded in actors' subjective orientations and beliefs about what is appropriate or morally correct," which determine whether the agents in question consider the institution legitimate and "voluntarily opt for its reproduction" on the grounds that it is "the right thing to do." With that in mind, Mahoney writes that "increasing legitimation processes are marked by a positive feedback cycle in which an initial precedent about what is appropriate forms a basis for making future decisions about what is appropriate" (523). As mentioned in this book's introductory chapter, the upshot is that "a familiar cycle of self-reinforcement occurs: the institution that is initially favored sets a standard for legitimacy; this institution is reproduced because it is seen as legitimate; and the reproduction of the institution reinforces its legitimacy" (523–24).

In this formulation, processes of "increasing legitimation" are endogenous in the sense that an agent's perception of what is "the right thing to do"—and, therefore, his or her decision to comply—is itself affected by the workings of the institutions subject to self-reinforcement. Exactly how or why this should take place, however, is far from obvious. Why, in particular, would the "standard of legitimacy" set by a particular institution *cause* anyone—but especially those least advantaged by its distributive consequences—to perceive it as legitimate and spontaneously act in ways that favor its reproduction? While Mahoney's (2000) brief treatment leaves the question unanswered, an explanation consistent with his reasoning can be pieced together from the literature. The exercise serves above all to assess the strengths and weaknesses of existing "legitimation explanations," the improved specification of which ranks among this chapter's main objectives.

Institutions and Their Normative Force

The key point, as previewed in this book's introductory chapter, is the notion that institutions have "normative force." Individuals are often motivated by the desire to "fit in"—possibly one grounded in emotional responses that are "genetically based" (Fukuyama 2011: 39; alternative evolutionary explanations for aspects of the phenomenon are found in Baumeister 2005: 135–59; Haidt 2012: 237–40; Sapolsky 2017: 456–62; Wright 1995: chap. 12)—in order to earn the approval of others as well as to protect or boost their own self-esteem. In this view, institutions shape behavior not primarily through the incentives and disincentives that dominate an opportunistic, instrumental calculus but through their provision of behavioral templates or models that suggest how one might go about "fitting in." Certainly, the fact that not all institutions have the same capacity to elicit quasi-voluntary compliance raises the question of what accounts for variations in their normative force. Following Fukuyama (2011: 440, 442–43), answering the question would seem to require that we take into account the "innate propensity" of human beings for "creating and following rules," which often come to be endowed with "intrinsic value," as well as the human tendency to form "mental models of reality" in order to "make the world more legible, predictable, and easy to manipulate." On that basis, institutions should most reliably encourage compliance when they embody some "shared mental model of reality"—in Fukuyama's words, "mental models and rules are intimately intertwined, since the models suggest clear rules" (443).

It almost goes without saying that these expectations are most straight-forwardly associated with the "logic of appropriateness" proposed by scholars belonging to the "sociological" branch of new institutionalism, for whom the legitimacy of institutions is in part a function of the degree to which they embody a society's norms, values, and beliefs (among others, see Berger and Luckmann 1966; Meyer and Rowan 1977; Zucker 1977; DiMaggio and Powell 1983; Suchman 1995: 574). Prominent rational choice institutionalists, however, have also deemed the congruence of institutions with the "subjective mental constructs" prevalent in society to be crucial to the effectiveness with which formal rules and procedures can be expected to structure behavior and, potentially, engineer desirable outcomes (North 1990). Reasonable though it may be, it must be noted, an answer of this kind furnishes an argument *against*—not *for*—institutions having normative force. Why? Because the "force" here is exerted not by the institutions but rather by the content of preexisting ideas, which determine the success or failure of particular institutions.

A possible fix is discussed in Beetham (1991: 17), for whom political institutions ("rules of power") are legitimate—and, therefore, are capable of eliciting spontaneous cooperation/compliance—to the extent that they are "justified in terms of beliefs shared by both the dominant and subordinate." Such justifications generally consist of (i) an argument for the justice of the inequalities produced by rules that regulate access to (and exclusion from) power and (ii) an argument for why the existing arrangements serve the common good. Certainly, whether or not subordinates accept these arguments can be a matter of how consistent they are with prior beliefs or a function of the extent to which the authorities can actively shape their beliefs. Beetham (1991: 60–63, 103–8), however, pointed out that an arrangement of power is reproduced most effectively not through persuasion or brainwashing but through its capacity to generate, by its own workings, the evidence required for its legitimation.

First, a relation of power whose attendant inequalities are justified by differentials of "merit" (however defined) may well benefit from propaganda that seeks to impress upon subordinates that those in power truly are more "meritorious." More useful still, per Beetham (1991: 60–61), is the likelihood that those excluded from power will find it hard to acquire or demonstrate the qualities that make someone "meritorious" enough to wield power, especially to the extent that subordinates fail to recognize that this is a by-product of rules that perpetuate existing inequalities. Second, the fact that, under the existing arrangements, the general interest can only be furthered by measures that also serve the interests of the powerful, whose superiority is sanctioned by the institutional framework currently in place, can lead subordinates to presume that the preservation of current differentials of power is the only (practical) way to serve the general interest (61). Third, institutions induce subordinates to take actions expressing consent for the underlying relation of power. Regardless of whether such expressions of consent are motivated by fear, interest, or genuine support, they boost the legitimacy of the arrangement by binding the agents to some future action, as well as by influencing others through their symbolic or declaratory force (18, 61–62).

Beetham's (1991) reasoning is useful to the specification of an improved legitimation explanation for the self-reinforcement of institutions because each of the three mechanisms by which institutions are said to exert their normative force—in other words, each of the ways in which an institution's legitimacy contributes to its reproduction—is endogenous in nature. While an institution's legitimacy does require that its workings are broadly justifiable in terms of prior or otherwise exogenously set beliefs, what drives the institution's reproduction is not the degree to which it matches the "subjective mental constructs" prevalent in society but rather the extent to which the outcomes it produces shape what actors end up considering "the right thing to do." What is more, the three mechanisms help to account for an institution's self-reinforcement by clarifying the recursive logic of increasing legitimation processes. On the one hand, what drives an institution's reproduction is its capacity to generate, through its own workings, the evidence required for its legitimation. On the other hand, an institution's capacity to yield outcomes consistent with its rationale for inequalities, to advance the common good, and to generate behavioral expressions of consent for the status quo should conceivably increase as the institution becomes more deeply entrenched or as it structures behavior with increasing regularity and effectiveness.

Alas, the descriptions provided for each of these mechanisms are not sufficiently clear about their workings at the individual level—and, partly as a result, not terribly helpful in setting out expectations about the circumstances likely to set them in motion. With regard to the first, why would subordinates fail to recognize that the "evidence" provided for the justice of the arrangement is simply a reflection of differential access to power and resources? With regard to the second, likewise, why would subordinates fail to recognize that, under the existing arrangements, the general interest is less the beneficiary of the underlying relation of power than it is a hostage to the interests of the powerful? On both of these points, the plausibility of Beetham's (1991) account rests on the identification of a common psychological mechanism that speaks to the tendency of individuals to interpret evidence in ways that reaffirm the justice and benevolence of the status quo, as opposed to finding fault with it. The same goes for actions expressing consent, with respect to which Beetham (1991) lacks a psychological mechanism for the tendency of the agents, as well as those who merely observed the behavior in question, to feel obligated to take further actions expressing consent for the status quo.

Even if one stipulates that the desire to "fit in" promotes the adoption of prescribed behavioral models, existing accounts of the normative force of institutions have little to say about the psychology that subsequently makes one convinced of the appropriateness or goodness of the prevailing rules. Of course, whether or not "outwardly" conformist behavior undertaken to avoid punishment or social sanction actually does "reach all the way down to the soul," causing the internalization of the norms, values, and beliefs that make it "the right thing to do," has been the subject of considerable dispute (Elster 2007: 372–75). The fact remains, however, that an adequate understanding of the normative force of institutions requires the specification of mechanisms accounting for the endogeneity of individual preferences to the workings of institutions and/or their development over time.

The Psychology of Increasing Legitimation Processes

The insights and findings produced in the fields of experimental psychology, cognitive neuroscience, and behavioral economics have been the subject of a multitude of popular books published over the last two decades. The title of one such book (McRaney 2011) memorably encapsulates an overarching lesson to be drawn from this body of work: *You Are Not So Smart*. Human beings are subject to a host of biases that distort the manner in which information is processed and decisions are made (e.g., Kahneman 2011), often as a result of the outsized influence that self-serving motivations exert on the cognitive process, all the way down to the "pre-conscious processing of visual stimuli" that "guides what the visual system presents to conscious awareness" (Trivers 2011: 142).

For our purposes, a useful starting point for the specification of individual-level mechanisms accounting for the normative force of institutions is the idea that, as social psychologist Elliot Aronson proposed, "man is a rationalizing animal" (Aronson 1973). As the vast literature on cognitive dissonance, self-affirmation, and self-justification has shown (Cooper 2007), people frequently rationalize their own behavior to satisfy their "obsession for righteousness" (Haidt 2012: xix) and uphold a sense of their "beneffactance" (Greenwald 1980)—that is, the notion that "I am nice and in control" (Pinker 1999: 423). As the almost equally large literature on self-categorization, social identity, parochial altruism, and intergroup conflict has shown, people frequently rationalize the ethnocentrism practiced by their own social groups by embracing a common set of stereotypes (Tajfel and Turner 1986) that justify in-group favoritism and out-group discrimination. And, as the more recent literature on "system justification" has shown, people frequently rationalize the existence of "systems" over which they have little or no control by embracing their legitimizing myths and ideologies, complete with "meritocratic explanations for economic inequality" (Tyler 2006: 284), as well as stereotypes justifying their own inferiority (Jost and Banaji 1994; see also Trivers 2011: 53, 65). Rather more speculatively, they are presumed do so to avoid the sense of "threat and anxiety" resulting from the acknowledgment that "one is forced to conform to the rules, norms, and conventions of a system that is illegitimate, unfair, and undesirable" (Kay et al. 2009: 422; see also Thorisdottir, Kay, and Jost 2009: 7–9; for a similar argument, see Moore 1978: 458).

Equally important, for our purposes, are findings pointing to just how susceptible human beings are to the influence of others. Beyond the influence exerted by authority figures (Milgram 1963) and fellow members of cohesive or like-minded social groups (Bond 2015; Galanter 1999; Sunstein 2011), the mere suggestion that "most other people" are doing something that benefits society has proven effective in motivating subjects to buy products (Cialdini 2009), pay back taxes (Thaler and Sunstein 2008), or even turn out to vote (Issenberg 2012). As a series of experiments conducted in the 1950s have demonstrated, moreover, subjects are often willing to "deny the evidence of their senses" to conform to grossly erroneous judgments rendered by an otherwise unanimous group, having generally taken their own departure from the consensus view as "reflective of some personal deficiency" (Asch 2012: 20). In turn, the desire to fit in and the cognitive dissonance one experiences upon engaging in counter-attitudinal speech or behavior have been shown in experiments from Sherif (1937) on forward to cause the internalization of judgments or ideas that subjects came to express as a result of peer pressure or "induced" compliance (Cooper 2007).

Viewed through the prism of these findings, the normative force of institutions appears, if anything, psychologically overdetermined. The all too human tendency to adjust one's attitudes, preferences, and beliefs retroactively to match one's behavior explains why people who act consistently with the behavioral models provided by an institution—whatever their motivation—subsequently rationalize their conduct by convincing themselves of the behavior's desirability and the legitimacy of the institution that elicited it. Of course, compliance does not necessarily imply or even signal consent (Levi 1997: 17). In the absence of incentives or disincentives, like the threat of physical coercion, that otherwise make it impossible to speak of "(quasi-)voluntary" compliance, however, the actor is likely to feel some pressure to rationalize his or her decision to comply as motivated by principled consent, as opposed to reasons of minor convenience, petty cowardice, and blind imitation. Ironically, the impulse might be strongest when the actor has complied with a rule or procedure that he or she had previously deemed unjust, the consciousness of which may threaten his or her self-image.

The process of self-justification also commits the individual in question to future actions that are consistent with the original behavior and the suitably adjusted underlying preferences, which are in turn gradually reinforced as the actor engages in further compliant behavior, sliding down a "pyramid of choice" through "a chain reaction of behavior and subsequent self-justification" (Tavris and Aronson 2007: 37). To the extent that the institution proves capable of generating high levels of quasi-voluntary compliance, moreover, actors who merely observed such behavior should also experience greater pressure to comply. As more of their fellow citizens and, especially, as more of their fellow group members join the ranks of the compliant, the desire to "fit in"—whether it is motivated by the impulse/need to impress others, reassure oneself of one's own adequacy, or negotiate a social reality where a certain institution has already established its collective "validity"

(Zelditch 2001: 44)—should also motivate a growing number of holdouts to follow the herd and revise their preferences accordingly. Even when compliance is initially insincere, the fact that people generally feel uncomfortable when self-consciously lying to those around them can, in time, induce them to adopt stances and beliefs antithetical to their original preferences (for an illustration, see Greene 2013: 92). Neuroimaging studies suggest that the desire for consensus is so strong and deeply ingrained that subjects tend to exhibit greater activation of the brain regions crucial to the representation of value when exposed to stimuli rated more positively by their peers than when exposed to stimuli they had themselves rated more positively (Zaki, Schirmer, and Mitchell 2011).

The notion that social conformism and dissonance reduction via self-justification shape individual preferences more effectively than indoctrination and propaganda helps provide psychological microfoundations—grounded in decades of experimental research (Bowles 1998: 78–81; Elster 2007: 373–75)—for some of the expectations set out in Beetham (1991). Specifically, the logic articulated thus far supports Beetham's (1991) emphasis on "actions expressing consent" as crucial to the legitimacy of institutions, supplementing his account with a more explicit and empirically grounded argument that ascribes the normative force of institutions to their capacity to elicit compliance, the rationalization of which subsequently boosts the institution's legitimacy and, in so doing, recasts the behavior promoting its continued reproduction as "the right thing to do." Contributing further to the institution's self-reinforcement is the likelihood that, as the institution in question is met with increasingly high levels of compliance, more and more people subject to its provisions will be motivated to seek out evidence of its usefulness and justice, in an attempt to justify their own behavior as well as the features of a system they can do little to escape or change.

As noted, whether or not an institution can produce the evidence required for its own legitimation depends, per Beetham (1991: 60–63), not just on its capacity to engender behavioral expressions of consent but also on its ability to produce outcomes that attest to its promotion of the common good as well as to the justice of prevailing inequalities. Given the ambiguity likely to characterize the available evidence of an institution's performance, as well as the counterfactual nature of plausible alternatives, individuals so motivated will have little trouble procuring information confirming that the institutional arrangement currently in place serves the common good. Much the same goes for the justice of prevailing inequalities. On this count, system justification has been found to account for people's tendency not only to equate "the way things are" to the way they are supposed to be, thereby overlooking evidence of the system's injustice and discrimination (Kay et al. 2009; see also Olson and Hafer 2001; Yzerbyt and Rogier 2001), but also actively to "ascribe traits to themselves as well as other people in such a way that the status or role they occupy is justified" (Jost and Banaji 1994: 13; see also Tyler 2006: 384–90).

Ironically, members of disadvantaged groups may turn out to be the status quo's staunchest supporters, insofar as they face the strongest need to justify their own deprivation (Jost, Banaji, and Nosek 2004: 909). Indeed, consistent with the expectations set out in Beetham (1991), Ross, Amabile, and Steinmetz (1977: 494) found that "people are apt to underestimate the extent to which seemingly positive attributes of the powerful simply reflect the advantages of social control." A series of more recent studies suggests that the belief that the "people who have more resources are 'better,'" which is crucial to the legitimation of material inequalities, tends to form rather quickly among the advantaged and the disadvantaged alike "when control over resources in a social setting is correlated with a salient categorical difference" (Ridgeway 2014: 3). Members of disadvantaged groups will themselves contribute evidence of the system's legitimacy to the extent that "people who are stereotyped tend to choose social roles for themselves that are consistent with the stereotypic expectations others have of them" (Jost and Banaji 1994: 13). More generally, work on "status construction theory" has shown just how easily consensual "status beliefs" consistent with structural inequalities can spread among dominant and subordinate groups through a process of interaction and observation, even in the absence of a centralized source of ideological production and dissemination (Ridgeway 2001). As multiple studies have shown, subjects "primed with social status information" tend to "develop stereotypes that justify that social ordering" (Tyler 2006: 388). Conversely, contemplating unstable societal hierarchies and other scenarios indicative of "social uncertainty" tends to be deeply, viscerally unsettling, resulting in the activation of brain regions responsible for alerting the organism of incoming threats (Sapolsky 2017: 430–42).

Institutional Reproduction and the Dynamics of Legitimation

Putting it all together, self-reinforcing sequences of institutional reproduction driven by the dynamics of legitimation may be rendered as follows.

Political institutions set models for the proper behavior expected of various actors. For reasons of material necessity, opportunism, or genuine support, or based on a desire to "fit in," a varying number of people comply with—and, insofar as their compliance is perceived to have been freely chosen, implicitly express consent for—the existing institutional arrangements. In their turn, cooperators adopt preferences and beliefs that reaffirm the desirability of the behavior and the legitimacy of the institution that elicited it, predisposing or even binding themselves to continuing cooperation. In so doing, these actors influence the behavior of others around them, who may also be expected to exhibit the conformist behavior that causes them retroactively to adjust their own preferences and beliefs accordingly and thereby to commit themselves to taking similar actions in the future.

If the process continues undisturbed, cooperation grows wider and deeper—reinforcing, in individual actors, the legitimacy of the status quo, the tendency to look at its consequences for evidence of its justice, and the commitment to further conformist behavior. Put differently, actions that contribute to an institution's deepening entrenchment endogenously give rise to—and subsequently reinforce—preferences and beliefs that bolster the institution's legitimacy, thereby increasing the perception that actions conducive to the institution's continued reproduction really do represent "the right thing to do." It is also worth pointing out that while this chapter has theorized institutional reproduction as an endogenous process, the dynamics of legitimation can also magnify the effect of exogenous contributions to the "value and stability" of institutions, by rendering individuals who are already motivated to rationalize their compliance, or the workings of "the system" as a whole, more receptive to public relations efforts devised in support of the status quo's legitimation.

Taken to its logical conclusion, the self-reinforcing sequence responsible for an institution's deepening entrenchment and growing legitimation conceivably produces something akin to a "spiral of silence" (Noelle-Neumann 1974; Pierson 2015: 137). As Kelman (2001: 58) pointed out, legitimation and delegitimation processes "generally operate in tandem," as an institution's increased legitimation is typically accompanied by the delegitimation of alternatives. Especially to the extent that the marginalization of opposing viewpoints is expected to continue in the future (Noelle-Neumann 1974: 45), people motivated to "fit in" should grow increasingly reluctant to voice their opposition publicly and will likely rationalize their silence by adopting the prevailing view. Put differently, increasing legitimation processes are subject to the same "coordination effects" and "adaptive expectations" identified as sources of increasing returns in "utilitarian" (Mahoney 2000: 517) accounts of path dependence (Arthur 1994: 112; North 1990: 94; Pierson 2000: 254). Ultimately, in the presence of a firmly entrenched status quo, a host of other psychological mechanisms (Eidelman and Crandall 2009) make it increasingly harder for people to even entertain alternative arrangements, while rendering the individual behavior responsible for the status quo's reproduction increasingly automatic, unconscious, and cognitively effortless.

Setting in Motion Sequences of Increasing Legitimation

Having specified a self-reinforcing sequence of institutional reproduction driven by the dynamics of legitimation down to its psychological microfoundations, the question that must be addressed now is the following: What accounts for whether and, in Mahoney's (2000: 515) words, how "rapidly and decisively" such sequences are triggered? The question is important because not all institutions can be expected to benefit from self-reinforcement, certainly not in equal measures. Indeed, the activation of self-reinforcing sequences of institutional reproduction is not the only conceivable result of an institution's entry into force, which has been shown frequently to engender psychological reactions of a completely different nature from those that drive increasing legitimation processes. The theory of "reactance" (Brehm and Brehm 1981), for instance, speaks to the possibility that human beings might respond negatively to limitations placed on their freedom of choice— their resolve to fight back hardened by the tendency to value newly restricted freedoms or alternatives more than they had before. If an institution produces a reaction of this sort, it is quite possible that the propensity of individuals to conform to the behavior of others, as well as to rationalize their own behavior, will actually lead to growing levels of *non*compliance, accompanied by a growing perception of the institution's *il*legitimacy. Complicating matters further, the same social groups might develop different responses to an institution, if subsets of their membership alternatively exhibit greater compliance or greater noncompliance.

Considerations of this kind speak to the importance of examining not just the conditions affecting *whether* self-reinforcing sequences of institutional reproduction will be triggered at all but also those factors affecting the possibility that "mechanisms of reproduction are not activated quickly or powerfully enough" (Mahoney 2000: 515) to prevail over countervailing forces working against an institution's reproduction. It almost goes without saying—given the rarity of established, lawlike explanations in the social sciences (Elster 2007: 32–35), the complexity of the causal relations involved (Fukuyama 2011: 23), and the possibility that the same combination of variables could lead to different outcomes in different sets of cases (Capoccia and Ziblatt 2010: 935)—that it may not be possible fully to account for the conditions responsible for setting off alternative developmental trajectories, in a way that completely eliminates the indeterminacy surrounding the fate of newly established institutions. It is nonetheless still worthwhile to examine the manner in which certain commonly observed circumstances, be they of a structural or a contingent nature, conceivably affect the outcomes of interest.

Maximizing Levels of Quasi-Voluntary Compliance

The analysis may begin by pondering what is perhaps the most obvious implication of the reasoning articulated in the previous section: *All else being equal, the likelihood that self-reinforcing sequences of institutional reproduction governed by the dynamics of legitimation will be set in motion should vary with the initial level of compliance an institution proves capable of generating among the agents subject to its provisions.* Before proceeding any further, it is worth stipulating upfront that initial levels of compliance are not entirely dispositive one way or the other. In principle, just as an entire crowd can be swept up in a riot as a result of the actions of a single "instigator" (Granovetter 1978: 1424), it is possible to envision a scenario in which it is enough for an institution to elicit the compliance of a single person for it to trigger a bandwagon effect that leads to the universalization of compliance and, according to the expectations put forth in this study, the emergence of a unanimous consensus regarding the institution's legitimacy.

The outcome in question, however, can only be described as improbable, based on at least two considerations. First, as Granovetter (1978: 1425) explains, the emergence of a bandwagon of this kind constitutes a highly unstable equilibrium, given its reliance on a particular distribution of individual "thresholds" for engaging in a particular behavior. Second, insofar as increasing legitimation processes are rooted in individual behavior motivated by the desire to "fit in," as well as in the tendency of human beings to rationalize acts of compliance by revising their underlying assessments of an institution's legitimacy, it is reasonable to expect that when an institution is met with widespread noncompliance, conformism and self-justification will combine to promote the opposite effect: namely, the diffusion of noncompliant behavior, rationalized on the grounds of the institution's illegitimacy. At any rate, the fact that human beings are "conditional cooperators"—as theorized by Levi (1988: 53), among others, and as shown in experimental findings produced by the literature on "behavioral economics" (Thaler 2015: 145–46)—should render members of a society reluctant to comply when most others are not. So while it is theoretically possible for the dynamics of legitimation to give rise to a self-reinforcing sequence of institutional reproduction in spite of initially low levels of compliance, the likelihood that increasing legitimation processes will be set in motion—and usher in an institution's rapid entrenchment—should conceivably increase with the initial levels of compliance generated by the institution.

As pointed out above, among the obstacles that might prevent an institution from generating high levels of compliance, as well as from giving rise to preferences that reinforce the institution's legitimacy, is the possibility that the institution in question features provisions that are met with "reactance." Under what conditions should reactance be expected to be the dominant psychological reaction to an institution's entry into force? One plausible answer zeroes in on the manner in which a new institutional arrangement is introduced and enforced. Laurin, Kay, and Fitzsimons (2012), for instance, presented experimental evidence in support of the proposition that, when confronted with a new constraint on personal freedom, the "absoluteness" of the restriction determines whether subjects respond by exhibiting reactance or by rationalizing the new status quo. When the restriction is "absolute"— that is, complete, certain, and permanent—subjects tend to respond by recasting restrictions in a positive light and by minimizing the importance of the freedoms being limited. Reactance, conversely, is more prevalent in circumstances of uncertainty or in the presence of a perceived chance that the restrictions will not come into force. This finding is consistent with system justification theory, which predicts that a future outcome will be valued more positively as it becomes more likely (Jost, Banaji, and Nozek 2004: 889), as well as with social identity theory, which predicts that challenges to the status quo will increase with its perceived instability and the readiness with which members of subordinate groups can imagine "cognitive alternatives" (Tajfel and Turner 1986: 22). A similar reasoning also appears in Thaler's (2015: 131–36) discussion of measures that change a transaction's established "terms of trade," which are said to engender the perception of a loss by violating the standard of "fair treatment" that people feel entitled to receive based on experience. As in the case of restrictions to personal freedom, Thaler (136) pointed to the inescapability of the measures (i.e., their wide adoption by the competition) as the key to whether consumers punish firms for practices deemed "unfair."

The result in question, however, is somewhat more difficult to square with the experimental findings cited by Scott (1990: 109) in support of the idea that a subordinate's original act of compliance produces attitudes sustaining further compliance "if, and only if, that compliance is perceived [by the agent] as freely chosen—as voluntary." Consistent with the emphasis that scholars of cognitive dissonance have placed on the element of choice that must be present for hypocritical or counter-attitudinal behavior to impel the adjustment of underlying attitudes (Cooper 2007: 34–35; see also Cialdini 2009: 80), Scott (1990: 110) argues that "the greater the force majeure compelling the performance, the less the subordinate considers it representative of his 'true self.'" But while it is to be expected that an "absolute restriction" would fail to engender rationalization if the penalties attached to noncompliance (or the rewards attached to compliance) are heavy enough, experimental studies of cognitive dissonance suggest that the *illusion* of choice is generally preserved even when compliance is "induced" through a great deal of social pressure (Harmon-Jones 2000: 191). In view of the fact that maintaining a sense of control is such a basic human need (Baumeister 2005: 93–103), it is not surprising that people—absent a compelling reason to deny responsibility for their actions (Cooper 2007: 76–77)—would cling to the belief that they are in control of their own behavior, at least to the extent that they are able to concoct a reasonable justification for the motivated belief. Proponents of the theory, moreover, expect the intensity of reactance to be lowest when the restoration of a restricted freedom is perceived as next to impossible— per Miron and Brehm (2006: 6), "just as a goal must lose the positive affect attached to it when it becomes impossible to achieve, so the motivation to recover freedom must disappear when the freedom is no longer viable."

Laurin, Kay, and Fitzsimons (2012: 209) also qualify their findings by cautioning that "some restrictions, even when absolute, might be too sudden or abhorrent to elicit rationalization." In practice, the tendency of institutions to be, as "sociological institutionalist" scholars describe them, "'isomorphic' with (i.e., compatible with, resembling, and similar in logic to) existing ones" (Thelen 1999: 386) should render the adoption of measures of this sort relatively infrequent, if not altogether unimaginable, in periods of "normal" politics (see also North 1990: 89). In these situations, the rationalization of particular outcomes or measures—including those with aversive consequences for the persons in question—has been found to hinge in part on "legitimacy appraisals" that are sensitive to "contextual cues that convey information about distributive and procedural justice" (Major and Schmader 2001: 182; see also Feygina and Tyler 2009; Levi 1997: 23–24; Tyler 2006), as well as cues that give people "even a minor, or illusory, sense that they have some control over, or voice in, their outcomes" (Major and Schmader 2001: 184).

Of course, such cues are unlikely to feature in the relations of power examined by Scott (1990), where subordinates are denied the most basic rights and live in fear of the humiliation and violence routinely meted out by superiors. In today's world, however, it is rare for political leaders utterly to neglect fostering the impression that their decision-making process is fair, inclusive, and inspired by the desire to improve the lives of those subject to their authority, however coercive or discriminatory the system of government over which they preside. Nationalist ideologies—especially those resulting from "an anticipatory strategy adopted by dominant groups which are threatened with marginalization or exclusion from an emerging nationally-imagined community" (Anderson [1983] 1991: 101)—often serve to convey precisely that impression, whether or not "the nation" is formally conceived as a "deep, horizontal comradeship" of equal citizens (15). The widespread tendency of dictators to adopt "nominally democratic institutions," too, conceivably reflects an attempt to bolster the perceived fairness of their decisions, in addition to their need to establish "forums" in which meaningful compromises with potential challengers are routinely hammered out (Gandhi 2008). Indeed, the younger Anderson (1976: 27–29) suggests that democratic institutions serve essentially the same purpose in the legitimation of the Western "bourgeois State" as well.

On that basis, the likelihood that a citizen will comply with and accept the legitimacy of an institution or set of institutions should conceivably increase with (i) the citizen's perception of the legitimacy of the process that ushered in the institution's adoption, influenced by considerations of procedural and distributive justice, from which the actor may derive a moral obligation to comply with the institution in question; and (ii) the citizen's perception of the legitimacy of the system as a whole, from which the actor may derive a moral obligation more generally to heed the decisions made by an authority deemed "entitled to determine appropriate behavior within a given situation or situations" (Tyler 2010: 34; see also Tyler 1990: 24–25). Having said that, however, it is worth keeping in mind that, in practice, causation may often flow in the opposite direction. For one thing, assessments of the legitimacy of the process that led to an institution's adoption, and perhaps to a lesser extent of the system as a whole, can be a consequence, as opposed to the cause, of one's decision to comply. More specifically, just as the need to concoct a principled justification for otherwise motivated acts of compliance often colors an actor's assessments of an institution's legitimacy, it is quite possible that self-justification will also drive his or her assessment of the legitimacy of the system as well as the process in which the institution originates. Similarly, to the extent that an actor is motivated by "system justification," appraisals of the legitimacy of the system—and the legitimacy of the process that ushered in an institution's adoption—are not so much "causes" contributing to his or her subsequent assessment of the institution's legitimacy as much as they are by-products of the same motivational process that causes the actor to seek out evidence of the institution's legitimacy.

Identity, Social Structure, and the Dynamics of Legitimation

Once again, while an institution's "isomorphism" with a society's existing assortment of formal rules and "informal constraints" (North 1990: chap. 5) should reduce the likelihood that it will be perceived as too "abhorrent" to be obeyed and rationalized, individual responses may be expected to vary with the institution's perceived significance to—and anticipated effect on—the social groups with which the persons in question identify. This expectation is at the core of what Simon and Oakes (2006: 112) have called an "identity model of power," which emphasizes "the relative salience of shared and differentiating identities" as the key determinant of the balance observed in a given power relation between elements of "consensus" (and influence) and elements of "conflict" (and coercion).

Certainly, the fact that institutions generally represent "political legacies of concrete historical struggles" (Mahoney and Thelen 2010: 7) or "contingent outcomes of conflicts" (Przeworski 1988) introduces the possibility that sizable constituencies, insofar as they were not comprehensively defeated or eliminated, might "abhor" institutional arrangements imposed at the conclusion of previous rounds of struggle, especially if the arrangements in question work effectively to relegate "losers" to a position of enduring inferiority or systematic disadvantage. As Thelen (2004: 32) pointed out, it is not always safe to assume that "losers" will simply reconcile themselves to the institutions imposed by (and for) "winners" and adjust their behavior accordingly, so as themselves to contribute to the institutions' reproduction. On the contrary, as part of the ongoing "struggle over the form that these institutions should take and the functions they should perform" (32), "losers" can often be expected to respond with more or less overt, sustained efforts to subvert the rules, interfere with their enforcement, undermine the coalition supporting the status quo, and engage in a host of other actions aiming to displace, modify, or otherwise prevent the institutions they oppose from working as intended (Mahoney and Thelen 2010). In turn, the determination to avert such a backlash is the reason why, as Tang (2011: 36) has proposed, superordinate groups might seek to "co-opt" or "bargain with" some or all of the mobilized groups on the "losing side"—or at any rate boost their members' perception of the procedural and distributive justice of the proceedings—by involving their representatives in the design of institutions or by ensuring that the new rules feature well-advertised concessions to their interests or demands.

In any event, given the propensity of individuals to assess the "subjective validity" of their attitudes and behavior by looking to other members of the social groups with which they identify (Turner 1991)—as Tyler (1990: 24) has put it, "Individuals look to their social groups for information about appropriate conduct"—whether or not one's social group conforms, in the main, to a behavioral model prescribed by a certain institutional arrangement can have a powerful influence on those who are contemplating resistance or have not committed themselves either way. When the group as a whole appears willingly to comply, these individuals may be brought along to the extent that they are motivated by the desire to fit in, according to the logic outlined above. Conversely, those contemplating resistance may draw greater courage to disobey upon observing significant noncompliance within their own social groups, as did the subjects of Solomon Asch's experiments who were provided a "partner" who disagreed with the consensus judgment expressed by the remainder of the study's confederates. In this scenario, moreover, individuals inclined toward obedience may themselves be successfully pressured to exhibit noncompliance, sometimes on pains of social ostracism and perhaps even physical coercion (Scott 1990: 27, 129–31; see also Tyler 1990: 23–24). The presence of significant opposition—an exaggerated perception of which may be favored by the prevalence of noncompliance among a person's associates (Granovetter 1978: 1429)—can also undermine the apparent "absoluteness" of an institutional arrangement, thereby depriving it of the air of inevitability that tends to favor its rationalization.

This reasoning suggests that self-reinforcing, increasing legitimation sequences of institutional reproduction are *most likely* to be set in motion in situations where opposition to a certain institutional arrangement on the grounds of "appropriateness" does *not* overlap with mobilized, politically salient social identities shared by a sizable portion of the population. This could happen as a result of either (i) an institution's intergroup appeal, which should increase with the extent to which meaningful concessions are made to the interests, aspirations, and values of mobilized social groups; or (ii) the absence of large, organized social groups whose members espouse beliefs concerning appropriateness that are starkly at variance with those enshrined in the institutional arrangement in question, given the intellectual "hegemony" of the dominant group, the purchase of shared "higher-level [e.g., national] identities" (Simon and Oakes 2006), or the multidimensionality of most citizens' politically salient lower-level identities, which has been found to temper the extremism generally associated with the mobilization of subnational, ethnic allegiances (Chandra 2005). Chandra (2005) has shown that even the most deeply divided societies can defuse the potential for ethnic extremism if the rules of the game incentivize the politicization and mobilization of multiple aspects of citizens' lower-level identities, citing India as the prime example.

In turn, the "rapidity and decisiveness" with which the dynamics of legitimation, once triggered, contribute to an institution's reproduction should be greatest in the presence of a social structure that combines a modicum of cohesion at the societal level—based on an overarching set of ideas and/ or a national identity shared by the members of most mobilized social constituencies—with low levels of social "fragmentation." As Granovetter (1973) has shown, social structures characterized by the presence of multiple, internally cohesive identity groups that are effectively walled off from the influence of others limit the reach of the "diffusion processes" such as those that drive the reproduction of institutions in a legitimation framework. By requiring that increasing legitimation processes contributing to the entrenchment of institutions be set in motion, separately, within each group, high levels of fragmentation may be expected to slow down the process of institutional reproduction, even when *none* of the groups involved holds beliefs that are incompatible with the institutional arrangement in question. Then again, more recent scholarship has shown that the diffusion of behaviors whose contagion is "complex" (i.e., "costly, risky, or involv[ing] some degree of complementarity" [Centola 2018: 7]) cannot rely on what Granovetter (1973) referred to as "the strength of weak ties." When "innovative behaviors" can only spread through repeated interactions and "contact with multiple adopters," their diffusion benefits from the presence of "closely knit, densely overlapping networks" (Centola 2018: 2, 6–9)—hence the reference made here to "a modicum of cohesion at the societal level."

Conversely, self-reinforcing sequences of institutional reproduction based on the logic of legitimation should be *least likely* to be triggered in contexts where beliefs in the inappropriateness of certain institutional arrangements are somehow bound up with mobilized, politically salient lower-level social identities, especially if (i) the groups in question are cohesive and the relative social identities occupy much of their members' "cognitive landscapes" (Taylor 2006: 40–41) and (ii) the beliefs in question are strongly held, in the sense that they have been reinforced repeatedly and are central to the network of ideas that defines a group's worldview (127–29). Generally speaking, the stronger the identification with a group—and, therefore, the greater the significance of group membership to an individual's sense of self—the greater the propensity of its members to blur the distinction between self- and group interest and therefore the greater their willingness to act in accordance with group norms as well as to exhibit the behavioral tendencies associated with "parochial altruism" (Choi and Bowles 2007: 636).

In these situations, insofar as the social groups opposing the new status quo *cannot* muster the strength and resources to fight back openly, the institution's reproduction may nonetheless be undermined by scarce (or low-quality) cooperation. As Scott (1985: xvii) pointed out, subordinates can make "utter shambles" of an institution by resorting to "everyday forms of resistance" masked by the public appearance of compliance, deference, and obedience. Given the risks involved in enforcing compliance through coercion alone, widespread noncompliance can also lead to nonenforcement (Levitsky and Murillo 2009: 121–22), which consigns an institution to a position of irrelevance or chronic instability. Insofar as the social groups opposing the new status quo *can* muster the strength and resources to fight back openly, however, the adoption of the institution could lead to organized reactions against it. Such reactions may lead to the restoration of the status quo ante. Or, if the groups supporting and opposing the institutional arrangement are more or less evenly matched, the initial reaction may set in motion temporal sequences other than those said to account for an institutional arrangement's reproduction. Whether such alternative developmental sequences take the form of a "balancing process" (Page 2006: 99–100), a "cyclical process" (Bennett and Elman 2006: 258–59), or a "reactive sequence" (Mahoney 2000: 526–27) is largely a function of the interaction observed in a particular context between the logics of legitimation and power, a synthesis of which is pursued in the next section.

Synthesizing the Logics of Power and Legitimation

For all its emphasis on the importance of ideas as "fundamental causes," this chapter's analysis of institutional reproduction in a "legitimation framework" has already highlighted just how untenable it is to theorize the dynamics of legitimation separately from the dynamics of power—that is, without making reference to the modulating effect that the distribution and the exercise of power have on the way the dynamics of legitimation affect outcomes of interest. The strained, artificial character of the separation between the logic of legitimation and the logic of power became all too apparent at the end of the last section, where it proved impossible to develop the most basic expectations about the competition between groups espousing different beliefs regarding appropriateness without referencing the way in which such groups are matched in terms of their "relations of power."

So closely intertwined are the logics of legitimation and power that some scholars do away with the distinction altogether. A case in point is the effort recently made by Pierson (2015) to clarify the logic of increasing returns to power by exploring the precise mechanisms by which "power begets power." In that context, Pierson (2015: 127) treats legitimacy as one of the dimensions of power. Accordingly, one of the key mechanisms accounting for the self-reinforcing nature of asymmetries of power is rooted in the possibility that the "winners" of previous rounds of struggle will seek to capitalize on an initial advantage earned over their rivals by manipulating "cultural institutions" so as to "alter discourse" in their favor. Echoing Schattschneider's ([1960] 1988: 66) contention that "the definition of alternatives is the supreme instrument of power," Pierson (2015: 127, 137–38) explains that the attempt to "alter discourse" entails the dissemination and inculcation of certain "views regarding what is desirable or possible," the suppression and marginalization of opposing viewpoints, and the imposition of boundaries delimiting the range of legally permissible or socially acceptable debate.

Pierson's (2015) discussion of the mechanisms accounting for the self-reinforcement of asymmetries of power provides an ideal basis upon which to assemble an integrated account of processes of institutional reproduction driven by the interaction between the dynamics of legitimation and the dynamics of power. Having already examined the process's reliance on the tendency of "legitimation to beget legitimation," while also stipulating its reliance on the tendency of "power to beget power," this section explores the manner in which self-reinforcing sequences of institutional reproduction also benefit from the tendency of "legitimation to beget power" as well as the tendency of "power to beget legitimation." Equally important, this section specifies alternative developmental sequences to which the logics of legitimation and power may give rise when their interaction *does not* follow a pattern of mutual reinforcement.

Power and Legitimation: The Logic of Mutual Reinforcement

The mutual reinforcement between the dynamics of power and legitimation may be said to operate according to the following logic. Consistent with Pierson's (2015) account, power typically involves the control of "resource stocks" and "resource flows" that an advantaged group can parlay into even greater power. One of the principal ways in which the group in question might go about doing so is by investing resources in the legitimacy of its privileged status as well as the legitimacy of the institutions responsible for regulating behavior in ways that perpetuate existing social hierarchies. On the one hand, as Pierson pointed out, advantaged groups can direct their efforts toward "foster[ing] beliefs in others (about what is desirable or possible) that serve the interests of the powerful" (127). More generally, the ideological work undertaken by superordinate groups may intervene on preferences (e.g., making conformity into a value in and of itself), beliefs (convincing subordinate groups of the justice or appropriateness of the status quo), or identities (reconfiguring the identities of subordinate groups, binding them more closely to the dominant ones). On the other hand, this chapter's specification of the dynamics of legitimation suggests that advantaged groups can most effectively boost the legitimacy of an institution or system of institutions by investing available resources into securing the public's compliance. In so doing, aside from reaping what benefits may flow from an institution's "power-distributional" aspects, advantaged groups can solidify their position, or entrench a cherished institution, by relying on the public's tendency to rationalize acts of compliance and to revise their underlying preferences and beliefs, at least insofar as the measures taken to maximize compliance are not so conspicuous as to dispel the impression (or the illusion) that compliance was meaningfully "chosen."

Based on the reasoning articulated in the previous section, the success of efforts made to shape the public's preferences and beliefs hinges on whether the rejection of the existing arrangements of power, or the rejection of an existing institution, is already central to the social identities of disadvantaged or subordinate groups, rendering them more resistant to official attempts to reshape their worldviews. Certainly, it is not entirely unprecedented for groups brought in line through coercion or material inducements eventually to support arrangements of power they previously deemed unacceptable. As Max Weber pointed out, "It is very common for minorities, by force or by use of more ruthless and far-sighted methods, to impose an order which in the course of time comes to be regarded as legitimate by those who originally resisted it" ([1922] 1978: 37). In turn, that may or may not have something to do with Tocqueville's proposition that "there is no more inveterate habit of man than to recognize superior wisdom in his oppressor" (cited in Elster 2007: 373), which Scott (1990) vigorously disputes. Even so, the available evidence lends credence to the idea that subordinate groups should most readily embrace an institution's legitimacy when (i) preexisting values, beliefs, and identities present no particular obstacle and (ii) compliance is obtained through means subtle enough not to disrupt the self-justification process that tends to produce a favorable reappraisal of the institution's appropriateness.

At any rate, when an advantaged group successfully manages, through the application of power, to bolster the legitimacy of an institution or system of institutions, it not only sets in motion the increasing legitimation processes that drive self-reinforcing sequences of institutional reproduction but also conceivably boosts its own power. If, as Pierson (2015) explains it, what generates power for an advantaged group is the transfer of "resource stocks" and the redirection of "resource flows" in its favor, increased legitimacy contributes to both by freeing up the resources otherwise required to monitor the public's behavior, incentivize obedience, and punish noncompliance. As a result, just as the application of power helps trigger increasing legitimation processes, increased legitimacy might help set in motion mechanisms of institutional reproduction driven by the dynamics of power, as the additional resources it makes available for advantaged groups can be invested in the pursuit of policies that further expand existing asymmetries of power. Far from being limited to the triggering phase, the mutual reinforcement between the dynamics of power and legitimation may actually intensify further downstream, especially if the growing entrenchment of a superordinate group and its institutions eventually activates the cognitive and behavioral tendencies associated with "system justification," which should in their turn enhance the "decisiveness" with which sequences of institutional reproduction lead to the entrenchment of the institutional arrangement(s) in question.

On the whole, the triggering of sequences of institutional reproduction driven by the mutual reinforcement between the dynamics of power and legitimation is easily the best-case scenario for a newly minted institution or system of institutions. Once again, however, in recognition of the fact that this outcome is far from guaranteed, it becomes necessary to identify the sorts of conditions in which mutual reinforcement is more or less likely to be activated, as well as to specify alternative developmental sequences where the interaction between the logics of power and legitimation takes a different form. Perhaps the most obvious alternative is a scenario in which the two logics work in a mutually exhausting, as opposed to a mutually reinforcing, fashion. Based on the considerations made above, this dynamic could be set in motion when an advantaged group's attempts directly to shape the public's preferences and beliefs, or to enforce compliance, are resented by subordinate groups as an undue imposition, damaging the legitimacy of an institution or set of institutions, thereby rendering the enforcement of compliance ever more reliant on conspicuous, expensive measures that threaten further to deplete an advantaged group's legitimacy *as well as* its power.

Once again, the likelihood that the dynamics of power and legitimation will work in a mutually exhausting fashion should be highest where the rejection of existing arrangements of power is already central to the social identities of subordinate groups. In these circumstances, political authorities may consider applying levels of physical coercion extreme enough to beat subordinate groups into complete submission, in the hope that this will afford them the time and space required to reshape their values, beliefs, and identities. Quite aside from the difficulty of doing so, which is all the greater in circumstances where subordinate groups exhibit high levels of awareness and involvement in politics, repression is only sustainable insofar as it is justifiable to the constituencies upon which the stability of the status quo is predicated based on their beliefs regarding what constitutes an appropriate use of power—or, failing that, based on their perception of a threat serious enough to warrant something of a "state of exception" (Agamben 2005). Rather than risk doing damage to the entire relation of power, advantaged groups may in practice find it prudent either to scrap or to scale back their enforcement of institutions that are met with an effective resistance campaign supported by groups that are too large or too powerful to be ignored.

Power, Legitimation, and the Road to Instability

Between the extremes represented by mutually reinforcing and mutually exhausting interactions between the dynamics of power and legitimation, it is possible to identify an array of intermediate developmental trajectories. One internally varied set of alternatives falls under the heading of "dynamic stability." In these situations, though the selection of an institution fails to trigger mechanisms of reproduction "quickly" or "decisively" enough to pre-empt an organized reaction, the arrangement's proponents enjoy enough of an advantage over their rivals to beat back successive challenges, through measures that potentially include legal or physical repression, a public relations offensive, the expansion of support coalitions, and/or adjustments to the institution that successfully neutralize the source of the arrangement's vulnerability. Depending on a variety of factors and contingencies related to the effects of both choice and chance, such measures could succeed in placing an institution on a path toward greater stability or could simply inaugurate a new round of conflict. It is also quite conceivable that an institution might generate self-reinforcement, perhaps not quickly enough to discourage all challenges from the start but still decisively enough to reduce gradually the severity of challenges over time.

Another category of "intermediate" outcomes features situations characterized by a varying degree of *instability*. Each of the three sequences identified in Bennett and Elman (2006) as alternatives to self-reinforcing sequences marked by increasing returns is set in motion when the reaction to an initial event—like the introduction of an institution—is vigorous enough to yield a different outcome, but not decisive enough to prevent a successful counter-reaction that leads to another iteration of the "reaction and counterreaction" cycle. As suggested above, the situations that fit this general pattern require a rough balance of forces between the opposing sides, whether the coalitions supporting alternative arrangements are stable or whether they change with every iteration of the process. In each case, continued instability is also conceivably accounted for, in part, by the nature of the institutional arrangement being fought over—specifically, the inability of an institution to alter the balance of forces by conferring upon one coalition or another a decisive enough advantage to trigger increasing returns processes. Beyond these common characteristics, however, the three following sequences describe different developmental trajectories, the triggering of which conceivably reflects the influence of structural as well as contingent factors.

By far the simplest of such sequences is referred to in Bennett and Elman (2006) as a "cyclical process." There, "successes by one constituency," such as the establishment of a favored institution, "result in the mustering of greater political forces by the other" (Page 2006: 99), and vice versa, ushering in the "cycling between two (or more) alternatives" (Bennett and Elman 2006: 258). Designating the alternatives favored by each constituency "A" and "B," therefore, cyclical processes are diagrammed as A→B→A→B→A. (Following this notation, self-reinforcing sequences would be diagrammed as A→A→A→A→A.) Ferrara's (2015: 34) work on Thailand's political development shows that the country's history of regime instability instantiates a sequence of this kind, as "each success scored by the forces of electoralism and majoritarianism" in the past century "has prompted those opposed to muster greater political strength, and vice versa, leading to the cycling of alternative regime types."

Aside from reflecting a rough balance of forces, as well as social divisions deep enough to prevent support for each institutional arrangement to spread widely enough to prevail over its alternative(s), cyclical processes conceivably require a degree of ideological polarization, wherein different groups have roughly equally intense preferences for different sets of institutions. So, while the committed following of their partisans accounts for the staying power of both institutional arrangements over successive iterations of the process, none of the alternatives in question successfully triggers mechanisms of institutional reproduction rooted in the dynamics of power or the dynamics of legitimation. On the one hand, neither set of rules, once established, carries significant enough power-distributional benefits—following Pierson (2015), neither causes significant enough transfers of "resource stocks" or "resource flows"—to trigger increasing returns to power. On the other hand, deep social divisions may prevent the establishment of one set of institutions from triggering, outside the confines of the groups already supporting it, the psychological reactions that drive increasing legitimation processes. On the contrary, each alternative may be plagued by "negative feedback." Aside from invigorating the opposition, the establishment of an institutional arrangement may diminish the support it enjoys among more moderate nonpartisans as well, whose reluctance to defend each set of alternatives may be fueled by fears of moving too far in one direction or another. Indeed, if they exist at all, moderate constituencies in these cases are likely not numerous, powerful, unified, and/or committed enough to impose a stable middle-ground solution but are rather cross-pressured into periodically shifting sides.

A different, albeit related, type of sequence is what Page (2006) and Bennett and Elman (2006) refer to as a "balancing process." In this case, the reaction to an institution and the subsequent counterreaction do not set off the cycling between the same two alternatives (say, "A" and "B") but rather trigger a process in which one institution ("A") is a recurrent equilibrium, whose restoration is met with a reaction that leads to the establishment of a different alternative ("B," "C," and so on) each time. In a balancing process (diagrammed as A → B → A → C → A), the initial success of the reaction to the recurrent equilibrium is said to be accounted by a period of increasing returns, after which negative feedback kicks in, ushering in the restoration of the recurrent equilibrium. Once again, a sequence of this kind would seem to require social divisions that limit the effect of social influence and conformism, as well as the inability of any of the alternative institutional arrangements to provide its supporters with a decisive enough advantage in terms of power. As in a cyclical process, moreover, moderates lack the capacity to impose a middle-ground solution.

Whereas balancing processes also require a rough *overall* balance of forces between the groups siding with the reaction or the counterreaction, however, what might explain the asymmetry in the staying power of the recurrent equilibrium and its alternatives is an imbalance in the organizational capacity of the opposing sides or in the intensity of their preferences. On the one hand, the fact that the reaction to the recurrent equilibrium rallies around different alternatives each time suggests that the groups involved are ideologically flexible enough to form different coalitions and/or strategically to endorse different alternatives to mobilize support. Indeed, to the extent that balancing processes may feature fluid as well as stable coalitional alignments, the scenario in question would seem to require the presence of groups available to join the reaction at one time and join the restoration of the recurrent equilibrium at another time, depending on whether the alternative that the reaction rallies around is judged better or worse given the groups' interests or preferences. Even so, the initial period of increasing returns accounting for the success of the reaction early on likely reflects the advantage that challengers may temporarily enjoy thanks to their greater cohesion and their more intense motivation to replace the recurrent equilibrium, relative to the opposing side. On the other hand, that the recurrent equilibrium is both chronically vulnerable and remarkably resilient to repeated iterations of the process points to the fact that its proponents, though powerful enough invariably to restore the recurrent equilibrium, are not sufficiently cohesive and ideologically committed to take the measures required to forestall predictable future challenges. As a result, they only act upon being confronted with the success of their opponents' reaction.

In these cases, the difference in the two alignments' cohesiveness may be explained by the possibility that while the recurrent equilibrium advances neither the interests nor the vision of its proponents in a particularly strong way, its proponents fear the workings of the arrangements supported by the opposition, the adverse consequences of which must nonetheless manifest themselves before they can spawn a counterreaction. The fact that the counterreaction always rallies around the restoration of the status quo ante, as opposed to the pursuit of a new alternative, is likely less a reflection of the ideological commitment to the recurrent equilibrium than it is a reflection of the breadth of interests and visions exhibited by the groups available to support the counterreaction, whose superior combined strength has the downside of making it impossible for them to agree on much other than the idea that they were doing better before. Bennett and Elman (2006: 258) cited "the persistence of the anarchic Westphalian state system" as an example of a balancing process in which "the state system is sustained by reactions against it."

The last of the three sequences identified by Bennett and Elman (2006) as alternatives to self-reinforcing processes is based on the concept of "reactive sequences," defined by Mahoney (2000: 526) as "chains of temporally ordered and causally connected events," where "each event in the sequence is both a reaction to antecedent events and a cause of subsequent events." Reactive sequences differ from any old "sequence of causally connected events" because they possess "an inherent logic in which one event naturally leads to another" (532). Unlike balancing or cyclical processes, moreover, reactive sequences do not feature one or more recurrent equilibria; instead, the "chain of tightly linked reactions and counter-reactions" (527) constantly moves the system in new directions. Consequently, reactive sequences may be diagrammed as $A \rightarrow B \rightarrow C \rightarrow D \rightarrow E$. While there is no self-reinforcement, early events are still crucial because "a small change in one of these events can accumulate over time and make a great deal of difference by the end of the sequence" (526).

That such "inherent logics" can vary a great deal complicates the identification of a precise set of conditions that cause an institution's entry into force to set in motion a reactive sequence. Even so, it is worth addressing two scenarios conducive to the triggering of reactive sequences characterized by different logics. The first is a situation in which the combination of deep social divisions and a rough balance of forces between large, competing groups prevents any of the institutional arrangements established along the way from achieving a modicum of stability. As in the sequences described above, the introduction of an institution favored by a group or coalition causes the intensification of the opposition to it, which succeeds in toppling and replacing the institution in question, only to cause a successful counterreaction, thereby setting the stage for another iteration of the cycle. In this case, moreover, both sides' lack of ideological commitment to a specific institution gives them the flexibility to experiment with different institutional arrangements and coalitional alignments to edge out the competition. The sequence, therefore, follows a logic of mutual adaptation, in which the adoption of a set of institutions "naturally" leads to another because it prompts the other side to intensify its mobilization and respond with institutional innovations of its own.

Another scenario that might give rise to a reactive sequence is characterized by high levels of social fragmentation, reflecting a society divided into multiple, relatively small but highly cohesive social groups that are fairly immune to the influence of others. In the absence of high levels of polarization, fragmentation leads to fluid coalitions that are constantly vulnerable to the defection of groups the other side can "poach" simply by offering a better deal. In this case, therefore, groups excluded from the initial winning coalition approach one of the groups supporting the existing set of rules, offering to replace the status quo with a new institutional arrangement that does more to further the group's interests or vision, only for their coalition and favored institution subsequently to succumb to the other side's counterreaction. The cycle of defections causes the prevailing institutional arrangements to change constantly, depending on the ever-shifting composition of minimum winning coalitions and based primarily on the interests/preferences of the groups that most recently switched sides.

While each of the three sequences discussed in Bennett and Elman (2006) is characterized by the failure of successive institutional arrangements to set in motion self-reinforcing mechanisms of reproduction, it should be pointed out that instability can itself be self-reinforcing, giving rise to something akin to the "institutional instability trap" (Helmke 2010; Levitsky and Murillo 2009: 123). The tendency of instability to beget instability has been highlighted in studies of regime instability in Latin America (Przeworski 2009) and elsewhere (Ferrara 2015), which have found that reversals from democracy to dictatorship by way of military coup heighten the instability of *future* democratic regimes, established upon the generals' return to the barracks. The phenomenon is rooted in the dynamics of power, as each reversal weakens pro-democracy forces and discourages investments in organizations and institutions that might otherwise increase the "quality" of democracy—thereby keeping the costs of toppling democratically elected governments low—as well as the logic of legitimation, as reversals to authoritarianism devalue constitutional rules and procedures, create a habituation to solving problems through extra-constitutional means, and compromise the support for democracy by making successive democratic regimes weak, inefficient, and constantly preoccupied with keeping existential threats at bay.

Similar dynamics can also conceivably provide cyclical processes, balancing processes, and reactive sequences with an element of self-reinforcement, the main consequence of which should be that establishing stable institutions becomes more difficult with each iteration of the cycle of reaction and counterreaction. In all three cases, overcoming instability requires the establishment of institutional arrangements capable of triggering mechanisms of reproduction that place the process on a different track. The deeper a set of institutions has traveled along a path of instability, however, it is reasonable to expect that changing course will require increasingly radical shifts in the organizational capacity, the incentive structure, and/or the preferences of the actors and groups involved, whether such changes are brought about by an "exogenous shock" or by cumulative, endogenous processes whose effect is negligible until a certain "threshold" or "tipping point" is reached (Pierson 2004: 82–86).

The Development of Institutions and the Issue of Enforcement

As a final note, it may be worth pointing out that the failure of an institution to trigger its own self-reinforcement may have as much to do with an organized challenge—the manifestation of which inaugurated each of the three sequences discussed above—as it does with the failure to enforce its provisions. As Levitsky and Murillo (2009) have noted, accounts of institutional reproduction in a path-dependent framework typically assume that institutions, once established, are actually enforced. Enforcement, in turn, is crucial to the emergence of the set of shared behavioral expectations required for institutions to structure social interactions. In practice, the assumption limits the applicability of theories of institutional development to a subset of wealthy countries governed by the "rule of law," where institutions more or less work as intended. In the rest of the world, conversely, a variety of reasons potentially account for the tendency of "parchment rules" (Carey 2000) to exist solely on paper. Institutions may be intentionally designed as "window dressing" in an attempt to bolster the domestic and international image of power holders who have no intention actually to submit to the rules in question. Alternatively, the failure to enforce the rules may be unintentional, reflecting either the lack of state capacity or, perhaps more commonly, the inability of actors vested with the formal authority to make the rules actually to enforce the compliance of privileged constituencies whose "real" (if extra-constitutional, unaccountable) power is leveraged to "evade laws or policies that allow disadvantaged groups to translate their political rights into claims for greater substantive equality" (Levitsky and Murillo 2009: 122, 120–22).

The prevalence of widely shared expectations that formal institutions will *not* be enforced, or may not remain in force for long, should undermine the capacity of newly established institutions to harness the dynamics of power and the dynamics of legitimation in their reproduction. Institutions that go unenforced are of no use in triggering increasing returns to power, for they confer no advantage that can be converted into greater power. Nor are they of any use in triggering increasing legitimation processes, as their likely failure to be met with high enough levels of compliance—or, at any rate, their perceived "*non*-absoluteness"—should prevent them from giving rise to preferences that reinforce the perceived appropriateness of the arrangement. Indeed, the mere expectation that an institution will not be enforced may be self-fulfilling, as the widespread noncompliance likely to result from it could render the enforcement of an institution too costly to be attempted in the first place.

For these reasons, societies where certain kinds of institutions have historically not been enforced should be expected to make it all the more difficult for newly adopted institutional arrangements ever to set in motion sequences of institutional reproduction. When the main obstacle is represented by the existence of groups whose "real," extra-constitutional authority or power exempts them from having to play by the rules, the stability of a country's basic institutional architecture is predicated on weakening the hold exercised by such groups. Incidentally, this consideration is at the heart of Tilly's (2007) argument that democracy can only take hold once "autonomous centers of power" are disbanded and government policies are effectively decoupled, in theory as well as in practice, from a society's prevailing "categorical inequalities." Even when no such groups are present, however, the expectation that institutions will not be enforced significantly complicates matters, for it renders the measures required to generate high levels of compliance necessarily more conspicuous and, therefore, more likely to invite a backlash. As Levitsky and Murillo (2009: 119) have argued, institutions that are not enforced may very well endure—indeed, they may endure precisely *because* they are not enforced. Even so, such institutions cannot be deemed to be meaningfully "stable," for the demise of something that exists only on paper is likely to necessitate nothing more than the stroke of a pen.

Institutional Reproduction: The Theory and Its Implications

Historical institutionalism first arrived on the scene of the study of political institutions in order to answer the "two fundamental questions" that North (1990: 92) asked with primary reference to economic institutions: "What determines the divergent patterns of evolution of societies, polities, or economies over time? And how do we account for the survival of economies"—as well as sociopolitical orders and regimes—"with persistently poor performance over long periods of time?" The mere fact that it raised such questions spoke to the distinctiveness of the approach, whose interest in *divergence* and *persistence* (the latter made problematic by patent inefficiency) marked a departure from traditions of inquiry that, for one reason or another, had predicted the convergence of social, political, and economic arrangements, as well as their tendency to exhibit growing efficiency over time, generally as a result of competition and learning.

The nature of the explanations that historical institutionalists provided for divergence and persistence further differentiated the approach from the existing alternatives. The parsimony of the explanation, as well as its capacity to make sense of the most disparate outcomes and phenomena, not only earned historical institutionalism a relatively large following but also assisted in the projection of the approach's influence beyond its adherents, as scholars in other camps were compelled to account for path dependence in their traditions' own terms, retrofitting their research programs so as to turn what they had not anticipated into something to be expected as a matter of course. Characteristically, leading historical institutionalists were eager to move on from the issues of divergence and persistence long before their audience was, perhaps in the knowledge that the approach's continued viability was predicated upon its capacity to explain more than just one aspect, however important, of the development of institutions. As noted, what followed was a marked shift in emphasis from stability to change and, with regard to the study of stability itself, a sustained effort to "put path dependence in its place" (Rixen and Viola 2014) by blaming on the concept's "stretching" and over-use the tendency of scholars to overlook the strategic adaptations and active maintenance often required to secure an institution's reproduction over time.

Partially because of the importance of stability in its own right and par-tially based on the widely accepted notion that explanations of institutional change must be built on a proper understanding of institutional reproduc-tion, this chapter revisited historical institutionalism's foundational concern in the hope of assembling an improved explanation accounting for the role played by the dynamics of legitimation as well as the dynamics of power. While foregrounding the mechanisms that govern the self-reinforcement of institutions, so as not to lose sight of the fact that their resilience is often the most striking aspect of a country's political development, the analysis carried out in this chapter placed a great deal of emphasis on what can go wrong, complete with an attempt to specify some of the alternative developmental sequences an institution's "failure to launch" might conceivably set in motion, most of which originate in a moderately successful, organized reaction to the institution's entry into force. The contribution made by the theory developed in these pages is arguably best assessed by means of a comparison with its principal rivals in the literature. Aside from verifying the extent to which this chapter's explanation of institutional reproduction does have, in Lakatos's (1978: 33–36) words, "some excess empirical content over its predecessor[s]," the goal is to establish whether "some of this excess empirical content is also corroborated."

One prominent alternative was articulated in Francis Fukuyama's bril-liant books *The Origins of Political Order* (2011) and *Political Order and Political Decay* (2014). In both volumes, Fukuyama (2011: 22–23, 446–48; 2014: 524–40) describes a "general mechanism of political development" whose workings resemble Charles Darwin's theory of evolution, equating moments of institutional choice with genetic "variations" that may or may not spread throughout a given population. Borrowing the logic that governs Darwin's mechanism of natural selection, Fukuyama (2011: 446) argues that the institutions best suited for the environments in which they operate—

"meaning those that could generate greater military and economic power"—have historically "survived and proliferated," displacing those that could not produce enough wealth and military might. What differentiates processes of political development from biological evolution is their openness and sensitivity to the effects of choice and purposive design, as well as the greater resilience generally exhibited by manmade institutions relative to "genetic traits." Fukuyama (447) attributes said resilience to the tendency of institutions, once established, to acquire "intrinsic value" in the minds of actors innately predisposed to follow rules, to reconcile themselves to social hierarchies, and constantly to seek out reassurances that they are doing "the right" (or, better yet, "the natural") thing. Elster (2007: 293–95) describes this type of evolutionary argument in the social sciences as combining "intentional variation" with "nonintentional selection." Indeed, it is worth pointing out that choice figures in Fukuyama's model during moments of institutional design/choice exclusively, as the adoption of a selection mechanism akin to natural selection *requires* us to assume that human agency plays no role in determining whether or not institutions will go on to "survive and proliferate" (Elster 2007: 274–78, 287–98). Beyond their promulgation, the fate of institutions is entirely a matter of how "suited" they are for the environment—and it is the environment itself, as opposed to the intentional agents who inhabit it, that *selects for* successful institutions or, rather, *selects against* the unsuccessful ones.

The theory of institutional reproduction assembled in this chapter repeatedly referenced Fukuyama's work, with which it shares, among other things, an emphasis on ideas as "fundamental causes," as well as a model of human motivation in which the desire for "recognition" often trumps considerations of material self-interest. Less compatible with the account presented in these pages is Fukuyama's "general mechanism of political development." It might be noted up front that Fukuyama's model suffers from the same issues highlighted in Elster's (2007: 295–98) general critique of evolutionary arguments purporting to explain the development of institutions and organizations. Just as in the competition between firms in market economies, choice is likely not as irrelevant to the development of institutions, beyond the design phase, as Fukuyama's evolutionary model *requires* us to assume. If, as Fukuyama (2014: 537–40) has argued, military competition did indeed serve as the engine of institutional development throughout most of human history, it seems reasonable to believe that human agency played a significant role in determining which institutions survived and which were eliminated. That is, while institutions may have needed to be minimally suited for their environment to survive, the ones that did survive may not always have been those that generated "greater military and economic power," especially if we consider that the fulfillment of an institution's potential on this count hinges on whether the relevant actors actually take advantage of the opportunities it provides. Similar considerations have led North (1990: 96) to observe that "throughout most of history the experience of the agents and the ideologies of the actors do not combine to lead to efficient outcomes." At any rate, whether or not the competition between societies actually did play out as Fukuyama has hypothesized at some point in the past, it is probably safe to say that an evolutionary argument of this kind has long since ceased to explain the development of political institutions. In a post-Westphalian and postcolonial world, economically backward and militarily weak nations are no longer in danger of being swallowed up by global or regional powers. Consequently, most no longer face the kind of evolutionary pressures Fukuyama has described.

Indeed, despite the unprecedented degree of "convergence of political forms" and the "higher rates of political change" made possible by the combination of economic development and modernization (Fukuyama 2014: 477), Fukuyama (2011: 454–57; 2014: 463–66) also highlights the persistence of "dysfunctional" institutions in contexts where actors or groups advantaged by the institution's distributive consequences remain steadfast in their defense of the status quo, when society as a whole would benefit from change. Another reason cited in Fukuyama (2011: 452; 2014: 463) for the persistence of "dysfunctional" institutions is the fact that formal rules and procedures tend to "reflect the cultural values of the societies in which they are established" (Fukuyama 2011: 14). Aside from the possibility that not all cultures hold values equally conducive to the accumulation of economic or military power, the conservativeness of most societies often stands in the way of efforts to retool institutions in the face of environmental changes responsible for a decline in their performance. Fukuyama (2014: 463) explains that "cognitive rigidity" often prevents relevant political actors from recognizing, or acknowledging, evidence pointing to the harmful consequences of institutions they treasure "for reasons that are not entirely rational," such as their perceived embodiment of values and beliefs deemed central to their countries' cultural distinctiveness and national pride.

In each of these respects, Fukuyama's account echoes North (1990), whose path-dependent explanation for "the divergent patterns of evolution of societies, polities, or economies over time," as well as the survival of institutions "with persistently poor performance over long periods of time" (92), emphasizes both (i) the fact that those with the power to design or reform institutions will often do so in an effort to promote their "own interest at the expense of the rest of society" (North 1990: 59; see also 99–100) and (ii) the crucial role played by the relevant actors' "historically derived perceptions" and "available mental constructs," which shape the choices they make by intervening on their desires—elevating the pursuit of certain priorities above others—as well as on the manner in which they "decipher a complex environment" to form their beliefs (95–96). "If the markets are incomplete, the information feedback is fragmentary at best, and transaction costs are significant," North (1990: 95) concludes, "then the subjective models of actors modified both by very imperfect feedback and by ideology will shape the path."

The theory of institutional reproduction assembled in this chapter improves on Fukuyama's (2011, 2014) as well as North's (1990) explanation for the persistence of institutions. In a world in which most countries' territorial integrity is guaranteed to the point of permitting some to dispense altogether with an armed external defense force—Costa Rica, which does not inhabit the friendliest of neighborhoods, abolished its military back in 1948—the domestic institutions most likely to endure are conceivably those that most "rapidly and decisively" set in motion self-reinforcing sequences of reproduction driven by the dynamics of power, the dynamics of legitimation, or, better yet, both dynamics working in a mutually reinforcing manner. For each of these dynamics, there is no reason to assume that the institutions best equipped to generate self-reinforcement are those that yield the best economic performance, the greatest military capabilities, or, for that matter, any outcome in which the interests of "society" as a whole trump powerful sectional interests. On the contrary, the explanation developed in these pages suggests that inefficiency and dysfunction are something more akin to the rule than the exception.

With regard to the dynamics of power, the contribution made in this chapter is limited to reaffirming the link that historical institutionalism has long drawn between path dependence and "potential path inefficiency" (Pierson 2000: 253). In particular, if the institutions most likely to endure are those that confer upon a certain social group or coalition a large enough advantage to provide them a motive to ensure the institution's reproduction, as well as an opportunity to institutionalize their position of advantage by leveraging increasing returns to power, the resulting perpetuation and expansion of asymmetries of power should conceivably produce greater levels of intergroup inequalities, as measured in wealth, status, and/or influence on the making of policy. In turn, the policies devised in that context and under such rules of the game are likely to promote the translation of "everyday categorical inequalities" (Tilly 2007: 111) into inequalities in the de facto enjoyment of variously significant rights of citizenship. And though inequality does have its principled apologists, the state's *active promotion* of existing inequalities cannot but engender dysfunction and inefficiency, to say nothing of "de-democratization." If properly enforced, more pluralistic, egalitarian institutions have themselves been found to benefit from endogenous self-enforcement or self-reinforcement (Acemoglu and Robinson 2012: 82–83, 302–34; North, Wallis, and Weingast 2009: 125–36; Przeworski 2006). Alas, institutions designed to promote greater equality in the access to power—or in the "rights and obligations" conferred upon the members of different social groups—often find it impossible to overcome the fierce resistance of privileged groups with the means to forestall the institutions' proper enforcement and gradual entrenchment (Levitsky and Murillo 2009: 122).

In this regard, then, while Tang (2011: 7) argues quite forcefully that a good theory of institutional development must account for the great progress achieved by human societies, the explanation assembled in this book—the point will be articulated more fully in the next two chapters—questions the existence of an evolutionary tendency *toward* greater progress. To be sure, the continuing exclusion of subordinate groups from their societies' arrangements of power may be expected more or less to guarantee that nondemocratic regimes will experience a degree of pressure for the development of more democratic, egalitarian, "inclusive" institutions, in measures that vary with the size of the discrepancy between the group's situation and its members' aspirations, as well as the resources the group has at its disposal to press demands of this kind. Moreover, the relative prosperity and freedom found in advanced liberal democracies remains something to which a great many people in the rest of the world still aspire. On balance, therefore, the diffusion effects regularly found in comparative studies (Brinks and Coppedge 2006; Gleditsch and Ward 2006; Weyland 2008) should continue to promote the adoption of democratic institutions in an increasing number of countries.

However, because the survival of these regimes and their capacity to promote greater equality rests on the defeat of elites opposed to majority rule, or the presence of elites who find it in their interest to grant, or reconcile themselves to the introduction of, such institutions, there are reasons to expect that their success will remain episodic. To the extent that "the arc of the moral universe," to use a celebrated formulation, does "bend towards justice," it is because the history of any given country is likely sooner or later to produce the economic conditions that help subordinates to displace old elites or to produce the political conditions where the adoption of democratic, "inclusive" institutions constitutes a workable settlement to the kind of conflict so prevalent in underdeveloped, unequal societies ruled by exclusive, "extractive" regimes. Then again, so long as the adoption of institutions that promote human progress rests, in essence, on having exhausted all of the alternatives, the diffusion of such institutions throughout the world is likely to remain as slow and as halting as it has been in recent decades. As Olson (1993: 573) memorably put it, "autocracy is prevented and democracy permitted by the accidents of history that leave a balance of power or stalemate—a dispersion of force and resources that makes it impossible for any one leader or group to overpower all of the others."

A more original contribution to the study of institutional reproduction was made in this chapter with regard to the dynamics of legitimation and their interaction with the dynamics of power. Broadly speaking, one of the main overarching lessons to be drawn from this chapter's analysis of the dynamics of legitimation is that institutions do not merely "reflect" shared cultural or ideological values and beliefs. Aside from their continuing capacity to produce, as Beetham (1991: 60–63) has proposed, the evidence required for their legitimation, the institutions most likely to benefit from processes of "increasing legitimation" are those that generate, by their own workings, the values and beliefs conducive to their reproduction, by structuring interactions in such a way as to yield high levels of compliance, encourage the diffusion of compliance by leveraging the conformist tendencies of those subject to its provisions, and activate "motivated" (Kunda 1990) cognitive processes of self-, group, and system justification.

The mechanism provided for the endogenous formation of preferences, values, and beliefs further differentiates the explanation assembled in this chapter from the theories of institutional development featured in Fukuyama (2011, 2014) and North (1990). Fukuyama (2011, 2014), for his part, does not consider this aspect of the normative force of institutions at all. And while North repeatedly cites the possibility that the "subjective mental constructs" informing individual decisions might be endogenous to the historical development of institutions (e.g., North 1990: 99), his account lacks a mechanism elucidating the recursive nature of the relationship between ideas and institutions, beyond passing references to "rationalization." This chapter's specification of the normative force of institutions down to its psychological micro-foundations, therefore, improves upon existing attempts to account for the causal force of ideas by demonstrating how the dynamic, recursive relationship between institutions and the relevant underlying preferences, values, and beliefs contributes to the institution's endogenous reinforcement or "self-reinforcement." Meanwhile, its exploration of the conditions in which the dynamics of legitimation are most likely triggered, as well as the conditions affecting the character of the interaction between the dynamics of power and the dynamics of legitimation, improves upon existing understandings of the manner in which frequently observed combinations of structure and contingency promote or hinder the reproduction of different kinds of institutions.

Once again, a key implication of the inquiry conducted into the dynamics of legitimation and their interaction with the dynamics of power is that the institutions most likely to generate self-reinforcement are not necessarily, nor perhaps even characteristically, those that produce the best outcomes for society as a whole. Insofar as institutional innovations result from a major shift in the main social groups' relative bargaining strength, as opposed to widespread changes in preferences, values, and beliefs (these are the two "sources of change" described in North 1990: 83), the values that such innovations are likely designed to promote are those that serve the interests of the group in question—that is, those designed either to increase support for the group's vision or to justify newly modified hierarchies of wealth, status, and power. As in the case of the dynamics of power, insofar as the institution does contribute to the diffusion of such ideas, the result is likely to be increased support for, or acceptance of, inequality, as well as for the translation of "categorical inequalities" into inequalities in the enjoyment of variously significant rights. Conversely, in places where elite, superordinate groups still command enough power and deference to mount effective reactions against the workings of institutions threatening their interests, institutions designed to actualize ideals of individual equality will find it especially hard to generate self-reinforcement or promote the diffusion of egalitarian ideas.

In this sense, the reason why ordinary people in developing nations often fail to defend democratic institutions, and in some cases participate in their demise, is not that such institutions *reflect* alien ideas incompatible with local values. It is rather that such institutions come into force in the presence of privileged constituencies that command a large enough reservoir of material resources and moral authority to prevent the diffusion of democratic values or the development of strong emotional attachments to democratic institutions. Popular support for democratic institutions can be undermined indirectly, by preventing democracy from working as advertised, or through direct appeals to local populations. But while the defense of "culture" often features prominently in public relations efforts designed to turn local populations against democracy, it is important to recognize that such efforts generally seek to emphasize not so much the *contents* of cultural values and beliefs, which are generally too ambiguous and contested to be dispositive one way or the other, but rather the sense of pride that local populations take in the presumed distinctiveness of their culture, said to face an existential threat in the diffusion of foreign ideas like those that democratic institutions are alleged to embody. More generally, to the extent that the institutions most likely to benefit from the workings of the dynamics of legitimation are those backed by the greatest amount of power—or, conversely, institutions that do not engender a reaction on the part of privileged constituencies determined to preserve existing inequalities—the logic of legitimation will in practice often benefit institutions that promote the interests and the values of a powerful minority, at the predictable expense of everyone else.

CHAPTER THREE

Institutional Decay

The Logic of Self-Undermining Processes

The development of an improved explanation of institutional decay—one governed by the dynamics of "power" and "delegitimation"—presents challenges of a different nature from those encountered in the analysis of institutional reproduction. Most obviously, while the literature seeking to account for the entrenchment and stability of institutions is so voluminous as to render the task of contributing original insights appear rather daunting, historical institutionalism has neglected the study of institutional decay to the point of requiring anyone interested in theorizing the phenomenon to formulate an explanation almost from scratch. Put differently, while the previous chapter sought to specify the microfoundations and triggering conditions for mechanisms of institutional reproduction driven by the familiar logic of "path dependence" and "self-reinforcement," no functional equivalent to these mechanisms exists in the literature on institutional decay. The reasons for the neglect extend beyond the long-standing tendency of historical institutionalists to overemphasize—and at times overstate—the stability of institutions. Indeed, the literature has largely continued to overlook the process of institutional decay in spite of its ongoing shift from the study of stability to the study of change. Certainly, the scholars involved deserve credit for redirecting the field's attention from "punctuated equilibrium" models to incremental, endogenous forms of institutional change. Even so, it is hard to justify the literature's continuing neglect of the process by which institutions come unstuck, whether or not their decay actually ushers in their replacement. For while institutional change does not require, or inevitably follow from, institutional decay, the incremental, endogenous process that potentially leads to an institution's breakdown is sufficiently important in its own right to merit an explanation, as scholars in different traditions of inquiry have long recognized (e.g., Acemoglu and Robinson 2012; Diamond 2005; Fukuyama 2014).

In that endeavor, there is every reason to expect that the analytical tools for which historical institutionalism is so well known will prove just as valuable as they have been in the study of institutional reproduction.

What might a "historical institutionalist" explanation of institutional decay look like? As a preliminary step, recall that this study has defined "institutional decay" as the opposite of "institutional reproduction"—that is, as the process by which institutions *lose*, as opposed to *acquire*, "value and stability," as reflected in their capacity to generate high levels of compliance as well as their vulnerability to threats to their continued existence. It follows from this consideration that institutional decay could be driven by temporal dynamics that reverse the logic said to govern mechanisms of institutional reproduction. As reiterated in the previous chapter, while the literature on historical institutionalism has recently highlighted the need to look beyond path dependence to explain stability, the fact remains that the extraordinary resilience frequently exhibited by institutions cannot be properly understood without reference to their capacity to generate self-reinforcement. In turn, having already adopted Rixen and Viola's (2014) definition of "self-reinforcement" as an endogenous, "increasing returns" process by which a certain outcome becomes increasingly entrenched over time, this study also derives a "general mechanism" of institutional decay from Rixen and Viola's (2014) treatment of "self-undermining" processes.

For the purposes of this book, a self-undermining process of institutional decay is an endogenous, "decreasing returns" process by which a particular institution becomes increasingly unstable or irrelevant to the behavior of actors subject to its provisions. More precisely, a self-undermining process of institutional decay is one in which an erosion in an institution's value and/or stability increases the probability of further deteriorations in the institution's value and/or stability, by endogenously modifying the behavior of relevant actors so as to reduce their compliance with the institution's behavioral prescriptions/proscriptions. This study's identification of institutional decay with the logic of self-undermining processes—in much the same way that self-reinforcing processes are conceived as the main engine of institutional reproduction—resonates with major works on the subject. Greif and Laitin (2004: 639), for instance, characterize self-reinforcing and self-undermining processes as temporal sequences where the range of situations in which the behavior associated with an institution is "self-enforcing" (i.e., it constitutes an optimal behavioral response from which none of the individuals involved has an incentive to deviate) expands or contracts, respectively. Fukuyama's

(2014: 469–71) description of the process by which institutions decay is also consistent with the logic of self-undermining processes described above.

The main contention articulated in this chapter is that, just as self-reinforcing sequences of institutional reproduction can be driven by temporal dynamics governed by the logics of power and legitimation, so can self-undermining sequences of institutional decay be driven by temporal dynamics that reverse the logics of power and legitimation. The full specification of a "delegitimation explanation" of institutional decay, as well as an integrated theory accounting for the interaction of the logics of power and delegitimation, will be taken on in the next sections. What is worth stating up front is that this chapter identifies the engine of a self-undermining process of institutional decay in the recursive nature of the relationship between growing levels of noncompliance with an institution's provisions and the institution's decreased capacity to produce the results (or "returns") necessary to sustain it, whether the returns in question are measured in terms of material benefits or the fulfillment of normatively (i.e., morally, ideologically, etc.) desirable objectives. Growing noncompliance causes an institution to produce fewer returns, thereby causing even greater levels of noncompliance.

When the self-undermining sequence is driven by the "dynamics of power," then, it is likely to take the following form:

(i)   Reversals or shifts in the distribution of power and/or material resources cause levels of noncompliance with an institution's behavioral expectations to increase, perhaps especially among constituencies disadvantaged by the institution's "power-distributional" consequences.

(ii) The resulting deterioration in the institution's capacity reliably to structure behavior undermines its capacity to deliver the returns required to reproduce prevailing asymmetries of power, preserve the cohesion of ruling coalitions, and administer the rewards/penalties that incentivize compliance.

(iii) As noncompliance becomes more generalized, it further harms the institution's performance and its capacity to contribute to the reproduction of existing relations of power, encouraging even greater noncompliance, and so on.

Conversely, when the self-undermining sequence is driven by the "dynamics of delegitimation," it is likely to take the following form:

(i)   Changes in preferences regarding an institution's appropriateness, and/or changes in the prevailing subjective assessments of the institution's performance, cause levels of noncompliance with an institution's behavioral expectations to increase among newly disillusioned constituencies.

(ii) The resulting deterioration in the institution's capacity reliably to structure behavior undermines its capacity to produce outcomes consistent with the needs and normative preferences of relevant constituencies, thereby eroding its legitimacy.

(iii) The institution's delegitimation leads to even greater noncompliance; increased noncompliance further undermines the institution's capacity to produce outcomes consistent with the needs and normative preferences of relevant constituencies, which erodes the institution's legitimacy and encourages even greater noncompliance, and so on.

It goes without saying that, in practice, a self-undermining process of institutional decay is likely to involve both dynamics working in conjunction with one another. For while an erosion in an institution's legitimacy undermines its capacity to generate the returns required to reproduce asymmetries of power, the disruption wrought on the institution's capacity to reproduce existing relations of power conceivably damages its legitimacy.

Having identified institutional decay with a self-undermining, decreasing returns process, the specification of a general explanation for the phenomenon can also be said to present challenges quite similar to those tackled in the analysis of institutional reproduction. On the one hand, with respect to the process of institutional decay as much as to the process of institutional reproduction, it is best to avoid the determinism for which explanations relying on path dependence and other temporal dynamics characterized by non-constant returns to scale are frequently criticized. In the specific instance, while institutions may well carry "the seeds of their own demise," the successful activation of "contradictions and challenges" with the potential to disrupt their "reliable reproduction" (Thelen 2006: 155) is far from inevitable. Nor are self-undermining sequences of institutional decay—once triggered—irreversible. On the contrary, the (in)capacity of institutions to avoid, withstand, or reverse self-undermining processes has a lot to do with the outcome of strategic interactions between the supporters and opponents of the status quo. Following the example set in recent historical institutionalist accounts of institutional change, this chapter emphasizes the actions of individuals and groups—whether they are motivated by power-distributional concerns or by considerations of ideology and/or social identity—actively engaged in attempts to destabilize undesired institutions and undermine their capacity to structure behavior, as well as the actions of individuals and groups engaged in efforts to shore up institutions whose "value and stability" is threatened.

On the other hand, the considerations made in the previous chapter with regard to the existing literature's failure fully to account for the manner in which the "dynamics of legitimation" contribute to the process of institutional reproduction also apply to the manner in which the dynamics of *dele*gitimation drive processes of institutional decay. As Mahoney (2000: 525) has explained, "institutional transformation" in a legitimation framework "results from changes in actors' subjective beliefs and preferences, not from changes in the power distribution of actors," as "inconsistencies in the multiplicity of cognitive frameworks that are predominant in society" provide "a basis for actors to adopt new subjective evaluations and moral codes concerning appropriateness," potentially leading to a "breakdown in consensual beliefs regarding the reproduction of an institution." Once again, however, a more satisfactory explanation for the phenomenon requires a finer-grained understanding of the mechanisms that drive it, as well as a sense of the circumstances most likely to set the process of delegitimation in motion, beyond Mahoney's observation that "the events that trigger such changes in subjective perceptions and thus declines in legitimacy may be linked to structural isomorphism with rationalized myths, declines in institutional efficacy or stability, or the introduction of new ideas by political leaders" (525). The remainder of this chapter addresses these issues in turn, before turning to the interaction between the dynamics of power and the dynamics of delegitimation.

A Delegitimation Explanation of Institutional Decay

In their landmark contribution to the literature on incremental, endogenous forms of institutional change, Mahoney and Thelen (2010: 5) singled out approaches that rely on the "logic of appropriateness" for having an especially difficult time accounting for disruptions to the process of institutional reproduction not attributable to "an exogenous entity or force," having largely failed to produce "a set of general propositions about what properties of institutional scripts make some of them, at some times, more vulnerable than others." Other approaches can hardly be said to fare any better on this count—by Greif and Laitin's (2004: 633) own admission, the assumptions upon which rationalist accounts are typically grounded also point to the "inescapable conclusion" that any disruption to a self-enforcing institutional equilibrium must have "an exogenous origin." Still, accounts that rely on behavioral models influenced by "culturalist" or "sociological institutionalist" assumptions are themselves bound to treat the notion of endogenous change as a "contradiction in terms," pending the formulation of a convincing explanation of how the values, norms, and beliefs responsible for informing considerations of appropriateness develop, over time, in the absence of exogenous pressures or shocks to the system. Fortunately, a number of propositions that identify potential vulnerabilities in the "properties of institutional scripts" *can* be derived from the existing literature. This section builds upon such insights in an effort to specify sequences of institutional decay governed by the logic of delegitimation.

How Institutions Come Unstuck: Erosions of Legitimacy

A useful starting point for the development of a delegitimation explanation of institutional decay is provided by the considerations featured in Beetham's (1991) analysis. Beetham (109) specifies two possibilities for how a relation of power—and the rules that govern said relation of power—might experience an "erosion of legitimacy" that threatens to usher in a crisis of authority. Both scenarios, each of which also features, in one form or another, in other well-known accounts of the issue, identify in the rationale for the existence of institutions their principal vulnerability. First, an institution or a system of institutions, such as those constitutive of a "political regime" (Skanning 2006: 13) or a "socio-political order" (North, Wallis, and Weingast 2009: 1), might become "chronically unable" to meet the interests of subordinates (similar arguments appear in Easton 1965: 230; Lenski 1966: 180–81; Levi 1988: 52–53; Tainter 1988: 27–28, 36–37). Second, an institution or a system of institutions might cease to produce outcomes reconcilable with official or otherwise prevailing justifications for existing inequalities or might begin routinely to violate its own principles regarding the ultimate source of authority, the manner in which authority is exercised, or the purposes for which authority is wielded (see also Lenz and Viola 2017).

While this chapter has identified processes of institutional decay with the logic of endogenous, self-undermining sequences, the "erosions of legiti-macy" responsible for setting the process in motion do not necessarily origi-nate in developments that are endogenous to the workings of the institutions involved. For one thing, institutions might become "chronically unable" to meet the interests of subordinates as a result of exogenous, environmental transformations that disrupt their workings or as a result of an exogenously driven shift in the manner in which subordinates define their interests, which might in turn lead to a proliferation of demands that the system was not originally designed or expected to meet. On this point, Huntington (1965; see also Fukuyama 2011: 450–53) famously emphasized the danger presented by the rigidity of institutions during periods of rapid social change, especially in circumstances where the institutions themselves are not flexible or adaptable enough to deal with a surge in the demands of subordinates. As Fukuyama (2011: 458) has put it, this was what Huntington believed "was causing insta-bility among the newly independent countries of the developing world during the 1950s and '60s, with their incessant coups, revolutions, and civil wars." Likewise, the legitimacy of institutions responsible for the reproduction of systemic inequalities in power, status, and/or wealth might suffer as a result of exogenous, environmental shifts that disrupt the institution's capacity to structure behavior as intended or as a result of exogenously driven shifts in the beliefs in terms of which the institution had previously been justified, which might raise questions about the justice of existing inequalities and, therefore, the desirability of outcomes that the institution continues to pro-duce. As Beetham (1991: 109) puts it, "The latter will happen when social changes taking place within the society, or the evidence available from other societies, reveals that what had previously been assumed to be a 'natural' form of social organization, or one based upon 'natural' differences, is in fact socially constructed."

Even so, "erosions of legitimacy" of the kind described in Beetham (1991) certainly can have endogenous causes. On the one hand, as Scott (1990: 105) pointed out, "the very operation of a rationale for inequality creates a poten-tial zone of dirty linen that, if exposed, would contradict the pretensions of legitimate domination." Saul Alinsky recognized in what Scott (105–6) referred to as "critiques within the hegemony" a crucial vulnerability for any relation of power, urging those who challenge the status quo on behalf of the "Have Nots" to take actions designed repeatedly to bait "the Haves" into vio-lating—or, better yet, into actually following—their own rules (Alinsky 1972:

128). On the other hand, an institution might lose the capacity to meet the interests of subordinates or to produce outcomes consistent with its founding principles, in part or in whole, as a result of its own latent "contradictions and challenges" (Thelen 2006: 155). Consider, for instance, a scenario in which an institution becomes "chronically unable" to meet the interests of subordinates as a result of a loss in a superordinate group's ability or will to serve the broader good—Gramsci (1977: 2012) appears to have had in mind a situation of this kind when he referenced the possibility that a dominant group might lose its "progressive" role in "mak[ing] an entire society truly advance," thereby precipitating a breakdown in its own ideological hold. While a host of exogenous factors can intervene to reduce a dominant group's capacity to deliver on the promises made to subordinates, the will to do so may decline simply as a by-product of the group's own success, which typically owes a great deal to the workings of the existing "rules of power."

More generally, Scott (1985: 338) has argued that "the most common form of class struggle arises from the failure of a dominant ideology to live up to the implicit promises it necessarily makes." For if these "implicit promises" are crucial to the legitimation of inequalities of power, reassuring subordinates that their interests will not be neglected, the normative order stipulated in a dominant or official ideology also provides subordinates "with the means, the symbolic tools, the very ideas for a critique that operates entirely within the hegemony." When such promises are broken, the status quo is left vulnerable to the charge that its failure to live up to its own "promissory note"—as Dr. Martin Luther King Jr.'s historic "I Have a Dream" speech characterized the vision of universal equality enshrined in the founding documents of the United States of America—constitutes a breach of the social contract serious enough to release subordinates from the obligation to provide continued consent and cooperation. While a more comprehensive analysis of the circumstances that might trigger erosions of legitimacy will be undertaken in the next section, it might be ventured up front—following Moore (1978: 35, 470; see also Scott 1976: 176–79; 1985: 236–40)—that the broken promises most likely to produce a backlash of this sort include those that had previously assured subordinates of a modicum of personal security and social order, as well as those that had previously guaranteed subordinates that they would have the means to provide for their families and "play a respectable role" in their communities, leading to the "collapse or partial breakdown of daily routines."

The Microfoundations of Increasing Delegitimation Processes

At first blush, the foregoing account of the manner in which "erosions of legitimacy" take place might appear somewhat difficult to reconcile with the psychology in which the theoretical framework elaborated in these pages is grounded. Specifically, if delegitimation is a process of "recategorization, whereby what was previously legitimate now becomes illegitimate" (Kelman 2001: 57–58), and if the legitimation of institutions really does rely, as suggested in the previous chapter, on the tendency of individuals to rationalize features of the system by overlooking evidence of its injustice, what does it take for the same individuals to start doing the opposite? After all, while the status quo's capacity to serve the interests of society and produce outcomes consistent with its own rationale for inequalities may occasionally become so obvious as to make it impossible for subjects to convince themselves otherwise, under normal circumstances the evidence of its failures should be a great deal more ambiguous and, therefore, susceptible to further rationalization. Indeed, Pierson (2000: 260–61) identified in the "complexity and opacity of politics"—which, among other things, makes assigning responsibility for a society's successes and failures prohibitively difficult for even the most informed citizens—one of the main reasons why path dependence is as prevalent in the realm of politics as it is in the economy. Similarly, Fukuyama (2014: 463) identifies in cognitive rigidity one of the reasons why human beings often fail to consider reforms in the presence of clear signs of an institution's growing dysfunction. As Lenz and Viola (2017: 951) have pointed out, "legitimacy judgments" tend to be "robust, up to a threshold," because the heuristics employed to navigate ambiguities and minimize cognitive strain make people quite conservative when it comes to processing new information, which tends to be "rationalized by existing schemata" (952).

Of course, the issue is relatively unproblematic in situations where significant transformations in the values and the beliefs in terms of which an institution is justified precede changes in the prevailing assessments of its legitimacy—perhaps as a result of social change and/or the rise of new leaders and movements—as the "motivated" (Kunda 1990) switch from positive to negative evaluations is likely to follow regardless. In cases where underlying values and beliefs have not undergone significant change, however, the switch from a positive to a negative evaluation of the status quo's performance—or its record of upholding prevailing standards of legitimacy—based on a dispassionate analysis of the evidence is likely to be complicated further by fears of social sanction or disapproval, especially in situations conducive to "pluralistic ignorance" (Elster 2007: 375–80). Worse yet, the switch may threaten the self-image of those with a history of cooperation and compliance, who are likely determined not to appear (in the eyes of others as well as their own) as turncoats or carpetbaggers.

As Trivers (2011: 141) has put it, the "psychology of self-deception" works "in service of maintaining and projecting a positive self-view." If an institution's delegitimation requires that those who deem it legitimate overcome the motivation to rationalize its existence, therefore, the switch should happen most readily when the social and psychological pressures to rationalize the status quo are somehow reversed, to the point that continued cooperation and compliance—and the maintenance of attitudes that define such behavior as appropriate—come to threaten one's social standing and self-image more than the adoption of positions and behaviors that are clearly at odds with one's previous stances and actions. Conceivably, the reversal in question might be expected to take place as a result of perceived changes in the attitudes and/or the behavior of peers, close associates, and authority figures. As Haidt (2012: 56) pointed out, people tend to change their beliefs less as a result of evidence-based arguments than as a consequence of the social influence exerted by recognized authorities and the social pressure applied by those whose approval they seek. Similarly, Kelman (2001: 58) attributes a crucial role to "the actions or pronouncements of authorities of one or another kind"—whose powers of persuasion, per Cialdini (2016: 165), are likely to stem from presumed trustworthiness and expertise—in triggering, or accelerating, the process. Within the "new institutionalist" literature, Garud, Hardy, and McGuire (2007) as well as Béland (2005, 2009) have focused on the way institutional/political "entrepreneurs" go about disrupting their audience's perception of existing institutions, often as a prelude to "the social construction of the need to reform" (Béland 2005: 11).

In turn, the "actions or pronouncements" devised in an attempt to delegitimize existing institutions are most likely to prove effective when they "draw on dispositions that are structurally or historically available within the society" (Kelman 2001: 59)—or, in Mahoney's (2000: 525) words, when they draw on "inconsistencies in the multiplicity of cognitive frameworks that are predominant in society." Aside from the fact that people are generally biased against messages that are completely at odds with preexisting values and beliefs (Petty and Briñol 2010: 228), the reason why appeals of this kind can effectively provide "a basis for actors to adopt new subjective evaluations and moral codes concerning appropriateness" (Mahoney 2000: 525) is that their familiarity offers the best hope that "the associations they trigger are favorable to change," as required for the success of all "influence attempts" (Cialdini 2016: 7). Better yet, to the extent that the target audience is in any way committed to the values and beliefs that make up the "dispositions" and "cognitive frameworks" referenced in the appeals, their recall and "amplification" (Béland 2009: 706) should predispose its members to embrace a message that helps them restore a sense of consistency between current attitudes and preexisting commitments (Cialdini 2016: 169). On a related note, to the extent that agents of change seek to discredit an existing institution by exploiting their target audience's susceptibility to a comparison with different societies, the effectiveness of the comparison has been found to be greatest when it involves very similar societies, as well as the selection of "target standards" that facilitate the recall of accessible knowledge most likely to bias a recipient's evaluation in favor of the messenger's preferred conclusion (Mussweiler 2003).

Once "predisposed" or made "open" to change, actors are most effectively motivated to shift their subjective evaluations of existing institutions, revise their appraisals of the appropriateness of existing institutions, or even adopt new standards of appropriateness as a consequence of appeals they find personally relevant (Petty and Briñol 2010: 228; Cialdini 2016: 110; Izuma 2013: 4). If, as previewed above, the main challenge before anyone wishing to delegitimize an institution or a set of institution is to reverse the social and psychological pressure to rationalize the status quo, success is likely predicated upon their ability to impress upon their audience the dangers that continued cooperation/compliance presents to *their* self-image and social standing, as well as the boost both are poised to receive as a result of changing course. Accomplishing the former conceivably entails heightening the recipients' fear of the social sanction and personal regret they are likely to experience if they remain steadfast in their support of the status quo; accomplishing the latter, instead, conceivably entails drawing the recipients' attention not only to the rewards that jumping ship will bring in terms of social approval and self-esteem but also to the inherent scarcity of such rewards—in other words, their tendency to diminish with every person that jumps on the bandwagon. In both cases, of course, the appeal can only be successful to the extent that a plausible case can be made that the status quo's demise is only a matter of time.

At any rate, once individuals are properly motivated to make the switch—and, if possible, publicly committed to doing so—they will have no trouble turning up evidence of the status quo's illegitimacy, given the tendency of motivation to bias our cognitive process in favor of information confirming whatever judgment we have already reached. Our "totalitarian ego" (Greenwald 1980) can generally be counted on to restore a sense of consistency after the fact, in a process likely to feature the revision, the suppression, or even the fabrication of memories (Trivers 2011: 143–45), possibly to the point that one might convince oneself never to have supported—at least not genuinely—the status quo. In this and other settings, the reason why victory has a thousand fathers and defeat is an orphan is likely not—or not exclusively—because people consciously misrepresent their past opinions or conduct in the pursuit of some social or material benefit. It is rather because human beings have an innate propensity to fool themselves "the better to fool others" (Trivers 2011; but, see also Elster 2007: 289). Studies of "recall error" (Joslyn 2003: 441; see also Smith 1984: 645) have also shown that a person's awareness of the popularity of certain policy positions tends to bias the recall of his or her prior attitudes—insofar as "people rely on heuristics to reconstruct their cognitive autobiographies," "the vision of popular preferences presented by the media can become a surrogate for one's prior preferences."

As it turns out, the process by which individuals may be expected to overcome the tendency to rationalize the workings of existing institutions bears out the emphasis that Beetham (1991), Scott (1990), Levi (1988), and others have placed on erosions of legitimacy as caused by an institution's failure variously to live up to its stated rationale. That is, if individuals are most susceptible to appeals that seek to leverage preexisting commitments, dispositions, and mental associations, one can hardly do better than craft a message that zeros in on the failure of institutions to deliver on clear promises, to work as advertised, or to uphold widely shared conceptions of procedural and distributive justice. Of course, at this point one might object that messages of this kind can be persuasive regardless of an institution's actual performance. But while it is quite right to expect that *perception*—and the motivations that drive it—matters more than the underlying reality, there is also good reason not to lose sight of the contributions that reality itself makes to the effectiveness of influence attempts.

Indeed, a battery of fairly recent experiments has confirmed that, to the extent that the introduction of new information can prompt an individual to change his or her judgment of a particular position, policy, or institution, its impact is strongest and most durable when the individual in question compares the newly available, discrediting information with the information that had previously justified his or her support (Albarracin et al. 2012). Crucially, however, the comparison only produces this effect when the new information is "difficult to argue against"—failing that, it can actually help reinforce the initial judgment (46). Lenz and Viola (2017: 952–53) also point to evidence that individuals are most likely to reexamine an institution's legitimacy when the information challenging existing judgments is sufficiently "new, strong, salient, and rapidly arriving" to trigger "negative emotions and cognitive conflict," as a result of which the individuals in question tend to be more "reflective" and "analytical." The increasingly "post-factual" nature of politics notwithstanding, appeals designed to delegitimize an existing institution by drawing the audience's attention to the discrepancy between its workings and its original rationale should, all else being equal, prove most compelling to the greatest number of people when supported by incontrovertible evidence of the institution's *actual* failings.

Whatever the reason behind the shift in values, preferences, and/or subjective appraisals, the actors in question may be expected to reconsider their compliance with the behavioral requirements of institutions they have come to regard as illegitimate—and all the more so "as dissatisfaction increases" (Levi 1988: 53–54). Whether or not this translates into actual noncompliance conceivably turns on a variety of factors. As Greif and Laitin (2004: 637) have noted, "There are good reasons that individuals would continue to follow past patterns of behavior." The tendency to let past behavior guide current behavior, the expectation that others around them will not change *their* behavior, and/or the difficulties involved in coordinating a behavioral change with like-minded people might cause actors to continue to act in compliance with an institution they no longer deem legitimate. Considerations of a similar nature led Beetham (1991: 109) to caution that "the possibility of communication with others and an autonomous space relatively protected from the influence of the powerful" is crucial to both the diffusion of attitudes and the coordination of behavior in opposition to the status quo. Likewise, Scott's (1990: 118–19) analysis underscored the opportunities for effective communication and coordination provided by the existence of a "space insulated from control and surveillance"—where, among other things, subordinates may develop a common meaning for shared experiences.

Assuming that such opportunities exist, continued compliance rests on the capacity of superordinate groups to compel it or otherwise incentivize it. The fact that an institution or a system of institutions can no longer count on the "quasi-voluntary" compliance of a sizable portion of the population, however, is likely to have far-reaching consequences regardless. Coercing the disaffected into complying with the requirements of an institution they had once willingly abided by requires the redirection of substantial resources away from other priorities. In turn, as the amount of resources required to ensure widespread, high-quality cooperation and compliance increases, so do the risks of further delegitimizing a society's institutions. Subordinates, in fact, are likely to resent the increasingly stringent measures enacted to monitor and sanction their behavior. At the same time, cracks might appear inside the ruling coalitions as portions of it object to the sacrifices they are asked to make to enforce the status quo, while the growing inefficiency with which the state's resources are allocated threatens the legitimacy the existing political order enjoys on the basis of its performance.

Institutional Decay and the Dynamics of Delegitimation

Given the contentiousness likely to characterize the selection of countermeasures, as well as the risks presented by the most effective among them, an institution's delegitimation will in practice often result in growing noncompliance or at any rate in the declining quality of cooperation. Regardless of whether the root causes of the institution's delegitimation are exogenous, endogenous, or a combination of the two, growing noncompliance can set in motion an endogenous, self-undermining process marked by "increasing delegitimation." As previewed in this chapter's introduction, higher levels of noncompliance cause the institution concerned to lose the capacity to structure behavior in the manner required for it to continue to work as intended. In turn, as institutions lose the capacity to satisfy the needs or the normative preferences of various constituencies, their legitimacy should deteriorate even further, damaging the institution's capacity to elicit compliance and deliver valued outcomes. If left undisturbed, the process ushers in the institution's thorough delegitimation, stripping away what "value" and "stability" it may once have enjoyed.

Aside from accelerating the process, the factors theorized in the last chapter to account for the "normative force" of institutions—namely, the tendency of individuals to conform to the behavior of those around them and to rationalize their behavior by retroactively adjusting their preferences and beliefs—may actually cause delegitimation to spill over to other institutional domains. Insofar as subordinates are not policed so aggressively—by the state or by their own social groups—as to effectively prevent them from expressing their views and from communicating with others, the social pressure to comply should conceivably attenuate as more people around them reject an institution's legitimacy. Indeed, as dissatisfaction grows more widespread, and as more and more people take actions that express or imply the *withdrawal* of consent, noncompliance should spread even to people whose underlying preferences and subjective evaluations have not changed. Among other things, "more people are likely to begin to break the law" as an increasing number of people "break the law and get away with it" (Levi 1988: 54) simply as a function of the fact that human beings generally dislike being "played for suckers." As noncompliance spreads, the same dynamics said to account for "spirals of silence" within fairly cohesive social groups might actually end up conspiring, in time, to make various constituencies appear more unified than they actually are in their *dissatisfaction* with the status quo.

What is more, to the extent that those who engage in acts of noncompliance feel the need to adjust their underlying preferences and beliefs accordingly, the process of self-justification can be expected to harden their perception of an institution's illegitimacy as well as the illegitimacy of institutions that are "isomorphic" with the one in question (Lenz and Viola 2017: 957). In this way, the process of delegitimation threatens to spill over to other institutions—its potential to snowball into the delegitimation of an entire political system conceivably determined by the degree to which the institutions concerned are central to the political system's institutional architecture. Certainly, the chain of events that leads from the delegitimation of a single institution to a full-blown crisis of authority that ends up threatening an entire sociopolitical order is neither inevitable nor irreversible. A full accounting of the available countermeasures, however, requires a better understanding of the circumstances in which delegitimation processes of institutional decay are set in motion, as well as a better appreciation of the workings of the interaction between the dynamics of delegitimation and the dynamics of power. The remainder of this chapter takes on these issues in turn.

Setting in Motion Sequences of Increasing Delegitimation

The specification of a self-undermining sequence of institutional decay driven by the dynamics of delegitimation also raises questions analogous to those answered with regard to processes of institutional reproduction. First, is it possible to identify a set of circumstances that reliably affect the likelihood that the dynamics of delegitimation will be set in motion? Second, is it possible to identify circumstances that reliably affect the "rapidity and decisiveness" with which said dynamics, once triggered, will bring about a decline in an institution's value and stability and possibly come to threaten the reproduction of "isomorphic" or closely related institutions, if not the entirety of a society's "rules of power"?

The previous section featured several references to the circumstances in question, reflecting the difficulty of examining causal mechanisms in isolation from the context in which they operate, but left it for this section to attempt a more systematic and more comprehensive treatment. At the cost of some redundancy, the same caveats made in the last chapter with regard to the indeterminacy surrounding the circumstances affecting whether, how rapidly, and how decisively the dynamics of legitimation are set in motion, as well as the effect that certain sets of circumstances have on the legitimacy of political institutions, also apply to this discussion. An additional caveat is that, as the discussion above has acknowledged, the process by which individuals turn their backs on institutions previously supported as legitimate requires that they be properly motivated to do so, which is only in part a function of "objective," evidence-based considerations about the manner in which the institutions in question operate and the results they produce. While some consideration will be reserved for the circumstances that affect the motivation to entertain arguments aiming to discredit existing institutions, the ways in which such motivations are formed are so varied and idiosyncratic as to foreclose the possibility of a full accounting.

From Legitimation to Delegitimation: General Considerations

The multiple references made in the previous section to circumstances conducive to the delegitimation of institutions point to the three major ways in which an institution's performance can set in motion endogenous, self-undermining processes of institutional decay driven by the dynamics of delegitimation. Each may be said to constitute a violation of the terms in which the existence of particular "rules of power" is justified and made acceptable to those least advantaged by their distributive consequences, in keeping with the expectation that widespread "moral anger" is most frequently observed as a consequence of "violations of the social contract" (Moore 1978: 493).

First, as noted above, processes of increasing delegitimation can often be traced back to an institution's or a set of institutions' failure to live up to their "implicit promises" (Scott 1985: 338)—that is, their failure to meet the needs of subordinates or their failure to limit the extent to which the outcomes they produce favor sectional interests at the expense of the interests of society as a whole. As others have recognized, the legitimation of the most exploitative and unequal of power relations typically requires that meaningful concessions be made to the general interest, as well as to the interests of subordinates, whose continued fulfillment requires that superordinate groups make genuine sacrifices and exercise of a measure of self-restraint, as opposed to simply "blow smoke" in the faces of subordinates (335; see also Scott 1990: 77, 103). Meeting such "output expectations," which can be of a material as well as a nonmaterial nature, imposes on a society's leadership "a never-ending need to mobilize resources" in order to maintain a level of support in excess of what the simple "manipulation of ideological symbols" can guarantee (Tainter 1988: 28). The chief sources of this sort of "output failure" (Easton 1965: 230) may be characterized, in Beetham's (1991: 135) words, as "manifest failure of performance" and "manifest particularity."

A second, alternative way in which an institution or a set of institutions may be expected to set in motion processes of increasing delegitimation is by violating existing norms regarding distributive or procedural justice. On the distributive side, Beetham (1991: 77–82) focused on the damage that the "rightfulness" of institutions sustain as a result of their failure to produce outcomes reconcilable with prevailing ideals regarding the sources of social inequalities—which he referred to as "principles of differentiation"—whether by empowering the presumed "undeserving" or by disempowering the presumed "deserving." On the procedural side, though different societies and different systems of government may be founded on different sets of principles regarding what constitutes equitable participation in the making of policies and rules, or their equitable enforcement, the violation of such principles should nonetheless contribute to discrediting an institution or system of institutions in similar ways. As Levi (1988: 52) has found, "The failure of rulers to live up to the prevailing norms of fairness undermines compliance."

Possibly deserving of being in a category of their own are those situations in which institutions violate prevailing ideas regarding what constitutes the proper "authoritative source of power." Once again, societies vary—and have varied historically—with regard to what is considered the ultimate source of (sovereign) power, as well as the rules and procedures that constitute the proper expression of particular sources of sovereign power. Famously, changes in beliefs concerning "the source of political authority"—above all, its location "in the people rather than in the historical pedigree of the ruling dynasty"—have had, as Beetham (1991: 134) puts it, "profound consequences for the territorial organization of states and for the spatial distribution of power within them, as well as for the rules governing access to political office itself." Messages alleging that the existing rules no longer work in accordance with a widely recognized source of authority, moreover, are a mainstay of the efforts often made by dissidents to assemble a critique of the status quo whose "within the hegemony" (Scott 1990: 105–6) nature can appeal to subordinates and members of the ruling coalition alike, while complicating efforts by the powerful to discredit or suppress the messenger.

The previous section made reference to a host of reasons why we should expect that increasing delegitimation processes will most frequently be set in motion in contexts characterized by the failure of an institution or a system of institutions to deliver the results promised to important constituencies, to live up to shared standards of distributive and procedural justice, or to operate in accordance with prevailing ideas regarding the ultimate source of authority. Of course, such "failures" on the part of institutions to work as required by the terms of something akin to a "social contract" only matter to the extent that there are leaders and organizations with the resources, capabilities, and communication channels required to make subordinates aware of the situation, develop an effective narrative against the status quo, and motivate target constituencies to engage in acts of noncompliance. Having said that, however, it is still worth asking what sorts of "events" and "facts" (or "states of affairs"; Elster 2007: 9) are most commonly responsible for each of the three forms of institutional failure listed above, at least insofar as the resulting search for less "proximate," more "distal" causes does not lead down the rabbit hole of "infinite regress."

If, consistent with the reasoning presented in this chapter, an institution's delegitimation is most commonly the result of its perceived failure to meet the needs of subordinates, to work in accordance with widely shared standards of fairness and justice, or properly to embody prevailing conceptions of the ultimate source of political authority, each of the perceived failures may conceivably stem from two types of developments. The first is a major disruption in an institution's actual workings, which prevents it from structuring behavior in the manner required and to the extent required, to satisfy the public's expectations on each of the counts listed above. In turn, based on findings produced in the field of behavioral economics (Thaler 2015: 131–36), the threat that the disruption in question presents to the legitimacy of an institution conceivably varies with (i) the extent to which the results it yields mark a departure from prior experience, which determines the magnitude of the sense of loss experienced by relevant actors; and (ii) the extent to which the discrepancy is judged to have been avoidable and/or to be rectifiable, which affects the propensity of loss-averse actors to respond to the "new normal" through reactance or rationalization.

The second is a major transformation in the manner in which important constituencies define their role in society (and hence their interests/needs), their notions of distributive and procedural justice, and/or their beliefs with regard to either the ultimate source of political authority or the proper way to ensure its expression in the workings of an institution or set of institutions. In the absence of a corresponding change in the workings of relevant institutions, major shifts in the identities, preferences, values, and beliefs of important constituencies will cause the institutions in question to fail to satisfy what the actors concerned expect of legitimate rules and procedures, thereby leaving "a society's established power rules intellectually unsupported, like a bridge whose foundations have been weakened by the slow processes of erosion" (Beetham 1991: 75). On this count, it may be ventured that the dissatisfaction caused by the widening gap between the performance of existing institutions and the expectations of particular constituencies varies with the discrepancy's perceived self-relevance—as François de La Rochefoucauld (cited in Alinsky 1972: 26) wrote centuries ago, "We all have strength enough to endure the misfortunes of others"—or, at any rate, with the degree to which the preferences, values, and beliefs in which the revised expectations originate have come to occupy a central role in an actor's sense of self and attendant "cognitive landscape."

Of course, as previewed in the course of specifying self-undermining sequences of institutional decay driven by the dynamics of delegitimation, major disruptions to the workings of political institutions and major transformations in the preferences, values, and beliefs of important constituencies can originate in developments that are (mostly) exogenous or (mostly) endogenous to the institutions concerned.

Changes in Social Structure and Economic Conditions

Among the varied set of (mostly) exogenous factors that may be expected to threaten the continued reproduction of institutions by undermining their legitimacy, the most important and far-reaching is arguably an assortment of developments generally labeled as "social change." Beetham (1991) characterizes "social change" as a potential catalyst for both (i) disruptions in the capacity of institutions to function in a manner consistent with the expectations of subordinates, prevailing standards of fairness and justice, and their own justificatory principles with regard to "differentiation" and the "authoritative source of rules"; and (ii) transformations in the preferences, values, and beliefs relevant to the assessment of an institution's appropriateness and performance. A form of "social change" that has long been hypothesized to produce effects of this kind is a phenomenon generally referred to as "modernization." Modernization, however, "is only one form of change in the conditions surrounding the institution that may lead to dysfunction" (Fukuyama 2014: 463). Indeed, Goldstone's (1991: 37) analysis of the "waves" of rebellions and revolutions that broke out throughout Europe, Asia, and the Middle East in the "early modern world" shows that "a social explanation of state breakdown need not attach primary importance to the growth of capitalism or class conflict," given the decisive role often played by ecological and demographic shifts.

Certainly, insofar as political institutions are a crucial determinant of economic development and other social transformations, social change is always at least partially endogenous to the workings of a society's existing political system. More generally, the effects of exogenous shocks or transformations are always mediated by endogenous factors, as the characteristics of institutions determine "the magnitude and nature" of the exogenous factors that can meaningfully affect an institution's development (Greif and Laitin 2004: 639). Even so, it makes sense to describe social change as (mostly) exogenous on account of the fact that the phenomenon is, indeed, exogenous to most of the institutions whose legitimacy it conceivably affects—or, at a minimum, that the challenge it presents to the workings of particular institutions, and/or for the maintenance of the preferences, values, and beliefs upon which the institutions' legitimacy rests, stems from developments not caused by the institutions in question. Modernization and other forms of social change conceivably affect the legitimacy of a society's political institutions—when not the legitimacy of entire political orders—in each of the ways listed above: namely, by interfering with their workings as well as by affecting the preferences, values, and beliefs based on which actors assess their appropriateness and evaluate their performance.

With regard to the actual functioning of institutions, Fukuyama (2014: 27) listed the "failure to adapt to new circumstances"—that is, the failure to adapt to a change in structural conditions that include but are not limited to socio-economic conditions—as one of the two main sources of "political decay." In developing his case, Fukuyama (47–51) also revisited the claim Huntington (1968) famously made about the threats that modernization presents to fragile governing institutions in much of the developing world, where a breakdown in political order was hypothesized to result commonly from the intensified mobilization of newly ascendant constituencies. Echoes of Huntington's hypothesis also resound in theories of ethnic conflict that focus on the competition for scarce "goods of modernity" as the catalyst for an escalation in the hostilities often blamed for the collapse of weak states (Bates 1983; see also Chandra 2004: 8). At any rate, while acknowledging that, "in light of recent work, Huntington's theory would have to be revisited in many ways"—not the least of which is the fact that political orders most frequently break down as a result of poverty as opposed to its alleviation—Fukuyama (2014: 48) also argues that "Huntington's basic insight" regarding the destabilizing potential of modernization "was nonetheless correct."

Political decay, however, is not the inevitable result of modernization and the attendant spike in social mobilization. Societies that benefited from fairly robust preexisting institutions, and/or the presence of a political class with the foresight and skills required to make the necessary adjustments, managed the transition without major incident. Fukuyama (2014: 49) also points out that "the huge transformation in global politics" that took place between 1970 and 2008—during which both global economic output roughly quadrupled and the number of electoral democracies tripled—"occurred on the whole remarkably peacefully." Even so, the reason why "social change" is so frequently the cause of institutional decay is that societies often fail to make adjustments they are otherwise quite capable of making (463–66; see also Diamond 2005: 419–40). Complacency and confirmation bias on the part of elites and others can prevent the timely acknowledgment of looming threats and challenges. Extrarational, emotional attachments to existing institutions can preclude the consideration of viable alternatives. And, finally, powerful constituencies whose interests are threatened by the prospects of reform can successfully obstruct attempts to retool a society's institutions or withhold from the state the resources required to stave off a crisis (Goldstone 1991: 10, 461–62). As Tuchman (1984: 381) concluded in her classic book *The March of Folly*, "Chief among the forces affecting political folly is lust for power, named by Tacitus as 'the most flagrant of all passions'" (see also Diamond 2005: 431).

Even when a society's institutions can weather its effects, constituencies that find themselves on the losing end of "social change" might seek to disrupt their operation. Modernization, globalization, and other "macro-processes" responsible for major changes in a society's socioeconomic structure produce "losers" as well as "winners." And, in some instances, such macro-processes can make losers out of otherwise quite powerful, resourceful constituencies. As Acemoglu and Robinson (2012: 83–87, 213–44) have shown, the ruling classes of premodern societies have often feared the "creative destruction" associated with the workings of capitalist, (post)industrial economies to the point of opposing developments that promised to increase their nations' overall prosperity. More recently, disillusionment with democratic institutions has grown as a consequence of increased automation and globalization, which caused global inequality to worsen even as middle-class and working-class incomes have stagnated or declined throughout the Western world (Lakner and Milanovic 2013).

As a result of these underlying changes, existing institutions might cease to produce outcomes that "losers" recognize as being in their interest. In turn, the delegitimation of existing institutions might cause such constituencies no longer to feel bound to play by the rules. Elites in fear of "creative destruction" have at times proven quite capable, at least for a time, of defending their interests and status through efforts designed to discredit and destabilize existing institutions (Acemoglu and Robinson 2012: 213–44). Less powerful constituencies such as the losers of globalization in the West may not be quite as effective in defending their interests or status in the face of social change, but their dissatisfaction nonetheless presents a grave danger to institutions no longer deemed capable of meeting their needs. Western democracies themselves face an existential threat in the perception shared by sizable chunks of their electorates that democracy has let them down, coupled with the apparent willingness of some to experiment with the alternatives offered by right-wing populists and demagogues.

Similar threats to the legitimacy of political regimes and their institutions have been hypothesized to stem from poor economic conditions, at least insofar as such conditions are unfamiliar, unexpected, and/or generally perceived to have been avoidable. As Beetham (1991: 146) points out, poor economic performance translates into the delegitimation of institutions—as opposed to dissatisfaction with the government in office at the time—to the extent that the political system, aside from failing to deliver on its promises of material prosperity, offers no way to replace the current government or, if it does, no hope of producing a government capable of taking the measures required to improve the situation. Similarly, Goldstone (1991: 8) has argued that a "state crisis"—defined as "a situation in which politically significant numbers of elites, or popular groups, or both, consider the central state to be operating in a manner that is ineffective, unjust, or obsolete"—severe enough to threaten "state breakdown" can stem from "actual failures of governmental performance" or "changing economic conditions or reckless governmental actions that cause elites or popular groups to lose confidence in, or withdraw their allegiance from, the state."

The threat that poor economic performance presents to the legitimacy of existing institutions may be hypothesized to vary with a society's overall wealth as well as the nature of the regime itself. With regard to the former, the empirical evidence showing that political regimes are especially vulnerable to economic crises in the presence of low levels of income (Przeworski et al. 2000) appears to be consistent with some of the basic tenets of behavioral economics. For if, as Kahneman (2011: 283) has observed, the rate at which individuals value losses over equivalent gains is highest in circumstances where losses are potentially most ruinous, it stands to reason that the same decrease in income would be most aversive—leading to the most intense disapproval of the status quo—among those whose livelihoods are most precarious. Moore (1978: 468–70) qualifies this expectation by noting that an increase in "the suffering of the lower strata" is most consequential in the following circumstances: (i) when it follows "a rapid improvement in a society's capacity to produce goods and services," which causes it to be perceived as problematic and avoidable; (ii) when it reaches levels "new and unfamiliar" and does so "rapidly enough so that people don't have time to become accustomed"; and (iii) when it is attributable to easily identifiable persons.

Among the reasons why conditions of low income render democracy most likely to collapse in times of economic crisis, moreover, is the possibility that the crisis might further inflame the social divisions often present in underdeveloped societies, whose characteristic vulnerability to "oligarchic domination" and "populist revolution" alike (Fukuyama 2014: 439) often stems from the difficulties involved in expanding local economies at a rate sufficient to prevent mobilized groups from starting to engage in centrifugal, zero-sum competition (Beetham 1991: 171–73). Notoriously, moreover, elites have the most to gain from replacing democracy with dictatorship in relatively impoverished societies (Przeworski 2009). So, too, are the usual insecurities of middle-class citizens over redistribution and loss of status likely to become all the more acute in bad economic times (Fukuyama 2014: 441–

42). The history of the last century, particularly as it relates to the genesis of fascism and other right-wing populist movements, provides ample evidence for just what anxious, flighty, impressionable creatures members of the middle class can be, whenever their heightened susceptibility to "fear of falling" (Ehrenreich 1990; see also Gidron and Hall 2020: 1034) is successfully activated or when they are effectively made to feel "squeezed" (e.g., Antonucci et al. 2017) from above and from below.

A change in socioeconomic conditions, however, threatens the perceived appropriateness of institutions, as well as the public's satisfaction with their outcomes and confidence in the fairness of their workings, even when it does not cause any disruption or change in the results they produce or the way they function. For one thing, social change can lead to the rise of new classes and social groupings whose increased capacities, wealth, and/or skills render their exclusion from power no longer justifiable based on existing rationales or whose growing demands cannot be met by the existing arrangements. The phenomenon sometimes referred to as the "revolution of rising expectations" is consistent with what has been described as a "general rule" of "motivation theory," according to which "getting begets wanting" (Baumeister 2005: 161). On that basis, Tajfel and Turner (1986: 12) have argued that the members of subordinate groups often find the motivation to challenge status hierarchies in circumstances where their "objective deprivation" is actually decreasing, while Levi (1988: 54) observes that "resistance" to perceived injustice and exploitation "is as likely—indeed, more likely—to come from those with resources as from those without." In practice, continued exclusion from power threatens to delegitimize existing institutions among the members of otherwise ascendant constituencies, now rather more inclined to believe that the rules and procedures currently in force—especially those responsible for perpetuating inequalities of power and status—no longer operate in accordance with acceptable standards of procedural and distributive justice or at any rate that their interests are not being served by the existing rules of power. In turn, just as a citizen may derive a sense of moral obligation to comply with a variety of institutions from his or her perception of the entire system's legitimacy, the system's delegitimation should erode the actor's moral obligation to comply, whether or not the institutions in question are in any way responsible for his or her dissatisfaction.

More recent work on modernization also shows that postindustrial economic development in general does render subordinate groups desirous of greater equality, self-expression, and emancipation from authority (Inglehart and Welzel 2005). The acquisition of these motivations should also increase the receptiveness of subordinates to "the introduction of new ideas by political leaders" (Mahoney 2000: 525) seeking to erode the belief systems upon which certain relations of power rely for their legitimacy, as well as evidence attesting to the fact that "what had previously been assumed to be a 'natural' form of social organization, or one based upon 'natural' differences, is in fact socially constructed" (Beetham 1991: 109). As Fukuyama (2014: 40) has observed, the "social mobilization" that generally results from modernization "entails different parts of society becoming conscious of themselves as people with shared interests or identities, and their organization for collective action."

The reason why such transformations are likely to have far-reaching implications for the legitimacy and the survival of traditional, nondemocratic political orders is that few political issues have greater personal relevance than upholding one's aspirations of equality and desire for recognition. Fukuyama (1992: 144–45) himself famously characterized the struggle for "recognition"—for "an intersubjective state of mind by which one human being acknowledges the worth or status of another human being, or of that human being's gods, customs, and beliefs"—as the centerpiece of a "nonmaterialist historical dialectic" capable of accounting for "the prideful and assertive side of human nature that is responsible for driving most wars and political conflicts." Accordingly, Trivers (2011: 65) proposes that "revolutionary moments often seem to occur in history when large numbers of individuals have a change in consciousness regarding themselves and their status." For an illustration, one need not look any further than the momentous implications that the rise of (authentic) nationalism—the origins of which have famously been located in the spread of capitalism (Anderson [1983] 1991)—has had for the external boundaries and the internal organization of countries the world over, as a host of subject constituencies found expression for their desire for "recognition" in the vision of a "nation" defined by principles of equal citizenship and popular sovereignty.

In each of these instances, socioeconomic change threatens to harm an institution's legitimacy to the point of setting in motion processes of increasing delegitimation—whether by undermining the capacity of existing institutions to meet the interests of variously powerful and sizable constituencies, by empowering constituencies pressing a variety of demands that existing institutions were not designed to meet, or by transforming the way in which subordinate groups define their rightful place in society; the proper distribution of wealth, power, and status; or the ultimate source of authority in ways not consistent with the stated rationale for existing institutions. And while the reasons why different forms of social change threaten the legitimacy of existing institutions are varied, the processes they set in motion may be expected to follow a similar logic: in brief, the disaffection caused by the perceived dysfunction of institutions motivates behavior that reinforces the institutions' dysfunction, leading in turn to even greater disaffection. This basic logic characterizes the events described in Goldstone's (1991: 94–102) analysis of the government's failure to resolve the fiscal crisis that led to revolution and state breakdown in seventeenth-century England, in Ferrara's (2015: 292) treatment of the ongoing decline of Thailand's royalist order, and in Fukuyama's (2014: 503–4) discussion of the "political decay" currently plaguing the democratic institutions of the United States. The process can be described as self-undermining to the extent that the institutions concerned become increasingly unstable and increasingly incapable of eliciting quasi-voluntary compliance over time.

The Crisis Tendencies of Inclusive and Extractive Institutions

While endogenous, self-undermining sequences of institutional decay driven by the dynamics of delegitimation can be set in motion by exogenous or mostly exogenous transformations to aspects of the environment in which the institutions concerned operate, such sequences may also be set in motion by developments that are themselves endogenous to the institutions' workings. To be more precise, an institution's delegitimation is characterized in these pages as "endogenous" if it stems from the effects the institution exerts on the behavior of individuals or the relations/interactions between social groups. In turn, insofar as institutions vary with respect to their legitimizing ideas, which are reflected in their treatment of particular situations, actors, and behaviors (Beetham 1991: 126–27), the endogenous developments most likely to result in an institution's delegitimation should also vary depending on the principles that govern the institution's functioning.

For the purposes of this discussion, it is useful to adopt the basic distinction that Acemoglu and Robinson (2012) have drawn between "extractive" and "inclusive" institutions—in other words, between institutions that promote the concentration of unchecked, unaccountable power in the hands of the few, while restricting participation of "the many" in political and economic activities, and institutions devised to distribute power more broadly, to foster the open, equal participation of all citizens in the political and economic arenas, and to compel even the most powerful groups and individuals to adhere to the rule of law. Inclusive institutions are typical of liberal-democratic regimes founded on principles of popular sovereignty and equal citizenship; conversely, extractive institutions are found in nondemocratic regimes where sovereignty cannot be said to rest meaningfully with "the people," while full citizenship is often reserved for the members of groups situated at the top of "natural" or otherwise "desirable" social hierarchies.

Acemoglu and Robinson's (2012) treatment of extractive and inclusive institutions also features a discussion of the crisis tendencies of each, upon which it is possible to develop expectations about the sort of endogenous factors most likely to set in motion an increasing delegitimation process. For their part, Acemoglu and Robinson (343–44) make the most of the tendency of extractive institutions to break down as a result of the infighting typical of political systems where the rewards attendant to the control of the levers of power are too high. The exceedingly high stakes involved—to say nothing of the absence of lawful, peaceful mechanisms of alternation—have often caused the competition for narrowly concentrated, unconstrained power to degenerate into violent, armed conflict. As Beetham (1991: 129) pointed out, political systems need not be "democratic" to qualify as "legitimate" or, for that matter, to command widespread support in society. Indeed, the previous chapter has shown that institutions responsible for instantiating and perpetuating highly unequal arrangements of power are in some ways more likely to benefit from mechanisms of institutional reproduction driven by the dynamics of legitimation, thereby bearing out the notion that the presence of a "consensually accepted status system" can make groups excluded from power rather tolerant of their own inferiority (Tajfel and Turner 1986: 12). Besides, as Acemoglu and Robinson (2012: 86–87) have themselves suggested, the development of a centralized state and a stable regime under extractive political institutions may be expected to follow one group's defeat of major rivals from power, while the exercise of unlimited, unchecked power can subsequently prevent potential rivals from developing the strength to challenge superordinate groups.

Even so, the fact that extractive institutions place few limits on the exercise of power can be a double-edged sword, for it makes the system's legitimacy contingent on the willingness of superordinate groups to practice the degree of self-restraint required to appear mindful of the common good, the needs of subordinates, or prevailing conceptions of fairness and justice. Conversely, the failure to exercise the requisite level of self-restraint, which is not altogether uncommon for those invested with absolute or near-absolute power, can render otherwise passive subordinates receptive to the argument that the system's "manifest particularity" (Beetham 1991: 136), having exceeded acceptable proportions, releases them from the moral obligation to comply with the institutions that sanction existing arrangements of power. To the extent that such recognition translates into the withdrawal of voluntary compliance, the enforcement of compliance through other means can be expected not only to antagonize the groups targeted but also to require the redirection of substantial resources away from more popular initiatives. What is worse, the resulting deterioration in the system's performance may further damage its legitimacy, which in turn requires that even more of the state's resources be repurposed toward the enforcement of obedience, and so on, until, potentially, the exhaustion of the system's legitimacy.

The stability and continued viability of inclusive institutions also face challenges arising from the manner in which such rules and procedures structure individual behavior and intergroup conflict. By their very nature, genuinely inclusive institutions threaten the interests of elites, whose power, status, and wealth stand to suffer from open participation and competition on a level playing field. When they are established in the presence of low levels of development (Przeworski 2009) and/or high levels of economic inequality (Acemoglu and Robinson 2006), elites frequently make use of the resources at their disposal to delegitimize inclusive institutions, undermine their performance, depress the willingness of subordinates to fight in their defense, and gradually set the stage for getting rid of them entirely. In this endeavor, elites have often enlisted the support of relatively privileged middle-class constituencies, who may prove susceptible to efforts to discredit and delegitimize the institutions typical of liberal-democratic regimes in circumstances where they do not constitute the majority of the population (Fukuyama 2014: 441–43). On the one hand, elites can heighten the messy, chaotic nature of democratic competition by refusing to accept its results and to play by the rules or can even exploit the limitations the system places on lawful, elected governments in order to create the conditions of lawlessness and disorder that have often caused middle-class groups to withdraw their support for democracy. On the other hand, elites can seek to exaggerate the threat that inclusive institutions present for the middle class's own wealth and status, while leveraging their tendency to deem "corrupt" any policy that benefits others (Beetham 1991: 144), in order to create a sense of moral outrage among middle-class

citizens against elected politicians and their more numerous (but less affluent) supporters. As Kurer (2020: 1978) has shown most recently, it is "a perception of relative economic decline among politically powerful groups—not
their impoverishment—[that] drives support for conservative and, especially,
right-wing populist parties."

A contemporary case in point is the recent dismantlement of democratic institutions in Thailand, where royalist elites have gotten much of the
urban middle class to reject the workings of the electoral process, largely on
account of the fact that democracy—for which urban middle-class citizens
fought and died in 1973 and 1992—now invariably rewards politicians capable
of appealing to a provincial electorate whose aspirations and self-images have
been thoroughly transformed by decades of economic development (Ferrara
2015). As Montesano (2010: 280) has written, "insecurities" over status have
"haunted the rank and file of the yellow [royalist] camp" to a far greater extent
than their counterparts in the "red" camp, which includes the supporters of
deposed prime minister Thaksin Shinawatra and others who have remained
in favor of electoral democracy throughout the country's protracted political crisis. Indeed, there is both anecdotal and statistical evidence suggest-
ing that while "Yellow Shirt" sympathizers generally enjoy somewhat higher
levels of income and job/life security—largely because, compared with the
lower-middle-class and working-class citizens who make up the bulk of the
"Red Shirt" movement, a greater proportion are employed in the formal sector of the economy—they are more likely to *feel* economically deprived and
insecure (Aphichat 2010). Given the emphasis that the economic policies
pursued by Thaksin and his democratically elected successors placed on the
informal sector, these citizens are said to have feared being forced to bear
the cost of the advancement of others, even as their own economic situation
stagnates or deteriorates (Nidhi 2010: 132–37).

Certainly, inclusive institutions may be designed with a view toward reassuring elites that their interests will not be unduly threatened by open participation and competition. As Ziblatt (2006: 313) pointed out, some of the
world's oldest democracies were established only thanks to accommodations
and compromises that were decidedly *un*democratic but that made it safe for
elites to let the process unfold. Indeed, North, Wallis, and Weingast (2009:
27) concur with Ziblatt (2017) that the protection of elite interests is crucial
to the success of a society's transition from a "limited access order" to an
"open access order." Alas, the fact that "the heavenly chorus" of the "pluralist
heaven"—to borrow E. E. Schattschneider's ([1960] 1988: 34–35) aphorism—

typically "sings with a strong upper-class accent" is not without cost. For while it might give elites little reason to overthrow the system, it also makes it too easy for the rich and powerful to "capture" or, in Fukuyama's (2014) words, "repatrimonialize" its institutions, causing them increasingly to neglect the general interest and the needs of subordinates, to violate prevailing notions of distributive and procedural justice, and eventually to make a mockery out of the system's commitment to popular sovereignty and individual equality. As democratic institutions are gradually hollowed out, the public's growing disaffection may induce more and more people to withdraw from its participatory institutions, providing elites with a chance to assert further their dominance of a political system whose workings are increasingly at odds with its lofty founding principles. Eventually, those alienated and excluded from the political process may become receptive to the argument that the problem is rooted in the very nature of inclusive, democratic institutions, as opposed to their dilution and subsequent hijacking, or may become susceptible to the appeal of "populist" demagogues whose promises to clean up (or blow up) the system most often boil down to measures designed to erode further the system's openness and inclusiveness.

Delegitimation as a By-Product of an Institution's Destabilization

The final, major category of developments that may be expected to set in motion processes of increasing delegitimation is composed of situations in which an institution or a system of institutions begins to appear, in the eyes of politically relevant constituencies, increasingly weak, unstable, and/or incapable of securing broad-based compliance, whether as a consequence of a perceived decline in a superordinate group's capacity (or determination) to impose its will on the rest of society or as a result of the growing currency enjoyed by plausible alternatives to the existing arrangements, whose ultimate replacement may come to seem inevitable.

The idea that the deterioration in an institution's capacity effectively to structure behavior might set in motion a self-undermining process—one in which the institution's perceived weakness or instability damages its legitimacy, leading relevant actors to engage in behavior that further weakens, destabilizes, and delegitimizes the arrangement—is consistent with a key tenet of "social identity theory," which predicts that members of subordinate groups are most likely to question the status quo, develop a "positive ethnocentric identity," and choose strategies of "social competition" in pursuit of equal or dominant status when the situation becomes unstable and cognitive alternatives become more readily imaginable (Tajfel and Turner 1986). Likewise, prominent accounts of revolution have long ascribed to rifts between the state and wealthy elites (Skocpol 1979), or to intra-elite divisions (Goldstone 1991), a key role in the emergence of organized, revolutionary challenges to regimes in which the vast majority of the population is excluded from power. Though skeptical of the notion that members of subordinate groups ever truly believe their domination to be natural and immutable, moreover, Scott (1990: 220) reservedly shares Moore's (1978: 458) emphasis on "the conquest of inevitability" as "essential to the development of politically effective moral outrage."

Once again, the fact that the delegitimation of existing institutions often stems from perceived reversals in established relations of power speaks to the tendency of the dynamics of power and legitimation to work in conjunction with one another in the decay as well as the reproduction of institutions, albeit this time in a mutually exhausting or mutually undermining fashion. While a more comprehensive treatment of the interaction will be taken up in the next section, it may be worth pointing out here that exogenous as well as endogenous factors can account for the (real or perceived) weakness of an institution. Exogenous factors conceivably include the "shocks" to the system inflicted by episodic, external events such as natural disasters, global economic downturns, pandemics of infectious diseases, and outbreaks of interstate war, as well as disruptions to the workings of institutions caused by the forms of social change discussed above. Also, insofar as social change causes subordinates to acquire greater confidence in their own efficacy, the latter may come to regard relations of power and institutions once presumed to be immovable as the proverbial paper tiger. As for endogenous developments, Mahoney's (2000: 523) discussion of the "dynamics of change" associated with "power-based explanations" of institutional reproduction lists two scenarios that recur in the literature: (i) one in which "the reproduction of elite-supported institutions may eventually disadvantage subordinate groups to the point that these groups successfully challenge the prevailing arrangements"; and (ii) one in which "the very process through which an institution empowers an elite group may eventually become a source of divisions for this elite group."

Presumably, one of the ways in which the challenges presented to the status quo by "united subordinate groups" and "divided elites" (Mahoney and Thelen 2010: 9–10) might "facilitate a transformation of the existing arrangements" (Mahoney 2000: 523), aside from inducing the groups concerned to withdraw their support, is by increasing the existing arrangements' perceived weakness as well as the plausibility of alternatives spearheaded by those challenging the system. A third scenario that might produce similar results is one where a subordinate group or its leaders manage to exploit the opportunities provided by the system's institutions and their unintended consequences to accumulate power at the expense of the dominant group. In these situations, the countermeasures that superordinate groups often take in response to the empowerment of previously marginal constituencies, or the rise of new political leaders, may themselves undermine the legitimacy of the existing arrangements, sometimes to the point of providing the sort of "focal" event that sparks off uprisings and revolutions (Karklins and Petersen 1993). A violent crackdown on the opposition not only threatens to strip away the pretense of benevolence that dominant groups are often so keen to maintain in their dealings with subordinates; under certain conditions, it can also be interpreted as a further sign of weakness, prompting more people to join opposition activities. Rigged or otherwise "stolen elections" are also known to carry a high risk of backlash, for they often not only violate expectations of fairness, expose the system's commitment to popular sovereignty as a fraud, project an image of desperation, or threaten to divide the regime's own supporters (Kuntz and Thompson 2009) but also effectively relegate a plurality of the electorate to the rank of second-class citizens, in what is likely to be perceived as an outrage against their status and dignity.

Either way, while a loss of power can motivate behavior that further weakens or destabilizes existing institutions, and thereby erode their legitimacy, the institutions' declining legitimacy can further undermine existing arrangements of power by inducing more and more people to withdraw their support and voluntary compliance, the loss of which also threatens to aggravate elite divisions and prompt the defection of influential constituencies in favor of previously disadvantaged groups. In turn, if perceived reversals of power can help set in motion an institution's increasing delegitimation, the fact that delegitimation can usher in a further loss of power suggests that the workings of the interaction between the two logics are of great importance to the other question raised at the beginning of this section, which spoke to the "rapidity and decisiveness" with which a self-undermining, increasing delegitimation process of institutional decay, once triggered, may deplete an institution's stock of legitimacy.

The Rapidity and Decisiveness of Delegitimation Processes

As previewed above, a more systematic analysis of the interaction and its consequences will be taken up in the next section. What is worth addressing here is the role that some of the factors previously hypothesized to affect the rapidity and decisiveness of increasing legitimation sequences of institutional reproduction may be expected to play in processes of institutional decay driven by the dynamics of delegitimation. Above all, one might hypothesize that processes of institutional reproduction and institutional decay are affected in similar ways by the structure of the societies in which they operate. The rapidity and decisiveness with which self-undermining, increasing delegitimation processes of institutional decay unfold, in particular, should also be greatest in the presence of social structures that combine a modicum of cohesion at the social or national level—based, once again, on an overarching set of ideas and/or a widely shared national identity—with low levels of social "fragmentation" (Granovetter 1973).

Conversely, the presence of multiple, internally cohesive social groups with a strong sense of their lower-level group identities is an obstacle to the diffusion of attitudes, beliefs, and behaviors responsible for driving increasing delegitimation processes. In the presence of fragmentation, moreover, some of the groups concerned might share strongly held beliefs about an institution's appropriateness, from which they might derive greater motivation to serve as a bulwark against the institution's growing delegitimation and its corresponding destabilization. Aside from their numbers, their cohesiveness, their status, and their available resources, the effectiveness with which such groups defend existing institutions should also turn on whether or not their members' commitment to the institution's continued existence translates into efforts to adjust their structure and workings so as to remedy the root causes of their delegitimation. Conversely, their opposition to any and all proposals for reform may well increase the probability of a crisis. For while the success of their obstruction ensures that nothing is done to address the sources of the public's growing dissatisfaction with specific institutions, such efforts also contribute to the diffusion of a more generalized disapproval for the nonresponsiveness exhibited by the existing arrangements, which heightens in its turn the propensity of other groups to withdraw their support for, and their (quasi-)voluntary compliance with, the rules and procedures that govern an entire relation of power.

Synthesizing the Logics of Power and (De)legitimation

Once again, the discussion above highlights the difficulties involved in the-orizing the "dynamics of (de)legitimation" in isolation from considerations of power, as well as the crucial role that the exercise of power in response to erosions of legitimacy plays in determining the fate of the institutions concerned. This chapter's introduction features a brief statement specifying self-undermining sequences of institutional decay driven by the dynamics of power. Such sequences are set in motion when reversals in a society's dis-tribution of power and/or material resources erode the capacity of super-ordinate groups to enforce the compliance of those disadvantaged by the distributional consequences of particular institutions. Increased noncompli-ance, in turn, undermines an institution's capacity to structure behavior and produce its intended outcomes, causing it increasingly to fail to generate the "returns" necessary to reproduce asymmetries of power, serve the interests it was meant to serve, and incentivize/enforce compliance. In cases where the institution's defenders lack the will, the capacity, or the opportunity to reform the institution, growing levels of noncompliance require them to choose between stepping up its enforcement—at the cost of redirecting scarce resources away from the pursuit of other priorities, which necessarily dimin-ishes the effectiveness with which power is wielded in other domains—or let-ting the process of decay take its devaluing, destabilizing toll. An institution that is increasingly incapable of producing the outcomes it was designed to produce is not only an increasingly less relevant or "valued" (that is, obeyed and enforced) institution but also an increasingly disposable, replaceable one.

Reversals in the distribution of power and material resources of the kind responsible for setting in motion processes of institutional decay might result from the strengthening of groups previously excluded from power or dis-advantaged by the workings of the institution concerned. Or, such reversals might result from the weakening of the coalition that supports the institu-tion's continued existence, the cohesion of which may be undermined by shifts in its internal balance of power. In each case, just as considerations of power were said to be crucial to the effects exerted by the dynamics of legiti-mation, so should considerations of legitimacy affect the extent to which, and the rapidity and decisiveness with which, the dynamics of power will result in an institution's declining value and stability. For instance, the degree to which reversals of power cause levels of noncompliance to increase conceiv-ably hinges, at least in part, on the extent to which compliance has heretofore been voluntary—or, conversely, the extent to which compliance has been dependent upon material inducements and coercion, both physical and legal. With that in mind, the remainder of this section theorizes the interactions between the dynamics of power and the dynamics of delegitimation to provide a more complete picture of the self-undermining sequences responsible for the loss in an institution's value and stability, as well as to shed light on the process by which an institution's decay might spill over into other institutional domains, potentially to the point of ushering in a more generalized crisis of authority.

Power and Legitimation: The Decay of Inclusive Regimes

Just as processes of increasing delegitimation were hypothesized to originate in different aspects of the workings of inclusive and extractive institutions, so should the genesis of sequences of institutional decay driven by processes of "decreasing returns to power"—as well as by the interaction between the dynamics of power and the dynamics of delegitimation—vary with the internal logic of institutions and their attendant vulnerabilities. As noted, inclusive institutions are most frequently threatened by the intensification of social divisions, as well as by the refusal of elites permanently to trade a position of systematic advantage for "open" competition on a level playing field. As Beetham (1991: 212) has argued with reference to democratic regimes, whose authority is grounded in the principle of popular sovereignty, "Here it is not so much the exclusion of society from the political process, as the consequences of its inclusion, that is the problem." To the extent that the inclusion of subordinate populations in the economic and political arenas threatens to undermine "traditional" hierarchies of wealth, status, and power, elites may seek to undermine the authority of elected governments—perhaps with the goal of inviting the armed forces' intervention—by exploiting "the system's freedoms of speech and association," to be "pushed to the limit" in disruptive actions designed to expose the government's "inability to secure the general interest" under inclusive arrangements (212).

The attempt to create conditions of disorder severe enough to threaten the continued existence of inclusive institutions might benefit from the interaction between the dynamics of power and delegitimation. As governments are forced to dedicate more and more resources to the defense of the political system, that is, the corresponding decline in the effectiveness with which power is wielded diminishes their capacity to meet the needs and expectations of crucial constituencies, while the resulting decline in the system's legitimacy further compromises the enforcement of social order by causing more and more people to withdraw their consent or give up on defending the system. Conceivably, elite-driven attempts to disrupt the workings of inclusive institutions—sometimes to the point of engineering their collapse—are most likely to prove successful when the non-elite groups otherwise inclined to resist such efforts are internally divided, especially if a sizable portion identifies more strongly with the country's elites than with other non-elite constituencies.

North, Wallis, and Weingast (2009: 116–17) have pointed out that "creative destruction" more generally represents a potential source of instability for inclusive institutions, insofar as the economy produces new "patterns of interest" that translate into changing political alignments. In some cases, moreover, the *beneficiaries* of "creative destruction" might themselves seek to exploit their temporary advantage in order to freeze the situation in place or otherwise make it impossible to dislodge them from their perch. Even in societies where there exists a fundamental, broad-based agreement about the desirability or appropriateness of inclusive political institutions, economic elites often favor the introduction of rules—sometimes under the guise of promoting "liberty"—that in practice restrict the system's inclusiveness or facilitate efforts to "capture" existing institutions to be repurposed in accordance with their private interest. For instance, the series of decisions by which the U.S. Supreme Court has dismantled most limitations on the influence of moneyed interests on the country's political system in the last two decades were ostensibly grounded in the First Amendment of the U.S. Constitution, which protects freedom of speech. Actions of this kind may effectively reverse the "virtuous circle" to which Acemoglu and Robinson (2012) ascribe the reproduction of inclusive political systems, based on the mutually reinforcing relationship between the workings of institutions that regulate power and the distribution of resources in society. More specifically, the "virtuous circle" describes a situation in which inclusive political institutions promote the equitable distribution of material resources, which empowers a varied set of constituencies effectively to pursue their interests through their participation in the political process, thereby further strengthening inclusive institutions.

Provided that the power grab is gradual or subtle enough to avoid triggering mass opposition, or that it occurs at a point in a society's political development when non-elites are either too complacent or not sophisticated enough to care or too divided or disorganized to do anything about it, the "capture" of existing institutions may itself set in motion a self-undermining sequence of institutional decay driven by the interaction of the dynamics of power and delegitimation. In brief, the de facto narrowing in the distribution of power weakens increasingly excluded or marginalized constituencies, diminishes the returns that non-elites may expect to receive from participation in the political process, and delegitimizes political institutions hollowed out of their inclusive content, while the resulting decline in levels of participation—and the increased irrelevance of competitive, participatory processes—facilitates efforts to narrow further the distribution of power and dismantle the limits formally placed on the exercise of power.

As the least powerful become increasingly disaffected—and gradually withdraw from the political process—access to power grows ever more limited, and its exercise ever more unrestricted, thereby emptying out the existing institutions of their inclusive substance. Once again, the sequence may devalue and destabilize inclusive institutions to the point of setting the stage for their replacement with institutions that are extractive in their form as well as their substance. Or, elites may prefer to avert the replacement or outright collapse of inclusive institutions, judging it in their interest to ensure that opportunities for political participation remain meaningful enough to prevent widespread disaffection, if not enough to threaten their wealth, status, and power. Indeed, one might venture that this is more or less the situation toward which some Western "democracies" are headed—the United States perhaps above all—as the result of the ongoing "re-patrimonialization" of democratic institutions (Fukuyama 2014). Whether or not the arrangement in question proves stable is another matter entirely, given its reliance on the willingness of elites to exercise enough self-restraint to avoid exposing it as an utter fraud.

In this and other situations, conflicts between the groups advantaged and disadvantaged by socioeconomic change may themselves become so polarizing as to threaten the survival of inclusive institutions, as attested by the rise of "populist," ethno-nationalist movements in parts of the Western world, as well as the relative ease with which such forces have gotten important constituencies to rethink their commitment to democratic politics (e.g., Hetherington and Weiler 2009; Armingeon and Guthmann 2014). In and of itself, excessive polarization can harm the legitimacy of inclusive institutions by causing those disgusted by the acrimony of the process to grow increasingly disaffected, as well as by decreasing the efficiency with which decisions are made and resources are mobilized in the service of national priorities. Economic change by way of "creative destruction" is conceivably one of the main reasons why societies with seemingly consolidated inclusive institutions might become so polarized as to threaten the underlying consensus over their appropriateness. If, in particular, the groups advantaged by socioeconomic change exploit their newfound strength in order to capture existing institutions or stand in the way of reforms designed to renew their capacity to promote an equitable distribution of resources and opportunities in the face of shifting economic conditions, subordinates may at some point withdraw their support for the institutions they deem responsible for consigning them to a position of permanent disadvantage.

In turn, these situations may trigger something of a vicious cycle. On the one hand, the increased willingness of subordinates to support extremists and demagogues produces greater polarization, worsening the performance of the existing arrangements. On the other hand, the rise of "anti-system" forces conceivably intensifies the mistrust between "elites" and "the people"—the latter increasingly disinclined to play by the rules of a system that the former are accused of having rigged in their favor. What is worse, if the declining legitimacy of existing institutions forces governments to dedicate more of their resources to policing discontent, maintaining public order, protecting scapegoated minorities, and arresting the rise of extremist movements, the likely unpopularity of these measures—and their pursuit at the expense of other priorities—pushes the system closer to the precipice of a full-blown crisis of authority.

Generally speaking, the threat presented by economic change to the value and stability of inclusive institutions—that is, its potential to set in motion self-undermining sequences of institutional decay driven by the interaction between the dynamics of power and delegitimation—should vary depending on the identity of "winners" and "losers." More precisely, it should hinge on (i) whether the distinction between winners and losers overlaps with existing social divisions—in other words, whether winners and losers share identities based on something other than their experience of economic change, which should both facilitate the mobilization of losers and heighten their sense of victimization and grievance; (ii) whether those who have suffered from economic change belong to relatively high-status constituencies historically unaccustomed to the status of losers; and (iii) whether those who have benefited from economic change are low-status constituencies, whose ascendance aggravates the status anxieties of relatively privileged groups.

Once again, the importance of these factors—that is, their potential to set in motion the decay of inclusive institutions—should be greatest in societies characterized by low levels of development and/or high levels of inequality, the combination of which is known to render relatively privileged constituencies nervous about the redistribution enabled by majority rule. When both of the conditions above are met, losers are not only likely to derive greater motivation to fight back from the experience of "resentment"—an emotion Elster (2007: 149) describes as "caused by the reversal of a prestige hierarchy, when a formerly inferior group or individual emerges as dominant"—caused by the ongoing transformation of "deviants into dominants" (Bowles 1998: 82); in these situations, moreover, losers are often better equipped to act on their discontent and seek redress for their grievances. The relatively privileged status (previously) enjoyed by these constituencies, in fact, not only gives them access to the skills and organizational resources required to make their voices heard but also makes it more likely that politicians, the media, and the public at large are willing to listen. On that basis, while it is to be expected that economic change will most likely lead to a backlash when it damages elites, it is also little wonder that the experience of the so-called white working class in the United States is politically far more significant than the plight of racial and ethnic minorities. As Beetham (1991: 231) has argued, "Seeking to rectify injustices is always more politically divisive than perpetuating them."

Power, Legitimation, and the Decay of Extractive Regimes

While the collapse of inclusive institutions generally results in their replacement with extractive institutions, extractive institutions are themselves most vulnerable to the infighting that typically takes place between groups vying for the control of a state vested with unchecked, unaccountable power, typically concentrated in the hands of an all-powerful executive. Aside from threatening the regime's legitimacy, authoritarian coalitions whose membership and internal organization are plagued by instability also carry the potential to set in motion processes of institutional decay characterized by the logic of "decreasing returns to power." As North, Wallis, and Weingast (2009: 39) have shown, the logic of "natural states"—that is, states based on nondemocratic, extractive institutions—requires the "dominant coalition" to be "constantly aware of the danger that a subset of the existing coalition will attempt to displace the rest and take control of the state." Indeed, conflict often stems from changes in the "relative bargaining position" of the coalition's own members, some of whom may seek "adjustments in the distribution of privileges and rents" in accordance with "the new balance of power," only to be met with the opposition of those determined to prevent the erosion of privileges that are "often inherent in the social identity of powerful elites" (40).

Even when the ascendant constituencies do not have the strength to seize power for themselves, the refusal on the part of their coalition partners to reform the existing arrangements in accordance with their demands threatens to set in motion a self-undermining sequence of institutional decay driven by interaction between the dynamics of power and the dynamics of delegitimation. As disgruntled elites withdraw their cooperation and support, causing existing institutions increasingly to fail to perform as intended, their defection could give rise to another vicious cycle, in which the loss in the ruling coalition's integrity—and, therefore, its power—makes it increasingly difficult for the institutions concerned to generate the returns required to reproduce prevailing asymmetries of power, keep authoritarian coalitions together, and provide elites with the means to enforce compliance among subordinates. In turn, the combination of growing elite divisions and worsening regime performance should further depress levels of "quasi-voluntary" compliance, whose enforcement requires that more and more resources be taken away from the "privileges and rents" promised to coalition members, to say nothing of the policies designed to meet the needs of subordinates or the pursuit of normatively desirable priorities upon which the system bases its claims to appropriateness and justice.

As quasi-voluntary compliance decreases, therefore, it forces the regime to take actions that threaten to aggravate elite divisions further and deepen the dissatisfaction of subordinates, potentially emboldening the status quo's original challengers. Once again, the sequence may be characterized as "self-undermining" because the decline in the value and stability of existing institutions is driven by an endogenous process in which the original reversal of power leads to greater noncompliance, which causes the institution to provide fewer returns for the actors involved, thereby reinforcing the initial decline in the dominant coalition's power. The process of decay is also likely to be compounded by the interaction between the dynamics of power and the dynamics of delegitimation. For while the destabilization in the ruling coalition—and its resulting failure to deliver on its promises—delegitimizes existing institutions in such a way as to decrease quasi-voluntary compliance, elite divisions may also embolden subordinates to intensify their fight in pursuit of alternative, more favorable arrangements of power. In other words, while the gradual loss in the dominant coalition's cohesion and power may be expected to set in motion the increasing delegitimation of existing arrangements of power, the delegitimation of existing institutions can itself help fuel processes of "decreasing returns to power" by requiring that more and more resources be expended on the measures required to enforce compliance.

Indeed, it is for good reason that some of the most prominent theories of revolution point to intra-elite division or intra-elite conflict as one of the major proximate causes of mass uprisings (Skocpol 1979; Goldstone 1991). Aside from the opportunities that intra-elite conflict presents for the mobilization of subordinate constituencies, it is also quite possible that the elite factions fighting for control of the state, or for a larger share of the "privileges and rents" disbursed by the state, will seek to "socialize" the conflict by involving segments of the subordinate, non-elite population (Schattschneider [1960] 1988). In the general public, to be sure, each elite faction is likely to find plenty of individuals eager to serve as hired hands or ready to be manipulated into sacrificing for a fight that is not their own. Even so, it is rarely appropriate to chalk up to bribery or brainwashing the involvement of ordinary people in struggles that originate in conflicts at the elite level. It is rather more often the case that the elites vying to mobilize various social constituencies must find a way to make the conflict "about something" beyond elite interest (4)—that is, to appeal to the aspirations and fears of ordinary people, perhaps especially those related to considerations of status and demands for "inter-subjective recognition."

Broadly speaking, the involvement of more and more groups in a conflict responsible for driving the decay of existing institutions should hasten the process that leads to a crisis of authority. For their part, the elite factions seeking change are likely to base their attempt to win over portions of the non-elite population on promises of a better future centered on the establishment of a political system that advances their interests and fulfills their desire for recognition. The articulation of a compelling vision for an alternative future, in turn, may motivate subordinates to engage in acts of noncompliance that contribute to the delegitimation of existing institutions and complicate their enforcement. Meanwhile, though the elite factions dedicated to the status quo's defense may occasionally succeed in mobilizing non-elite constituencies to their side by leveraging their fears of social and political change, promising to keep things as they are is generally unlikely to motivate individuals and groups largely excluded from current arrangements of power to fight in their defense. Instead, conservative elite factions may themselves contribute to the decay of existing institutions in the likely event that the mobilization of non-elites requires them not only to *promise* better terms and conditions but also to scale back the enforcement of rules and procedures that sanction the inferiority and exclusion of the groups targeted for mobilization. In other words, the involvement of non-elites on the conservative side of the struggle may also require measures that end up delegitimizing existing institutions and strip them of the capacity to generate the returns—or achieve the goals— for which they were designed.

As for the conditions that render extractive institutions vulnerable to sequences of institutional decay characterized by the interaction between the dynamics of power and the dynamics of delegitimation, whatever makes the dominant coalition more cohesive should also attenuate the destabilizing potential of infighting, as should the presence of "higher-level" national identities shared by elites and non-elites alike. Conversely, the potential for infighting should be most severe when the dominant coalition is made up of groups with distinctive social identities and, therefore, little allegiance to one another beyond considerations of immediate convenience. It is in these circumstances that intra-coalitional shifts or reversals of power are most likely to prompt the advantaged groups to reorganize the ruling coalition, likely engendering a reaction of former allies facing increased marginalization and exclusion.

Another variable that conceivably affects the stability of dominant coalitions, albeit in potentially contradictory ways, is the relative strength and unity of the groups excluded from power. The indeterminacy stems from the fact that while the weakening of groups excluded from power removes a potential threat to the status quo, ruling coalitions can become more cohesive when presented with a realistic threat from below, which could motivate them to close ranks in order to establish institutions and organizations capable of withstanding revolutionary challenges (Slater 2010). Perhaps it may be hypothesized that the effects vary with the dominant coalition's own makeup. When the dominant coalition is rather cohesive, the system's stability is likely to benefit from the weakness and fragmentation of the subordinate population. It is when the dominant coalition is itself heterogeneous and internally divided that the stability of the system might actually increase with the unity of the subordinate opposition—or even the radical nature of its demands for redistribution or recognition—in the absence of which relatively privileged groups may lack the motivation and unity of purpose required to build strong, durable institutions. The presence of "divided elites" and "divided subordinates" may also serve to heighten the system's vulnerability to intra-coalitional reversals of power, as a result of which elites may be tempted to "socialize" disputes at the risk of destabilizing existing arrangements of power.

Institutional Decay and the Collapse of Political Order

Historical institutionalism's foundational concerns with the stability of institutions and the divergence of paths of institutional development have been pursued at the expense of the study of institutional decay *as well as* the study of institutional change. Alas, whereas the tradition has recently rediscovered the importance of long-neglected forms of institutional change, its move away from "breakdown and replacement" models (Thelen 2004: 29–30) has come at the cost of further neglecting the study of processes by which institutions gradually lose what value and stability they once enjoyed, which has largely remained the preserve of scholars working in other traditions. This chapter's basic premise is that the neglect, however regrettable, also presents the opportunity to theorize an important phenomenon anew—not from scratch, exactly, but with a set of analytical tools rarely deployed for this purpose—in the hope that the concepts and mechanisms that have proven so valuable in the study of stability might prove, with some fine-tuning, just as useful to the study of *in*stability.

The effort began with the provision of a general mechanism of institutional decay, identified with an endogenous, self-undermining process whose workings invert the logic often said to account for the process of institutional reproduction, and continued with the specification of the temporal dynamics that might drive it. As in the previous chapter, the effort proceeded by evaluating claims made by scholars in other traditions for their consistency with established findings about individual-level motivation, cognition, and behavior. The insights developed as a result were subsequently integrated into an account of the increasing delegitimation processes responsible for the decay of institutions. The analysis of the dynamics of delegitimation was followed by a wide-ranging attempt to identify the conditions in which such dynamics are typically set in motion, as well as to understand how the interaction between the logics of power and delegitimation drives the process further downstream. Given the paucity of alternatives, the contribution made in this chapter is rather easily stated: compared to Huntington (1965, 1968) and Fukuyama (2011, 2014), the explanation developed in this chapter features a more formalized concept of institutional decay, a more fully specified theory of the temporal dynamics that drive it, and a more systematic, comprehensive analysis of the conditions that set the process in motion.

Perhaps, then, it makes more sense to dedicate this chapter's concluding section to pondering the analysis's implications and extensions, as opposed to revisiting its contributions. Above all, some considerations are in order regarding what happens when self-undermining sequences of institutional decay, having gone unaddressed for some time, spread from one institutional domain to another, potentially to the point of destabilizing an entire political order. The issue is especially significant in regimes built on extractive institutions, for while the breakdown of inclusive regimes most often leads to their replacement with an extractive one, the collapse of extractive regimes might conceivably give rise to a broader range of outcomes.

Once again, Goldstone (1991: 8) defines a "state crisis" as the product of "a shift in elite or popular attitudes toward the state," in which "politically significant numbers of elites, or popular groups, or both, consider the central state to be operating in a manner that is ineffective, unjust, or obsolete," whether as a result of "actual failures of governmental performance" or "changing economic conditions or reckless governmental actions that cause elites or popular groups to lose confidence in, or withdraw their allegiance from, the state." In turn, "state breakdown" occurs "when a state crisis leads to widespread overt conflict," ushering in "a collapse of state authority" as well as "elite revolts, popular uprisings, and widespread violence or civil war" (10–12). In Goldstone's (1991) account as well as other prominent accounts of similar situations, the mass mobilization of subordinate groups in opposition to the state is necessary before a political order enters a crisis of this kind. For that to happen, however, as Beetham (1991: 109–10) reminds us, "something else is needed" beyond the delegitimation of the state's institutions, namely,

> the possibility of communication with others and an autonomous space relatively protected from the influence of the powerful within which to do so; and the imagination to conceive of a different set of rules and relations for the fulfillment of basic social needs from the existing ones. In other words, the subordinate have to acquire an institutional facility (formal or informal means of communication, movement, organization) that is independent of, and a level of consciousness or conceptual position that transcends, the established power relations, if they are to develop the impetus to transform them. . . . And when such a transformatory consciousness impels the subor-

dinate to action, to the active withdrawal of consent, to the delegitimation of power . . . , then the authority system enters a period of crisis, which may be resolved by reform, repression or revolution according to the circumstances and the relative balance of forces.

Other writers disagree with the need, perhaps most famously asserted by Gramsci (1977: 41, 311–12), for anything like a "transformatory consciousness." For Moore (1978: 476), subordinate classes are generally "backward-looking," their actions inspired by the desire "to revive a social contract that has been violated." Similarly, Scott (1985: 345–49) explains that the typical revolutionary crisis is not brought about by a new revolutionary consciousness but rather by "thwarted demands" that "appear to lie within the normative framework of the existing order." Even so, actions inspired by specific grievances, specific violations of the social contract, or the desire to restore a previous moral order, as opposed to the fulfillment of a radical vision of an alternative future, can still lead to episodes of rebellion, insofar as subordinates can develop a "politically effective identity" (Moore 1978: 87) by exploiting the opportunities for communication and coordination provided by the existence of some "space insulated from control and surveillance," in which a common meaning is given to shared experiences (Scott 1990: 118–19). The first public declaration of the "hidden transcript" of resistance, often in the form of symbolic acts testing "whether or not the whole system of mutual fear will hold up" (227), can set in motion "a crystallization of public action that is astonishingly rapid," for it might only be then that subordinates "recognize the full extent to which their claims, their dreams, their anger is shared" (223). Even when such opportunities are restricted by the workings of extractive authoritarian regimes, the process of institutional decay may erode the state's capacity for surveillance and repression to the point of making it possible for subordinates to mount an organized challenge.

As Beetham (1991: 110) suggests, the appearance of mass resistance plunges the system into a state of crisis that "may be resolved by reform, repression or revolution according to the circumstances and the relative balance of forces." Among the key factors that define "the circumstances and the relative balance of forces" is the extent to which subordinates can rely on pre-existing organizations as well as social identities that are sufficiently strong to preserve the movement's cohesion—and motivate its members to sacrifice on its behalf—but not so incompatible with higher-level, national identities as to make their defeat a matter of life and death for superordinate groups or as to make it impossible for the movement to win over elements of the dominant coalition that might otherwise be available to enter into an alliance with subordinates (Moore 1978: 471). What can also affect "the circumstances and the relative balance of forces" is the degree to which the crisis triggers a more generalized change in individual preferences and attitudes relative to the status quo: for different reasons, theories of institutional change based on the logic of social appropriateness as well as the logic of instrumentality predict that the uncertainty that accompanies the breakdown of existing institutions also makes individuals more willing to rethink "how power should be distributed" (March and Olsen 2009: 16) or "experiment and risk deviating from past behavior" (Greif and Laitin 2004: 639) in search of alternatives to the existing arrangements of power.

Certainly, the sequence of events that leads to a full-blown "state crisis" is not irreversible, especially when one considers the resources and opportunities superordinate groups might deploy in their response to processes of institutional decay. In some cases, elites may also have the good sense to cut their losses and agree to a package of meaningful reforms, however painful, before it is too late (Fukuyama 2014: 423–25). Unfortunately, there are also factors that militate against the timely resolution of conflicts driving the decay of extractive institutions. Even if those in power understand the risks involved, leaders forced to choose from an array of bad options are known frequently to exhibit risk-seeking behavior. Indeed, as Kahneman (2011: 319) has observed, the tendency to accept the risk of a large loss in exchange for some hope of avoiding a smaller one is what often turns "manageable failures into disasters" and motivates "the losing side in wars" to fight "long past the point at which the victory of the other side is certain." It may also be noted, based on "social identity theory," that the groups whose superiority is challenged, at least to the extent that they still perceive it as legitimate, will often "react in an intensely discriminatory fashion" (Tajfel and Turner 1986: 22) and redouble their efforts to defend the status quo. At any rate, given that the ideological work required to restore previously held beliefs and the adjustments required to improve the performance of the existing institutional arrangements are likely to take time to yield the intended effects—and, in any event, are likely to be viewed with suspicion by those who increasingly disbelieve—the options available to the status quo's defenders may in practice be limited to making concessions and stepping up their repression.

In a context of decay, both options can be double-edged swords. Concessions—which perforce involve a change in the rules that govern power,

even if only informally—can help defuse more radical challenges, but concessions can also signal weakness and embolden oppositions to press forward. In
turn, the legitimacy of a relation of power might suffer further, for if actions
expressing consent increase the likelihood that the individuals involved will
justify their behavior by adopting beliefs supportive of prevailing arrangements of power, actions expressing *dissent* increase the likelihood that the
agents will convince themselves of the injustice of prevailing arrangements
of power. Similarly, applying repression in a context of declining legitimacy
can lead to a vicious cycle—a "death spiral"—in which the loss of legitimacy
resulting from the unpopularity of repression only increases the need for
repression, which further harms the legitimacy of the existing arrangements
of power, the cohesion of dominant coalitions, and, potentially, the unity of
the security forces (Beetham 1991: 217). The effectiveness of repression would
seem to hinge on two factors: (i) whether or not it takes place early in the
sequence, before noncooperation and beliefs about the inappropriateness of
the status quo become widespread; and (ii) where the dissatisfaction originates from and which groups it has already reached: marginal groups can be
demonized and repressed most easily, while repressing the former partisans
of a relation of power, or the constituencies on which the status quo bases
its support, generally requires a violation of existing rules of power, which
further undermines the legitimacy of the arrangement and the cohesiveness
of ruling coalitions.

Ultimately, whether a "state crisis" causes elites to succumb to revolutionary change, accede to reforms, or opt for more repressive, reactionary
arrangements depends on a variety of factors—in Goldstone's (1991: 10)
words, it "depends on the flexibility of state authorities, on the unity and
organization of elites, on the mobilization potential of popular groups, and
on the precise relationships among these actors, including their financial,
organizational, military, and ideological resources." Whatever the exact circumstances, Gramsci (1977: 311) portentously warned that the "most varied
morbid phenomena" generally characterize "the interregnum" in which "the
old dies and the new cannot be born."

CHAPTER FOUR

Institutional Change

The Incremental Logic of Political Development

The idea that "the study of institutional change does not come easy to institutionalists" (Conran and Thelen 2016: 51) is by now widely acknowledged
by scholars in each of the traditions of inquiry that form the theoretical and
methodological mainstream of "new institutionalism." For different reasons,
each of these approaches has identified in their "resistance to change" a defining attribute of institutions. Indeed, though it is no doubt the case that institutions, if they survive long enough, commonly undergo changes both large and
small, reforming rules and procedures that have become "entrenched" after
a sustained period of reproduction can be a prohibitive task. In most places,
most of the time, rules and procedures that may be described as "institutionalized"—in Huntington's (1965, 1968) sense of the word—*do* exhibit a pronounced resistance to change, as the persistence of a firmly established status
quo is overdetermined by reasons of structure, culture, economic interest,
and psychology. Among other things, the emphasis that all major approaches
to the study of institutions have placed on the resilience of established rules
and procedures is reflected in the enduring popularity of "punctuated equilibrium" models, on the basis of which the development of institutions is presumed to feature long periods of stability interspersed with occasional crises
most commonly expected to result from exogenous "shocks" (Krasner 1988).
Though it has long since become apparent that major varieties of institutional change do not comport with the expectations of punctuated equilibrium models (Thelen and Steinmo 1992: 15–18), alternatives remain decidedly
undertheorized. After decades of research, "new" institutionalism has yet to
produce an explanatory theory capable of accounting for change in as comprehensive or as granular a fashion as the stability of institutions.

Having said that, the literature does feature theoretical insights and
empirical findings that may assist in the development of an improved theory

of institutional change. Indeed, the starting point for the inquiry conducted in these pages is North's (1990) identification of the two main "sources" of institutional change, which echoes the distinction made throughout this book between explanations rooted in the logics of "power" and "legitimation." By ascribing institutional change to (i) "fundamental changes in relative prices" or (ii) "a change in tastes," that is, North (1990: 84) identified its most immediate causes in events or processes responsible for shaking up a society's distribution of power and material resources to the point of placing a new set of actors in a position to reform a society's institutions, as well as shifts in the values, preferences, and beliefs held by actors with the power to change existing institutions. Put differently, while the previous chapter showed that institutional *decay* commonly results from the actions of individuals or groups who are resourceful and powerful enough to prevent existing institutions from functioning as intended but who lack the strength or the will formally to replace them, institutional *change* requires the presence of actors with the *power* as well as the *motivation* to modify the existing rules of the game. It follows from this consideration that an explanation of institutional change must account for the processes by which (i) actors committed to reforming existing institutions acquire enough *power* to enact their designs and (ii) actors who occupy positions of power acquire the *motivation* to reform existing institutions. Crucially, the implication is that processes of institutional change call for an explanation rooted in what this book has described as the logics of power and the logics of legitimation, respectively—once again, the difference being that "legitimation explanations" trace institutional change back to "changes in actors' subjective beliefs and preferences, not changes in the power distribution of actors or changes in the utility functions of actors who are assumed to have constant preferences" (Mahoney 2000: 525).

Whatever its source, institutional change may conceivably take place quickly, all at once, or more gradually, in a series of incremental reforms enacted over an extended period of time. In each case, the underlying shifts in the distribution of power or preferences may themselves occur rapidly or as a result of a "slow-moving" process. Following Pierson (2004: 79–82), therefore, sequences of institutional change may be expected to take on one of the following temporal structures:

(i) Quick cause, quick effect: A sudden shift in the distribution of power and material resources, or in the values, preferences, and beliefs of relevant actors, rapidly leads to change.

(ii) Quick cause, slow effect: A sudden shift in the distribution of power and material resources, or in the values, preferences, and beliefs of relevant actors, sets in motion a process of gradual, incremental change.

(iii) Slow cause, quick effect: A gradual, incremental shift in the distribution of power and material resources, or in the values, preferences, and beliefs of relevant actors, only leads to (rapid) change once a certain threshold is met.

(iv) Slow cause, slow effect: A gradual, incremental shift in the distribution of power and material resources, or in the values, preferences, and beliefs of relevant actors, sets in motion a process of gradual, incremental institutional change.

The punctuated equilibrium model so prevalent in the literature refers to situations where institutional change occurs rapidly, in bursts interspersed between lengthy periods of stability. While the periodic disruption and rapid replacement of stable institutional equilibria are most commonly explained with reference to equally abrupt "exogenous shocks"—as in scenario (i) above—instances of rapid change can also result from slow-moving causal processes, as in scenario (iii) above. In these cases, incremental, cumulative shifts in the underlying distributions of power or preferences only perturb the status quo's stability upon reaching a threshold or tipping point, causing the release of pent-up pressures explosive enough to precipitate the rapid transformation of existing institutions. In this regard, Weyland (2008: 313) has argued that "bursts of profound change" typically follow long periods of "*relative* stasis" (emphasis added) because incumbents have a tendency to allow problems to accumulate until they reach "crisis level," at which point the prospect of an irreparable, catastrophic loss prompts them to enact bold, drastic reforms. Similarly, Lenz and Viola (2017: 13–16) contend that the "legitimacy judgments" often responsible for bolstering the stability of institutions are "robust, up to a threshold"—the "negative emotions and cognitive conflict" triggered by the accumulation of "disruptive information" in measures exceeding what a particular actor can rationalize or ignore can prompt said actor to engage in a process of "active reflection" that leads to the revision of legitimacy judgments affecting the stability of a whole range of institutions. In other instances, radical institutional change may be caused by "a decisive change of political power, usually (though not always) after a violent struggle" (Tang 2011: 43) that took time to reach its denouement or, as described in the last chapter, as a result of a protracted, "self-undermining" process that ushers in the collapse of political order.

This chapter's main focus is on processes of "gradual" institutional change, as outlined in scenarios (ii) and (iv) above. Notoriously, the institutionalist literature writ large has had the most trouble accounting for incremental, gradual forms of institutional change. What progress has recently been made on this front has taken place thanks to attempts to theorize the phenomenon in a "power-distributional" framework (Mahoney and Thelen 2010). Meanwhile, even as some of the leading historical institutionalists have rediscovered the significance of ideas to the development of institutions (Lewis and Steinmo 2012; Blyth, Helgadottir, and Kring 2016; Hall 2016), to date no real effort has been made to formulate a general theory of institutional change centered on the values, preferences, and beliefs of relevant actors. Once again, this chapter takes on the challenge of specifying a legitimation explanation of gradual institutional change—one that seeks to close the gap that separates "ideas-based," legitimation explanations from "power-based" explanations, as well as to ensure that the latter themselves rest on more robust foundations (Blyth, Helgadottir, and Kring 2016: 158).

In this connection, however, it must be noted that while this book's treatment of institutional reproduction and institutional decay derives power-distributional theories of both phenomena from the existing literature—in the analysis of institutional decay, the logic of "increasing returns to power" was reversed—in this case the literature has also yet to produce a fully-fledged, power-based explanation of gradual institutional change. Even Mahoney and Thelen's (2010) "theory of gradual institutional change" is less of an effort to develop a causal explanation of the phenomenon than it is an attempt to distinguish between the types or "modes of change" (see also Rixen and Viola 2014: 20, fn. 11) most likely to be observed in different contexts, depending on the degree of discretion involved in the enforcement of existing institutions as well as the extent to which the status quo's defenders remain powerful enough to veto institutional reforms. What is missing from Mahoney and Thelen's (2010) treatment—and, more broadly, from the literature on historical institutionalism, whose theoretical models have been criticized for the tendency to "walk a blurry line between description and explanation" (Rixen and Viola 2016: 17)—is an attempt properly to account for the way in which agents of change develop the strength to challenge existing arrangements of power, as well as an effort to identify the combination of structural variables and individual choices that conceivably *explain* the nature and magnitude of the resulting transformations. It is for this reason that this chapter seeks to develop an improved power-distributional explanation of institutional change—one that emphasizes how previously excluded or marginalized actors acquire the power to enact change—*before* turning to the development of a legitimation explanation. As in previous chapters, an effort is also made to theorize how the interaction between the logics of power and legitimation affects the direction, the rate, and the transformative potential of institutional change.

By way of preview, *the main contribution made in this chapter is the specification of mechanisms of gradual institutional change that combine the logics of the "self-reinforcing" and "self-undermining" sequences previously hypothesized to drive processes of institutional reproduction and institutional decay.* Whether it is made possible by shifts in the distribution of power and material resources or by reversals in the values, preferences, and beliefs of relevant actors, the main claim developed in this chapter is that a major transformation in a society's institutional architecture can occur, gradually, when agents of change parlay an increase in the material resources available to them, or in the popularity of their ideas, into institutional reforms, however seemingly minor, that both (i) expand their power and/or influence, thereby affording them the opportunity to enact institutional reforms that make even greater contributions to the growth of their power and/or influence; and (ii) interfere with the workings of preexisting institutions in such a way as to prevent them from producing the "returns" crucial to their stability. By disrupting the reproduction of preexisting institutions—and, if possible, by helping to set in motion processes that cause them to decay and unravel—agents of change not only undermine the capacity of the status quo's defenders to veto or reverse increasingly transformative reforms but also weaken their commitment to institutions that no longer guarantee the reproduction of differentials of power and legitimacy. The magnitude of change conceivably reflects the degree to which the self-reinforcing and the self-undermining processes set in motion by incremental reforms catalyze the diffusion of "isomorphic" rules and procedures, both *within* and *across* institutional domains.

A Power-Based Explanation of Institutional Change

Ideally, a power-based explanation of institutional change is one that accounts for (i) the process by which actors who are motivated to reform or replace existing institutions—whether as a matter of principle or in the expectation that different institutional arrangements will have distributive consequences more congruent with their interests—acquire enough bargaining power to enact at least some of the desired changes; (ii) the process by which actors make use of their improved bargaining position in order more or less gradually to change the existing rules of the game in accordance with their preferences; and (iii) the circumstances or contexts that affect just how much, and how rapidly, political institutions are likely to change as a result of shifts in a society's distribution of power and material resources. In this section as well as the next, where similar questions are addressed in an effort to assemble an ideas-based, legitimation explanation of institutional change, the goal is to develop, as Mahoney and Thelen (2010: 7) have put it, "a general model of change . . . that can comprehend both exogenous and endogenous sources of change"—in other words, to specify sequences of institutional change activated by events or processes of an exogenous as well as an endogenous nature.

At the heart of "a general model of change" governed by the logic of power must be the proposition that institutional change happens when the transformations set in motion, exogenously, by structural/environmental shifts or, endogenously, by the workings of a society's own institutions—perhaps most commonly, by the interaction of the two—disproportionately benefit the material well-being of one or more groups, having engineered conditions that render the groups' distinguishing traits, often the very traits that had previously caused their members to be branded as outcasts or "deviants" (Fromm and Maccoby 1970: 232; see also Bowles 1998: 82), uniquely conducive to the accumulation of wealth and power.

In some cases, the reversal of fortunes may be profound enough suddenly to afford its beneficiaries the power to change existing institutions at will. More plausibly, instead of waiting for social change to confer upon them the power to overthrow and replace the old order at once, ascendant groups may find it necessary or expedient to proceed incrementally. In these instances, that is, the best available option may be for such actors to parlay their improved bargaining position into reforms that modify the workings of existing institutions in a way that helps them accumulate *even more* wealth and power, thereby facilitating efforts to press for gradually more expansive reforms designed further to improve the material well-being of the status quo's challengers, while interfering with the workings of existing institutions so as to damage the material interests of the status quo's defenders. The extent of the resulting change conceivably hinges on the capacity of ascendant groups, as determined by contingent as well as structural/environmental factors, to translate their improved bargaining position into the enactment of reforms capable of setting in motion the kinds of self-reinforcing and self-undermining processes that generate increasing returns to power for themselves and decreasing returns to power for the opposition—or, in other words, their capacity to harness mechanisms of institutional reproduction and institutional decay in order to promote the diffusion of the desired institutions.

The Power to Change: Sources of Power-Based Change

Acemoglu and Robinson's (2012) concept of "institutional drift," not to be confused with the "mode of change" to which Mahoney and Thelen (2010) assign the same label, provides a good example of an endogenous process of gradual institutional change set in motion by exogenous forces. While Acemoglu and Robinson (2012) make extensive use of the concept of "drift" in their attempt to explain "between country" institutional differences—more precisely, the concept serves to explain why the same exogenous events or processes, largely as a result of their interaction with local conditions, can place different societies onto diverging paths of institutional development, causing them to "drift apart" institutionally—their analysis can also inform the specification of a "within country" explanation.

Acemoglu and Robinson (2012: 106–7) define the "critical junctures" that may be spawned by exogenous "shocks" to the system rather consistently with standard historical institutionalist accounts (Capoccia and Kelemen 2007; see also Capoccia 2015)—that is, as periods in which "a major event or confluence of events disrupts the existing balance of political or economic power in a nation," removing at least some of the "formidable barriers" normally responsible for thwarting or discouraging attempts to change political institutions. However, in recognition of the fact that the disruptions in question are rarely so thoroughgoing as to produce a tabula rasa, Acemoglu and Robinson (2012: 107) emphasize the role played by "initial conditions"—most commonly identified with the surviving institutions still affecting the behavior of relevant actors—in determining a society's response to an exogenous shock, as a result of which "relatively small institutional differences" may set in motion "fundamentally different development paths." Certainly, it remains true in Acemoglu and Robinson (2012) that the outcomes produced by critical junctures are "related stochastically to initial conditions" (Goldstone 1998: 834), for while such conditions affect the *likelihood* that a society will undertake alternative developmental paths, what ultimately determines the outcome are the choices that the actors involved make within the constraints set by the structural and institutional context in which they operate. In their words, "the exact path of institutional development" that takes shape during critical junctures is not "historically predetermined"; on the contrary, "it depends on which of the opposing forces will succeed, which groups will be able to form effective coalitions, and which leaders will be able to structure events to their advantage" (Acemoglu and Robinson 2012: 110).

It is worth noting up front, in the interest of developing "a general model of change . . . that can comprehend both exogenous and endogenous sources of change" (Mahoney and Thelen 2010: 7), that while Acemoglu and Robinson (2012: 106) focus on disruptions to "the existing balance of political or economic power in a nation" that originate in exogenous events or processes, equally momentous ruptures can result from endogenous processes. Indeed, "critical junctures" with the potential of setting in motion alternative paths of institutional development can also originate in "the internal inconsistencies and contradictions of an institutional arrangement" (Campbell 2010: 92). Broadly speaking, major reversals in a society's distribution of wealth and power may be expected to take place, endogenously, when the actors responsible for designing or spearheading the establishment of a given set of institutions fail to anticipate the possibility that such institutions' "net," "long-term," or "steady-state" consequences could end up serving a set of interests quite unlike those favored by the same institutions' "partial," "short-term," or "transitional" effects (Elster 1988), potentially to the point of allowing an entirely different set of actors to accumulate wealth and power in sufficient measures to challenge the status quo. Pierson (2004: 108–9) lists a series of reasons why, in practice, "we might expect significant divergences, or gaps, to emerge over time between the preferences of designers and the functioning of political institutions" as a matter of course.

Having said that, is it possible to formulate more precise expectations about the sorts of variables or processes—whether exogenous or endogenous in origin—typically responsible for setting in motion sequences of institutional change? While stopping short of attempting a general explanation, Acemoglu and Robinson (2012) have cited a number of factors said to account for why otherwise similar societies at some point embarked upon developmental courses that led them to drift apart institutionally. Perhaps most prominently, they credit the fourteenth-century Black Death for steering different societies onto developmental trajectories that explain the advent of more "inclusive" institutions in parts of Western Europe and more "extractive" institutions in parts of Eastern Europe. Similarly, Acemoglu and Robinson (2012) ascribe to the massive expansion in world trade made possible by the "discovery" of the Americas the emergence of an inclusive economic and political order in England and a decidedly more extractive regime in Spain. The different roles played by these events in the political development of European nations are explained by their varying impact on the demographic and socioeconomic structures of the societies they affected, depending on their interactions with the structural/institutional conditions that survived the disruption of previous arrangements of power. Such events contributed to the emergence of more inclusive regimes when their effect was to render the skills or traits of subordinate groups more scarce, more valuable, or otherwise more conducive to economic success. The same events promoted the development of more extractive regimes when their effect was either to deepen differentials of power and wealth between a society's ruling class and its subordinate population or to confer upon a subset of a country's ruling class an advantage significant enough to build an even narrower coalition, through the exclusion of constituencies with which they had previously been forced to share power.

More generally, the exogenous events or processes commonly responsible for major disruptions in a society's balance of power may be hypothesized to include those that either (i) reconfigure a society's demographic structure, whether as a result of catastrophic, mass casualty events—examples include an armed conflict, the genocide or "cleansing" of a subnational group, an epidemic of infectious disease, a natural disaster, and a famine brought about by an environmental calamity or an economic collapse—or as a result of waves of mass immigration/emigration or as a result of major changes in the rates of fertility/mortality of various groups, as caused by shifts in their economic and/or cultural practices; or (ii) reconfigure a society's socioeconomic structure through the diffusion of industries or technologies (broadly defined as any new application of knowledge, in any field of human activity) that produce a dramatic improvement (absolute and relative) in the material condition of particular groups.

Once again, it is worth pointing out that demographic and socioeconomic transformations of these kinds can be driven by endogenous as well as exogenous forces. For one thing, though fluctuations in rates of mortality and population growth have been characterized as "a major independent force in history" (Goldstone 1991: 30), many of the developments responsible for producing large demographic shifts not only commonly feature endogenous causes as contributing factors but can at times be attributed to endogenous forces entirely. In other words, the workings of a society's political and economic institutions—and the policies to which they give rise—may on their own be responsible for rendering a society more aggressive on the international stage, for increasing domestic ethnic/ideological tensions, for incentivizing violence as a means of resolving internal or international disputes, for destroying the environment, for causing economic collapses leading to famines, for creating the conditions that induce large numbers of people to migrate in and out of different countries, and for altering the economic incentives or the cultural practices of particular groups in such a way as to cause a gradual divergence in their fertility rates. Similarly, a country's institutions may themselves engineer the conditions that facilitate change by incentivizing innovations, or generating opportunities, that disproportionately redound to the advantage of one group or another.

The impact of demographic and technological change on a society's balance of power may be expected to vary with key features of the political and socioeconomic context in which the shifts take place. During mass casualty events, to be sure, the underprivileged are almost guaranteed to do most of the actual dying. As evidenced in Acemoglu and Robinson's (2012) discussion of the Black Death, however, though a spike in its rates of mortality may very well harm a group's capacity to organize in defense of its interests, the group's bargaining power may improve with the growing scarcity of its skillset or manpower. Similarly, while the privileged are often in a better position to exploit the diffusion of new industries and technologies, history is replete with episodes in which a society's elites, having grown too conservative, complacent, or risk averse to do so, allowed other groups to derive from these innovations the material benefits that fueled their economic as well as their political ascendancy. Arguably the best example is provided by the Industrial Revolution and the emergence of market capitalism, whose main beneficiaries were almost invariably the members of groups several rungs down the socioeconomic ladder from the European landed aristocracy.

On this count, it may be hypothesized that a major demographic shift can be conducive to the development of more extractive or more inclusive institutions depending on the shift's nature/magnitude (i.e., which groups it causes to increase/decrease in size and by how much) and its economic import (i.e., its effect on the supply of labor and valuable skills), as well as on the capacity of various groups to exploit the resulting opportunities to their benefit or to defend their interests and status from the attendant threats. As Capoccia and Ziblatt (2010: 937) have pointed out, the development of political institutions is driven by "strategic interactions" between the leaders of organizations, such as political parties, who often exercise "a significant degree of independence from underlying socioeconomic conditions or class alignments." In practice, therefore, the capacity of subordinate groups to press for more inclusive institutions, or resist attempts to establish more extractive institutions following a major shift in the distribution of power and material resources, should hinge on the effectiveness of the preexisting organizations operating in their defense or the rapidity with which such organizations can be assembled in a critical juncture, depending on the material resources at the groups' disposal as well as the degree of inclusiveness or autonomy guaranteed by the workings of surviving institutions.

Similar factors should conceivably affect the capacity of superordinate groups to impose more extractive institutions, or resist intensifying demands for more inclusive institutions, in times of demographic and socioeconomic change. As the examples above suggest, superordinate groups are better equipped to take advantage of the opportunities created by demographic shifts, or neutralize the threats arising therefrom, when levels of development are low, economic inequality is pronounced, and the surviving institutions are already highly extractive in nature. The same should go for the diffusion of new industries and technologies. For while low levels of development, high levels of inequality, and highly extractive institutions make it all the more likely that superordinate groups will translate the resulting opportunities into an additional source of wealth and power, each of these factors also mitigates the consequences of their potential failure to do so, limiting the capacity of subordinates to seize the opportunities for themselves. Of course, the record also abounds in episodes in which elites adopted particular innovations—whether political/administrative or economic—to increase their wealth and power, only to unleash processes that accomplished precisely the opposite, empowering groups that would later bring about their downfall. Indeed, miscalculations of this kind arguably rank among history's principal catalysts for the development of inclusive institutions.

The Logic of Power-Based Sequences of Institutional Change

Depending on the circumstances, sequences of institutional change set in motion by the disruption of a previously stable balance of power may conceivably resemble each of the "modes of change" described in Mahoney and Thelen (2010). Arguably most common are sequences of gradual institutional change whose workings approximate the logic Mahoney and Thelen (2010) have ascribed to processes of (gradual) "displacement" and "layering." The strategies associated with each of these "modes" of change are typically chosen in contexts where the actors seeking change do not yet have the power to enact wholesale reforms to the existing rules of the game—hence, the necessity to proceed incrementally, through the introduction of new rules and procedures that work alongside preexisting institutions or are layered on top of the institutions already in place in the form of "amendments, revisions, or additions" (16–17). The choice of one strategy or the other is said to hinge on the strength of the status quo's defenders—specifically, their capacity to veto the introduction of new rules and procedures standing in direct competition with the existing rules of the game. As Mahoney and Thelen (20, 16–17) have explained, there are instances in which "powerful veto players can protect the old institutions" but "cannot necessarily prevent the addition of new elements" that might end up tilting the balance in favor of the rules layered on top of the old institutions or fail to stop modifications that change "the ways in which the original rules structure behavior" or "compromise the stable reproduction of the [institution's] original 'core.'"

Either way, the significance of these incremental, seemingly minor reforms stems from their potential to set in motion a "self-sustaining" process that might eventually usher in major forms of institutional change. As Vermeule (2007: 3) has shown, "small institutional changes" can produce "large effects" in situations "where discontinuities in important variables occur" as a result. Aside from their capacity to generate "increasing returns" for ascendant actors and groups—empowering them to secure further reforms—the success of newly established rules and procedures conceivably increases with their capacity to interfere with the workings of preexisting institutions, so as to compromise their "stable reproduction" (Mahoney and Thelen 2010: 17) and possibly cause them to unravel by way of a self-undermining process. In this scenario, the deterioration in the capacity of existing institutions reliably to structure behavior translates into greater noncompliance; increased levels of noncompliance, in turn, further undermine the capacity of preexisting institutions to produce the returns required to reproduce prevailing asymmetries of power, to preserve the cohesion of ruling coalitions, and to administer the rewards and penalties that incentivize compliance.

As this reasoning suggests, self-sustaining processes of institutional change may be expected to combine the logics that this book has ascribed to processes of institutional reproduction and institutional decay. The difference, as noted, is that the processes of institutional reproduction and institutional decay specified in this book refer to the *depth* of institutions, or their *value* and *stability*, which may be said to increase (or decrease) when the features that an institution possesses at time t_1—such as the support it enjoys among a particular constituency or the effectiveness with which it structures behavior in a given institutional domain—become "more (or less) robust to change" at t_2 (Rixen and Viola 2016: 19). Conversely, processes of institutional change refer to the *scope* or *breadth* of an institution, achieved through the addition, subtraction, or modification of an institution's features. Processes of change, therefore, may be characterized as self-sustaining to the extent that the modifications made to an institution's features between times t_0 and t_1 increase the likelihood that the institution will undergo further modifications of a similar, "isomorphic" nature between t_1 and t_2. In other words, a self-sustaining sequence of institutional change governed by the logic of power is one where successive rounds of reforms, enacted at the behest of the actors and organizations representing constituencies that have benefited from increased access to material resources, produce outcomes that further empower the same actors to shape the rules of the game in ways that reinforce the original shift in the underlying distribution of power. More precisely, the reforms' contribution to the ultimate displacement and/or replacement of preexisting institutions should vary with their capacity to generate "increasing returns" for the groups spearheading change and "decreasing returns" for the groups supporting current arrangements of power.

Whether the reforms in question give rise to rules and procedures that work separately from, or "are attached to" (Mahoney and Thelen 2010: 16), the preexisting institutions they are intended to supplant, the effectiveness and the rapidity with which incremental reforms promote major institutional change should hinge on the degree to which their entry into force modifies the outcomes produced by the institutions that govern a given field of human activity, whether by serving as the source of new incentives affecting the decisions of relevant actors or "by changing the ways in which the old rules" themselves "structure behavior." The potential for incremental reforms to usher in major institutional change, that is, hinges on the returns—measured in terms of access to material resources—the reformed institutions deliver to ascendant groups, as well as on the extent to which the reforms disrupt the preexisting institutions' capacity to produce the returns required for conservatives to preserve established relations and asymmetries of power. Consistent with the logic of self-undermining processes, the more effectively the incremental reforms undermine the reproduction of existing institutions, the more difficult it is for conservatives to prevent the emergence of institutions serving an entirely different set of interests.

Over successive iterations, ascendant groups may parlay the power afforded to them by the appropriation of "resource stocks" and the redirection of "resource flows" (Pierson 2015) once controlled by the status quo's defenders into reforms conducive to the accumulation of even greater wealth and power. Within particular domains, each step taken toward the replacement of one set of institutions with another makes further steps in the same direction more likely insofar as it successfully expands the range of situations or behaviors affected by the new institutions at the expense of the old's. Ascendant groups, however, also have the option of redirecting the wealth and power accruing from the displacement and replacement of the institutions governing a particular domain into the diffusion of rules of the game whose workings are conducive to their empowerment *across* institutional domains. Consistent with the reasoning articulated in this book's analyses of institutional reproduction and decay, the rapidity and smoothness of the process hinge on the ease with which the newly established rules and procedures can generate high levels of compliance, undermine compliance with the institutions they are designed to displace, and whenever possible induce large numbers of people to "defect" (Mahoney and Thelen 2010: 16) from one to the other. All of that should be more likely to take place when relatively low levels of social fragmentation remove potential obstacles to the diffusion of new behaviors and practices.

Power-Based Processes of (De-)democratization

Depending on the character of the preexisting institutions as well as the nature of the constituencies whose empowerment drives the process, sequences of institutional change governed by the logic of power can contribute to the emergence of increasingly extractive as well as increasingly inclusive regimes. Certainly, the empowerment of subordinate groups features in the literature as one of the principal catalysts for democratization, especially in the developing world. Consistent with the reasoning articulated in this section, Acemoglu and Robinson (2012: 308–10) have ascribed the emergence of inclusive institutions to a self-sustaining, "virtuous circle" in which the empowerment of a segment of the subordinate population leads to increased pluralism and more stringent limitations on government power, thereby allowing an even broader array of non-elite constituencies to participate more effectively in the political process, press for the establishment of institutions yielding more equitable distributions of incomes and opportunities, and support independent media organizations whose reporting keeps the public abreast of gathering threats to their interests and freedoms, all of which helps nudge the system in a more inclusive direction.

Under what circumstances are sequences of gradual institutional change most likely to contribute to the development of inclusive institutions? The question is worth asking because the road to the development of stable, fully inclusive regimes is strewn with obstacles that render the system vulnerable to sliding back into more extractive arrangements. Above all, the tendency of inclusive institutions to threaten the interests of elites has been recognized as their chief vulnerability, especially in societies that combine low levels of development with high levels of inequality. Indeed, while the role of elites has often been overlooked in works where democratization is credited to the mobilization of workers and middle-class citizens, a good case can be made, based on the findings generated as a result of the "historical turn" recently observed in democratization literature (Ziblatt 2006; Capoccia and Ziblatt 2010; Ziblatt 2017), that the development of inclusive institutions is typically predicated on the willingness of a society's elites to allow it or their failure to deploy the means at their disposal to stop the process in its tracks.

Perhaps most importantly, the likelihood that a viable democratic regime will result from the mobilization of non-elite constituencies may be expected to vary with the institutional and socioeconomic context in which their empowerment takes place. With regard to institutional context, it seems reasonable to hypothesize, in keeping with Linz and Stepan (1996: chap. 4), that processes of democratization are least likely to bear fruit where each of the institutions necessary to a functioning democratic regime must be built from scratch, for the multiplicity of the tasks involved heightens the potential of something derailing the process. Once again, matters are complicated further by conditions of underdevelopment and inequality. Aside from motivating elites to act in order to avert the establishment of inclusive institutions, whose redistributive tendencies are conceivably most threatening to elites where the gap separating them from the rest of society is wide and the size of the overall "pie" available for (re)distribution is small, societies characterized by endemic poverty and massive wealth disparities are most likely to feature elites with the means to scuttle, hijack, or reverse the process before it does substantial damage to their interests.

The emphasis placed throughout this account on the difficulties involved in consolidating inclusive institutions in contexts of underdevelopment and inequality squares with a rather large body of evidence accumulated over the past two centuries about transitions to minimally "democratic" regimes. Przeworski's (2009: 21) review of the evidence in question highlights two "general facts" that help make sense of why countries whose first experience with inclusive, democratic political institutions came "early," relative to levels of development, may end up enjoying a semblance of pluralism and democracy "less frequently"—indeed, why they may have trouble building a stable regime of any kind. First, "the probability that, once in place, a democracy survives increases steeply in per capita income, converging to certainty when income is sufficiently high" (21; see also Przeworski and Limongi 1997). Second, both democracy and non-democracy tend to be more unstable in countries that previously experienced at least one episode of failed democratization. Putting the two together, a democratic regime established in conditions of underdevelopment may be expected to face a high probability of failure. In the probable event that such a regime does founder, all else being equal, future regimes, whether democracies or non-democracies, will also be less likely to endure. In contexts where income levels remain flat, therefore, the country in question may experience multiple democratic transitions and authoritarian reversals, each of them rendering future regimes more unstable. As incomes rise, however, spells of democracy should become longer in duration, until income crosses a threshold whereupon democracy, once established, is effectively "impregnable" (Przeworski 2009: 23).

What accounts for these empirical regularities? As is typical of rational choice approaches (Thelen 1999: 381–82), Przeworski takes the stability of democracy to hinge not on the elimination of alternatives, accomplished through a historical process that renders their adoption effectively unimaginable, but on the capacity of democratic institutions to coordinate and structure behavior in equilibrium. When democratic institutions are established in the presence of low levels of development, their subsequent evolution can unfold along a broad range of alternative developmental courses. Przeworski (1988) himself argued that democracy, which emerges as "the contingent outcome of conflicts," can succeed at any income level; while its chances of success rise in income, low income is never dispositive of its failure. Even so, the varying capacity exhibited by democratic institutions to establish themselves as "self-enforcing" is rooted in the incentives that guide elite behavior at different income levels. In Przeworski's (2009: 27–29) view, that is, democracy is more stable at higher levels of development because, as a society grows wealthier, democracy's redistributive tendencies become less threatening to elites, while dictatorship simultaneously becomes less appealing to those with the means to overthrow the regime.

Two additional factors may be said to contribute to making democracy more stable at higher levels of development. The first is that relatively wealthy societies generally feature non-elite populations that are more committed, if not to the abstract principles of democracy, at least to their own liberty and inclusion, as well as better equipped to organize in their own defense, the combination of which renders unlawful usurpations of power more likely to engender a coordinated response. The second has to do with the role of the middle class and its trademark ambivalence toward inclusive political institutions. In brief, the fact that affluent societies are generally "middle-class societies"—that is, societies where the middle class represents the majority of the population—reduces the effectiveness of appeals emphasizing the threat that the subordinate population's inclusion presents to the interests and status of middle-class citizens (Fukuyama 2014: 442–43).

What happens when democratic, inclusive institutions succumb to authoritarian reversals? Przeworski (2009: 27; see also Cheibub 2007) justifies the expectation that a democratic regime's failure makes future democratic regimes more unstable with reference to a "military legacy" that could be said to reproduce itself through the tendency of asymmetries of power to become larger over time (see also Pierson 2004: 36–37). Up to the last few decades, during which democratic institutions have increasingly proven vulnerable to the dictatorial ambitions of duly elected leaders (Levitsky and Ziblatt 2018: 3), authoritarian reversals most frequently took place as a result of military intervention. Though military regimes tend to be more short-lived than other forms of dictatorial rule, each military intervention strengthens the armed forces and weakens the oppositions targeted for repression, thereby increasing the likelihood of future military interventions. No less important, the dysfunction likely to plague democracies with a history of coups often works to justify the military's ongoing tutelage, up to and including the removal of elected governments that fail to guarantee the requisite degree of "order." As Huntington (1991: 116) puts it, "One successful military coup . . . makes it impossible for political and military leaders to overlook the possibility of a second."

The result is that the failure of each democratic regime makes *future* democratic regimes, reestablished periodically each time the generals return to the barracks, more likely themselves to prove unstable. In Przeworski's (2009) account, the tendency of regime instability to become more and more intractable is neutralized by rising incomes. Indeed, the argument that democracy becomes "impregnable" beyond some level of income suggests that, ultimately, economic development allows countries to shake off the influence of their past. Once certain (high) levels of income are achieved, democracy is self-enforcing because all major actors find it in their material interest to comply with the rules—losers are better off heeding the results of competitive elections, while the winners have, on balance, less of an incentive to dismantle the system in order to make themselves into dictators.

Just how rapidly should we expect inclusive institutions to stabilize in response to rising incomes? Conceivably, several factors help determine the relationship's elasticity and the likelihood that inclusive institutions will assert themselves as "the only game in town." All else being equal, relatively low levels of economic inequality and the presence of "higher-level" identities shared by every major social constituency may attenuate popular demands for more inclusive political institutions (Acemoglu and Robinson 2006) but could also render a country's elites less motivated to resist the system's growing inclusiveness—in practice, this combination of factors may be said to reduce the threats to the stability of the regime that happens to be in place at the time, whatever its exact nature. Conversely, high levels of economic inequality and stark differences between the social identities of superordinate and subordinate groups should render extractive as well as inclusive political orders more unstable, for while such factors conceivably make subordinates more determined to fight for the system's inclusiveness, they also increase the motivation and, possibly, the capacity of a country's elites to defend extractive institutions. The subordinate population's fragmentation into a varying number of relatively cohesive groups with distinctive social identities could also delay the stabilization of inclusive regimes in response to rising income levels, as elites may find it easier to drive a wedge between groups that otherwise share similar interests and/or to exaggerate the potential for these differences to lead to violence under more permissive rules of the game, so as to discourage subordinates from seeking their own inclusion. It should also be noted that elites are unlikely ever to accede to the establishment of an inclusive political order if they are not in a position to compete or otherwise protect their interests once they are out of power. Such is the case of personalized dictatorships

(Huntington 1991: 120) and "ethnocracies" or "racial oligarchies" where ruling classes represent a permanent minority of the population (111).

Alas, it is becoming increasingly clear that wealthy democratic societies are themselves in danger of backsliding into less democratic arrangements, especially to the extent that growing levels of economic inequality afford elites the opportunity to "repatrimonialize" the system (Fukuyama 2014) and set in motion a "vicious circle" by which a society's institutions gradually become more extractive, whether in form or in substance (Acemoglu and Robinson 2012: 343–44). Indeed, recent developments throughout the Western world—above all, a generalized increase in levels of economic inequality, the decline of moderate center-left parties, and the rise of right-wing "populist" leaders with clear authoritarian proclivities—raise unsettling questions about whether democracy truly is "impregnable" beyond certain levels of income.

In fairness, it must be noted that Przeworski's (2009: 19–20) expectations refer to a limited, "electoral" form of democracy. At any rate, insofar as the inclusive regimes of Europe and North America are threatened most severely by the dissatisfaction of their own electorates (Foa and Mounk 2016), or by the erosion of norms of "mutual toleration" and "forbearance" (the practice of restraint in the exercise of one's institutional prerogatives) (Levitsky and Ziblatt 2018), their destabilization calls for an explanation that is at least partly ideas based. For now, it will suffice to say that the data attesting to the stability of democratic regimes at high levels of income do not in any way inoculate the West's inclusive political orders against the danger of degenerating into more "exclusive," extractive arrangements: the fact that no wealthy democratic regime has collapsed to date is no guarantee that every last one of them will live on forever, especially in view of the epochal nature of the social transformations in which the threats to the stability of affluent democratic polities appear to originate. At the very least, the uncertainty surrounding the viability of democracy in an increasingly unequal, automated, globalized world suggests that it is prudent to adopt Tilly's (2007: xi) view of "democratization" as a process that "always remains incomplete and perpetually runs the risk of reversal—of de-democratization."

A Legitimation Explanation of Institutional Change

As previewed in this chapter's introduction, an ideas-based, legitimation explanation of institutional change is one that traces the "fundamental causes" of change back to reversals in the distribution of values, preferences, and beliefs held by the actors and social constituencies vested with the power to change the existing rules of the game, whether directly or through representatives. The first step in developing an explanation of this sort, therefore, is the specification of the causal processes by which powerful actors/constituencies acquire the *motivation* to enact major reforms or to support the efforts made by others to achieve change. Consistent with the discussion featured earlier in this book about the reasons why ordinary people conform, "quasi-voluntarily," with the behavioral prescriptions of institutions, the process that brings powerful actors to endorse institutional change may be expected to be driven by considerations of perceived interest as well as by moral judgments regarding an institution's legitimacy or by subjective assessments of its capacity to uphold prevailing standards of procedural and distributive justice—in other words, by the logic of instrumentality and the logic of appropriateness.

The Motivation to Change: Sources of Ideas-Based Change

In the former case, decision makers are motivated by the expectation that there is something to be gained in reforming the rules of the game—or, perhaps more commonly, given the way human beings are known to respond to perceived threats and opportunities (Kahneman and Tversky 1979), by the determination to avoid the costs feared to attach to the failure to reform existing institutions. Aside from the relatively straightforward situations in which officeholders are essentially bribed, more or less (il)legally, with campaign contributions, emoluments, and perquisites of various sorts, in most circumstances it is safe to assume that a society's "lawgivers," however (s)elected, are most concerned with threats and opportunities bearing on the amount of power they wield and the security with which they hold the positions in which said power is rooted. In relatively inclusive, representative democracies, rules are often tinkered with to maximize incumbents' chances of retaining powerful offices or to make it harder for the competition to access power. Under more extractive, authoritarian rules of the game, where competition is restricted and lawmaking powers are concentrated in the hands of a narrower set of actors, incumbents regularly craft institutional responses to the threats and opportunities stemming from each of the problems that Svolik (2012: 2–13) has credited for defining "the politics of authoritarian rule." With regard to the problem of "authoritarian power-sharing," the fact that no ruler, however "absolute," governs alone periodically calls upon incumbents to modify the rules, or the way the rules are enforced, in order to protect the integrity of ruling coalitions or to neutralize challenges presented by factions therein. With regard to the problem of "authoritarian control," a regime's determination to govern legitimately, with minimal recourse to physical coercion, periodically requires a willingness to adjust the rules that govern a relation of power, sometimes in recognition of changes in the capabilities, aspirations, or worldviews of subordinate constituencies.

More problematic—and, for the purposes of assembling a legitimation explanation of institutional change, a great deal more interesting—are situations where the actors vested with the power to change the existing rules of the game come to the conclusion that doing so is "the right" or "the appropriate" thing to do, in the absence of compelling instrumental reasons. Snyder and Mahoney (1999: 104) have cited the issue of "incumbent failure" as "a core problem of regime change," enumerating the difficulties the existing literature has faced in explaining why "incumbents who have a vested interest in the regime's survival fail to protect it." For our purposes, the question is why would incumbents—and the members of the constituencies to which they owe their positions of power—ever choose to enact institutional reforms, in the knowledge that the proposed adjustments will adversely affect their interests and very possibly embolden their rivals to seek even more transformative, more damaging reforms?

The theory developed in this study points to two possibilities. First, the values, preferences, and beliefs of powerful actors are also susceptible to revision through "self-justification," which may cause them retroactively to adjust their attitudes toward institutions in order to rationalize their public behavior. The tendency to engage in self-justification conceivably extends to situations where actors in positions of power pursue institutional reforms for reasons of necessity or advantage, in the course of which they should also experience a degree of psychological pressure to bring their underlying values, preferences, and beliefs in line with their public acts or pronouncements, so as to reassure themselves (and others, if possible) of their principled, upstanding nature. Presumably, powerful actors also share with the rest of the species the all too human tendency more or less readily to accept that which they cannot change, including reforms they have come to regard as inevitable. Second, incumbents may become convinced, without apparent regard for self-interest, that changing the rules is "the right thing to do" as a result of changes in processes of "cultural transmission" (Bowles 1998) that are driven by—and that, in turn, help drive—the "increasing delegitimation" of status quo institutions and the "increasing legitimation" of potential alternatives.

As in the previous section, a "general model of change" governed by the logic of legitimation may be said to revolve around the proposition that institutional change happens when the developments set in motion, exogenously, by structural or environmental shifts or, endogenously, by the workings of a society's own institutions not only disrupt the consensus regarding the legitimacy or appropriateness of the existing rules of the game but also disproportionately promote the diffusion of values, preferences, and beliefs consistent with particular kinds of reforms, especially within a society's most powerful and culturally influential constituencies.

Once again, though the previous chapter's discussion of the process by which individual preferences and subjective evaluations change focused for the most part on the groups least advantaged by the distributive consequences of existing arrangements of power, much of it also applies to more privileged actors and groups. For the privileged and the underprivileged alike, the reassessment of an institution's legitimacy is likely to be driven by "negative emotions and cognitive conflict" (Lenz and Viola 2017: 953). Accordingly, the members of superordinate groups may also be expected to change their assessments of an institution's appropriateness or performance when confronted with information that cannot be "rationalized by existing schemata" (952). So, too, should these individuals revisit values, preferences, and beliefs bearing on the legitimacy of existing institutions when changing conditions cause a reversal in the social and psychological pressures to rationalize the status quo, to the point where continued cooperation and compliance—and the maintenance of attitudes that define such behavior as appropriate—become a greater threat to their social standing and self-image than the adoption of positions that are clearly at odds with their previous stances and actions. It also seems reasonable to expect that the switch will often take place as a result of perceived changes in the attitudes or behavior of associates and authority figures.

Indeed, while the benefits they derive from existing institutions should generally render incumbents—and the constituencies that support them—more resistant to changing preferences with clear implications for the status quo's legitimacy, most of the exogenous and endogenous sources of preference change singled out in the previous chapter should remain operative in this analysis. With regard to (mostly) exogenous factors, relatively privileged actors are also subject to the influence that social change has on the way individuals more generally define their place and role in society. In other words, their values, preferences, and beliefs are also likely to be affected by the increased availability of information rendered possible by technological innovations, just as their subjective assessments of the performance of institutions are likely to be impacted by the disruption that exogenous forces might cause to the workings of existing institutions. With regard to (mostly) endogenous processes, the values, preferences, and beliefs held by members of superordinate groups are also subject to revision as a result of perceived violations of the terms in which certain "rules of power" are justified, of the failure of existing institutions to live up to their own "implicit promises," or of the systematic infringement of norms of procedural/distributive justice. Insofar as the relatively privileged support or oppose prevailing institutional arrangements for reasons that transcend self-interest, moreover, their attitudes and behavior may also be affected by the "manifest particularity" (Beetham 1991: 135) that often characterizes the workings of extractive institutions, as well as by the hijacking or "re-patrimonialization" of formally inclusive political orders.

The Logic of Ideas-Based Sequences of Institutional Change

Gradual institutional change in a "legitimation framework" may be expected to mirror the logic hypothesized to govern power-based processes of change. In this case, however, the sequence is driven by the diffusion of values, preferences, and/or beliefs that are clearly at variance with the ideas serving as the intellectual and moral foundations of existing institutions. As previewed above, in most circumstances the main obstacle to institutional change is represented by the tendency likely exhibited by the actors who benefit from the status quo to hold—and hold on to—preferences that are consistent with their past statements and public behavior, to say nothing of their material self-interest. Even in a democracy, the fact that an institutional reform proposal enjoys the support of a majority of the electorate is no guarantee that it will even come up for a legislative vote—in the United States, for instance, powerful sectional interests and organizations such as the National Rifle Association routinely prevent Congress from considering legislation supported by large majorities of the American people—as the intensity with which reformist preferences are held is often insufficient to overcome the resistance of a committed minority intent on defending the status quo or to override the veto of a society's political and economic elites.

Consequently, aside from blocking any attempt that conservatives might make to arrest the diffusion of ideas that threaten the status quo and/or to restore the capacity of existing institutions to deliver on the goals they were intended to serve, the best option available to agents of change is often to parlay the increased resonance of their ideas into organized efforts to extract relatively minor, incremental reforms to existing institutions. In this endeavor, challengers may benefit from the willingness of incumbents to countenance minor reforms as a way of remedying an institution's declining capacity to generate "quasi-voluntary compliance." As pointed out above, a set of institutions' continued reproduction may periodically require that their workings be adjusted in response to changing conditions. Incremental reforms undertaken for that purpose, however, can have the opposite effect—increasing the likelihood that even more transformative reforms will be enacted—if they cause an intensification in the diffusion of values, preferences, and beliefs undergirding demands for change, if they compromise the capacity of existing institutions to elicit the general public's compliance, or if they undermine the cohesion of ruling coalitions.

Much like the power-based sequences of institutional change specified in the previous section, self-sustaining processes of institutional change in a legitimation framework extend the logic said to account for self-reinforcing and self-undermining sequences of institutional reproduction and institutional decay, respectively, to the "scope" or "breadth" of institutions. In both instances, institutional change takes place when the institutional innovations resulting from successive rounds of reforms reproduce themselves at a faster rate than the original "core" of preexisting institutions—and, potentially, interfere with the workings of preexisting institutions so as to disrupt their "stable reproduction" or cause them to unravel (see also Mahoney and Thelen 2010: 17). Once again, the mechanisms by which institutions "reproduce themselves" or "unravel" in a legitimation framework are driven not by the transfer of "resource stocks" or the redirection of "resource flows" from the "winners" to the "losers" of previous fights over institutions (Pierson 2015) but rather by the diffusion of values, preferences, and beliefs that are inconsistent with the ideas forming the intellectual and moral foundations of existing institutions. Crucial to the magnitude of the transformations that will ultimately be wrought upon a society's political order is the capacity exhibited by agents of change to secure incremental reforms that fuel the diffusion of values, preferences, and beliefs consistent with their preferred alternatives, while aggravating the status quo's delegitimation and attendant instability, all of which facilitates subsequent efforts to obtain further, more expansive reforms.

Consistent with the reasoning featured in previous chapters, where an institution's legitimation was shown to hinge on its capacity to generate high levels of compliance, the gradual replacement of one set of institutions with another may conceivably be caused by, and may in its turn help cause, the diffusion of values, preferences, and beliefs supportive of institutional change. In other words, each step taken in the direction of replacing one set of institutions with another increases the likelihood of further steps in the same direction—in accordance with the "dynamics of (de)legitimation" previously hypothesized to drive sequences of institutional reproduction and decay—insofar as the reforms in question change the behavior of relevant actors and increase among them the perceived likelihood of even more thoroughgoing change, prompting those involved to adopt values, preferences, and beliefs that strengthen their support for further reforms as a means by which to justify their public behavior, the actions of those around them, and their revised expectations. Correspondingly, as each round of reforms makes existing institutions less effective in serving the purposes for which they were designed, the public may grow more supportive of reformist initiatives, while incumbents may prove less and less willing to oppose institutional change, having come to the conclusion that further resistance is futile—when not downright harmful to a political order's legitimacy—and/or that the continued enforcement of increasingly unpopular rules could alienate important constituencies. As intimated above, the status quo's defenders may themselves adopt the sorts of values, preferences, and beliefs that justify going along with reforms increasingly perceived as inescapable, especially when the institutions in question are not central to the workings—and the survival—of the entire political order.

Ideas-Based Processes of (De-)democratization

Like their power-based counterparts, processes of institutional change governed by the logic of legitimation can proceed in multiple directions. Put differently, such processes may take the form of temporal sequences that Acemoglu and Robinson (2012) refer to as "virtuous" and "vicious" circles, depending on whether the values, preferences, and beliefs driving the process are consistent with greater or lesser inclusion, freedom, and/or equality of rights and opportunities. On this point, while it is rather typical of individuals socialized in postindustrial, democratic societies to presume that the development of increasingly inclusive political orders, though subject to growing pains and temporary setbacks, has the force of "history" behind it, a degree of skepticism is warranted, given the ease with which one can imagine the idea lending itself to wishful thinking. Indeed, while the logic of power has been shown reliably to pull human societies in the direction of greater inequality during "normal" times—as Scheidel (2017: 6) has shown most recently, "narrowing the gap between rich and poor" typically requires a "violent shock" to disrupt the political and economic inequality that almost invariably develops in periods of stability—the tendency of human beings to become more tolerant and inclusive minded as they become more "modern" may not be strong enough reliably to function as an adequate counterweight. Modernization may well increase the propensity of human beings to demand *their own* emancipation (Inglehart and Welzel 2005), without rendering them any more interested in securing the emancipation of others. And while the tremendous improvements that modern societies have registered in terms of "human welfare" are often downplayed in theories of political development— whose emphasis on the conflictual aspects of the process can come at the cost of overlooking the ways in which "welfare-improving institutions" have prevailed over alternative arrangements (Tang 2011: 9, 44–45)—the laborious, uneven nature of progress underscores the severity of the obstacles in the way of making lasting improvements to the human condition.

As implied in the last section's concluding passages, much of the literature on the subject points to the redistributive tendencies ascribed to alternative regimes as the main reason why subordinate groups frequently support inclusive, democratic institutions, as well as the main reason why elites often seek to preempt, block, or reverse their societies' democratization. As Fukuyama (2014: 423) has observed, "classical Marxists" and "contemporary economists" alike tend to look "at the struggle for democracy as a fight between rich and poor." One version of this narrative proposes that elites are only willing to accede to their societies' democratization in the presence of a serious revolutionary threat from below: it is the prospect of being overthrown that makes it in their interest to make the system more inclusive (Acemoglu and Robinson 2006). Another version hypothesizes that elites will oppose democratization unless the political forces representing subordinate constituencies are weak enough to remove the threat of radical redistribution; the presence of a serious revolutionary threat from below, conversely, is expected to induce elites to strengthen authoritarian coalitions (Rueschemeyer, Stephens, and Stephens 1992; see also Slater 2010). As noted, some of this literature suggests that democratic regimes are self-enforcing at high levels of income because prosperous societies drastically reduce the benefits that elites can reasonably expect to derive from the replacement of inclusive with extractive institutions (Przeworski 2006), while making democracy's redistributive tendencies less threatening to the wealthy. Higher levels of development are also conducive to stable democracy insofar as they are associated with lower levels of inequality, which are expected to reduce the threat of redistribution (Boix 2003).

Missing from this literature (for a review, see Ziblatt 2006) is any indication that those with the power to change existing institutions spend much time or energy at all contemplating what course of action constitutes the "right" or the "moral" thing to do. But though it seems reasonable to expect that considerations of material self-interest are foremost on the minds of powerful actors in high-stakes situations, the historical record raises questions about the notion that conservative elites will *only* support the replacement of extractive with inclusive institutions when it is in their material, pecuniary self-interest to do so—in other words, when the weakness of their positions leaves them with no choice but to accede to democracy or be overthrown or when democratization poses no threat to their interests. It almost goes without saying that, for democracy to be viable, elites must be given a chance to protect their interests. As Ziblatt (2017) has shown most recently, the acquiescence of the old regime's elites—made possible, above all, by a country's "long tradition of robust, organized, and pragmatic conservative parties" (2017: xii)—played a crucial role in determining whether European nations followed a "settled" or "unsettled" path to democratization. Beyond that, however, Fukuyama (2014: 423–26) points out that "conservative social groups can interpret their self-interest in a variety of different ways," often rooted in deeply held values and beliefs, "some of which are more conducive than others to nonviolent transitions to democracy."

Put differently, ideas can orient the behavior of conservative elites in ways that hinder as well as promote the development of inclusive sociopolitical orders. In some instances, to be sure, superordinate groups may have developed values or identities that caused them to give up on the defense of extractive institutions when it was still in their material self-interest to keep such institutions in place. In other cases, however, the enduring purchase of reactionary worldviews has motivated conservative elites to fight for the continued acknowledgment of their superior status well past the point where it made good "material" sense to do so. In this connection, proponents of social identity theory have long highlighted the tendency of dominant groups to react to perceived threats to their sense of superiority "in an intensely discriminatory fashion" (Tajfel and Turner 1986: 22). Similarly, Baumeister's (1996) study of "evil" concluded that the most gruesome episodes of violence are frequently perpetrated as a reaction to threats perceived to have been leveled against the self-image or public reputation of people with a high (as opposed to a low) opinion of themselves.

What is worse, if the key to the success of the efforts made by agents of change to convince various constituencies of the appropriateness of the desired institutional reforms is their capacity to craft appeals that draw on "inconsistencies in the multiplicity of cognitive frameworks that are predominant in society," which provide "a basis for actors to adopt new subjective evaluations and moral codes concerning appropriateness" (Mahoney 2000: 525), those seeking to build support for institutional arrangements founded on the rejection of values of inclusion, liberty, and equality often enjoy a cultural as well as a psychological advantage. Struggles over a political system's inclusiveness typically feature the juxtaposition of narratives centered on what the cognitive linguist George Lakoff refers to as the "Moral Order" and "Reverse Moral Order" metaphors (2009: 98–99). The Moral Order metaphor is, in essence, the idea that the spontaneous, organic emergence of hierarchies of status and power over the course of history makes such hierarchies "natural" and therefore "moral" and legitimate. In the Western as well as the Eastern variants of this worldview—typically based on selective interpretations of religious texts that have long assisted in the legitimation of hierarchies of wealth, power, and status in Judeo-Christian (Walzer 1982: 153–54, 171–75) as well as Islamic, Confucian, Hindu, and Buddhist societies—the morality of an individual's conduct is judged on the basis of whether he or she performs the "duties" that come with his or her position in society, respects authority and obeys "natural" superiors, sacrifices freedom for the sake of "unity," and venerates "traditional" symbols, norms, deities, and institutions as sacred and hence beyond questioning. Conversely, the Reverse Moral Order metaphor is a mainstay of narratives crafted by groups that challenge existing status hierarchies, whose purpose is generally to equate "superiors" with "oppressors," whom "the oppressed" have a duty to challenge to rid the system of exploitation and injustice.

While most of the world's "cultures" feature ideas that are consistent with each of these "moral" metaphors (e.g., see Sen 1997), the fact that human beings throughout the species' recorded history have lived in hierarchical societies under extractive regimes ruled by groups fiercely opposed to values of inclusion, liberty, and equality provides the enemies of inclusive political institutions with a veritable arsenal of symbols, myths, and slogans that may festoon even the crudest forms of tyranny with the trappings of "history," "culture," and "tradition." Ironically, though appeals of this kind are generally most effective in relatively underdeveloped societies, "modernization" may at first serve to render them more, not less, resonant. As Bowles (1998: 101) pointed out, the "school-transmitted" cultures brought about by the advent of territorially vast markets and centralized nation-states have historically rendered processes of cultural transmission "markedly more conformist, as cultural models were selected from (or by) dominant groups and a society-wide socialization system intruded into what was once an entirely local learning process." In addition, the projects of "national integration" made possible by the combination of economic development and the centralization of state power are often identified with the production and dissemination of "national cultures" dominated by the worldviews of high officials and elites.

Decades of fieldwork conducted in northern Thailand by Engel and Engel (2010) illustrate the point rather compellingly. Their analysis of dozens of "injury narratives" demonstrates that the tendency of ordinary people to ascribe episodes of personal injury and misfortune to poor karma or loss of "merit" became more, not less, pronounced in the second half of the twentieth century, despite (or perhaps because of) decades of economic development. Indeed, Engel and Engel (2010) point out that in the past—that is, before processes of modernization and national integration really got underway—the average provincial citizen had been far more likely to explain accidents of fate with reference to the mood of local spirits or ghosts, as opposed to employing "delocalized" reasoning rooted in Thailand's state-sanctioned Buddhism or in the "official nationalism" produced and propagated in defense of the country's royalist political order since the 1950s (Ferrara 2015).

With that in mind, under what conditions are legitimation sequences of institutional change that approximate the logics of virtuous and vicious circles most likely to be set in motion? Once again, political systems are conceivably most vulnerable to the spread of ideas that threaten to undermine compliance with inclusive institutions—and hence facilitate their replacement with more extractive rules and procedures—in situations where levels of development are low and levels of inequality are high. As noted, these conditions may be expected generally to heighten fears of redistribution among the relatively privileged as well as the receptiveness of middle-class citizens to the anti-democratic appeals crafted by elite "intellectuals" to justify reforming the existing political institutions in a more authoritarian direction or to rationalize their refusal to establish inclusive political orders in the first place. Ironically, these effects may be strengthened, in the short term, by economic crises *as well as* by economic growth. On the one hand, while the social transformations resulting from sustained economic growth can contribute to the diffusion of ideas that make inclusive political systems more resilient and extractive regimes more vulnerable in the long run, in the short term economic development may cause privileged constituencies to redouble their efforts to protect old social hierarchies. On the other hand, if the threat that economic crises present to the survival of political regimes generally—especially in circumstances of low development—is in part owed to the capacity of these events to trigger, or to accelerate, the diffusion of values, preferences, and beliefs that undermine the status quo's intellectual and moral foundations, low levels of development make inclusive political orders more vulnerable to economic crises than extractive regimes because (i) the survival of democracies is more dependent on the consent of the governed; (ii) the free flow of information helps the diffusion of anti-system values, preferences, and beliefs; and (iii) the purveyors of anti-democratic ideas in developing nations typically have greater material resources at their disposal than the advocates of democratic ideas in Third World dictatorships.

Another set of structural conditions likely to affect the vulnerability of inclusive and extractive political orders to processes of institutional change governed by the logic of legitimation relates to a society's configuration of cleavages based on ethnicity and other relatively unchanging forms of social identification. Three aspects of these cleavage structures are relevant to this discussion: (i) the degree of fragmentation caused by these cleavages; (ii) the internal cohesiveness of the groups in question; and (iii) the extent to which identity-based cleavages overlap with, and reinforce, divisions produced by inequalities of wealth, power, and status—or, put differently, the extent to which identity-based cleavages cut across existing social hierarchies, thereby potentially undermining within-class solidarities. Once again, there is reason to believe that a subordinate population's fragmentation hampers the emergence of the common front required effectively to fight *for* the establishment of inclusive regimes or *against* elite-led efforts to subvert such regimes. At the same time, the presence of such a common front among subordinates could render inclusive political orders more threatening to a nation's elites, thereby inducing them to fight harder to prevent or undermine transitions to inclusive forms of democracy.

Conceivably, the absence of significant fragmentation among subordinates should favor the development and consolidation of inclusive political orders depending on the extent to which subordinate and superordinate groups share higher-level identities. The subordinate population's fragmentation, conversely, should most hamper the development and consolidation of inclusive political orders in the presence of a cohesive ruling class capable of exploiting the situation to "divide and conquer." Conditions more favorable to the development and consolidation of inclusive regimes are arguably found in societies where the ruling class's internal cohesiveness is also undermined by the presence of significant divisions, especially in contexts where subordinate and superordinate populations are internally divided along similar, cross-cutting cleavages, which may attenuate the elites' opposition to everyone else's inclusion. A more comprehensive discussion of the conditions that temper or heighten the vulnerability of inclusive and extractive political systems to sequences of change approximating the logics of vicious and virtuous circles, respectively, appears in the next section, which addresses the interaction between mechanisms of institutional change governed by the logics of power and legitimation.

Synthesizing the Logics of Power and Legitimation

Just as in the study of institutional reproduction and institutional decay, any attempt to theorize the manner in which the logics of power and legitimation drive processes of institutional change should feature an analysis of the interaction between the two dynamics of change. Once again, while the distinction drawn between power-based or power-distributional and ideas-based or legitimation mechanisms of institutional change remains useful from an analytical standpoint, real-world sequences of gradual institutional change should most commonly feature both dynamics working in conjunction with one another.

On the one hand, shifts in a society's distribution of power and material resources are virtually guaranteed to affect the prevalence of values, preferences, and beliefs with implications for the legitimacy of the status quo and potential alternatives. For instance, Bowles (1998) explains that when formerly "deviant" or excluded groups experience a substantial increase in their wealth and power—a development identified as crucial to the activation of power-based mechanisms of institutional change—convictions, worldviews, and practices associated with the newly ascendant tend to spread throughout the rest of society. In the short run, newly empowered, economically successful groups are likely subject to a great deal of imitation. In the longer run, ascendant groups can build on the advantage conferred upon them by a major shift in the distribution of power by asserting their control over the means by which a society's culture is produced and disseminated, likely by reserving for group representatives the authority to write "the learning rules that make up the processes of cultural transmission itself" (1998: 82) and by ensuring that group members are "disproportionately likely to occupy privileged roles as teachers and other cultural models" (83). On the other hand, when shifts in the values, preferences, and beliefs of powerful actors give rise to institutional change, the attendant transformations in the power-distributional consequences of a society's rules of the game may benefit the same actors in such a way as to afford them the opportunity to enact further reforms, as well as to promote—through their growing influence on processes of "cultural transmission"—the further diffusion of values, preferences, and beliefs consistent with their reformist designs. Conceivably, the process's transformative potential is greatest when institutional change is driven by the mutual reinforcement between the dynamics of power and legitimation.

With that said, this section focuses most intently on the manner in which processes driven by the logics of power and legitimation affect transitions from extractive to inclusive political orders, as well as processes of "de-democratization" (Tilly 2007) by which inclusive political systems become increasingly extractive. While this chapter has already examined a host of factors and circumstances hypothesized to affect sequences of institutional change in various ways, this section also focuses on the role of preexisting institutions, whose importance derives from their continuing capacity to "define strategic contexts that constrain the behavior of incumbents and challengers" as well as their "constitutive" effect on the "self-images, goals, and preferences" that explain the behavior of the actors involved—in other words, their contribution to shaping the configurations of political forces on both sides of the struggle (Snyder and Mahoney 1999: 113).

Power and Legitimation: From Extractive to Inclusive Regimes

By definition, the political orders described in this book, as in the literature, as "nondemocratic," "limited access," or "extractive" exclude the vast majority of their societies' adult citizens from the decision-making processes through which laws are promulgated, amended, and repealed. In these settings, political institutions are in various ways and measures designed to foreclose truly competitive, participatory mechanisms of government alternation; to forestall the mobilization and organization of mass-based political forces operating outside the regime's control; to narrow the range of topics that can be safely and legally broached in public debates (and, in extreme cases, in private conversations as well); and to deny most everyone the chance freely to speak their minds on "sensitive" political issues without fear of retribution or punishment, whether judicial or extrajudicial in nature. In these societies, key channels of the "cultural transmission" processes through which individuals acquire many of their values, preferences, and beliefs (Bowles 1998) are also regulated, monitored, and policed by state agencies and officials tasked with the promotion of conformity ("unity"), quiescence ("peace"), and obedience ("order"); the dissemination of self-serving historical narratives; and the suppression of information calling into question the appropriateness of prevailing arrangements of power or the quality of their performance. Special emphasis is generally placed on the design and implementation of school curricula, as well as on the programming of the news and entertainment media. Beyond this, political orders characterized by low levels of "inclusion" differ from one another in important respects, which may be expected to influence how previously marginal constituencies can acquire the power to implement a reformist agenda, as well as the ways in which powerful actors or groups might themselves be convinced that reforming the existing "rules of power" in a more "inclusive" direction is, indeed, "the right thing to do."

In the wake of the last major "wave" of democratization (Huntington 1991), Linz and Stepan (1996) formulated a typology of political systems that identified five "major regime ideal types"—four of them nondemocratic (*authoritarianism, totalitarianism, post-totalitarianism,* and *sultanism*). The analysis conducted in these pages only considers three of the four dimensions utilized by Linz and Stepan (1996), for while nondemocratic regimes generally seek to discourage or suppress forms of popular mobilization that might allow segments of the population to challenge the status quo, the extensive *mobilization* of ordinary citizens "into a vast array of regime-created obligatory organizations" is exclusive to a regime type—*totalitarianism*—that has all but disappeared from the world's political map. As for the remaining dimensions, it is worth reiterating that while a regime's "defining characteristics" may affect the development of institutions in clearly identifiable ways, it is possible that some might not do so consistently in one direction or the other. Aside from emphasizing the contingency of the process, the analysis focuses on the interaction between the "defining characteristics" of nondemocratic regimes and the contexts in which such regimes operate, in an attempt to as much as possible reduce the indeterminacy that invariably characterizes explanations of phenomena as complex.

Arguably the most consequential among the "defining characteristics" of nondemocratic regimes identified by Linz and Stepan (1996: 44–45) is the degree of "pluralism" tolerated in a country's political as well as economic, social, and cultural realms. On this count, *authoritarian* regimes stand out for their capacity to accommodate "limited," if still short of "responsible," "political pluralism," as well as for their "often quite extensive social and economic pluralism." Depending on just how decisively they have moved beyond the legacy of *totalitarianism*—where by definition all organized forms of collective action must take place within, and in the service of, the state—a degree of pluralism in the social and economic arenas may also be found in *post-totalitarian* societies, as well as in emerging *sultanistic* regimes where civil society has not yet been entirely stamped out in the process of developing a personalized dictatorship. In the interest of clarity, a regime is characterized by "limited but not responsible" forms of political pluralism when groups outside the state are to some extent capable of forming organizations that mobilize followers in political activities based on an alternative vision of a society's past, present, and future, the absence of truly competitive elections notwithstanding.

In these situations, "extensive economic and social pluralism" may still prove to be a source of potential instability for the regimes in question. On the one hand, prevailing relations of power—and the ideas that support their legitimation—are threatened by the "creative destruction" typically associated with institutions that guarantee genuine competition between firms and organizations. Insofar as economic and social competition improves the material well-being of groups historically excluded from power, moreover, socioeconomic development undermines nondemocratic institutions by bolstering such groups' bargaining strength, as well as their commitment to ideals of equality and freedom. On the other hand, while intense competition for the public's loyalty to particular brands or products in the economy or to particular civil society organizations is bound from time to time to result in the airing of ideas that more or less directly challenge the status quo's legitimacy, their diffusion throughout the population is facilitated by the open debate permitted under "limited" political pluralism.

Certainly, it is possible to envision scenarios—especially those defined by

conditions of relatively high development or sustained economic growth—
where the degree of pluralism that already characterizes these systems helps
to defuse the destabilizing potential of reformist ideas, whether by blunting
the sense of dissatisfaction experienced by the general public or by allowing the status quo's defenders to point to the benefits guaranteed by existing
rights and freedoms in order to dispute the necessity or the urgency of further
reforms. Linz and Stepan (1996: 78), however, have also pointed out that "prolonged economic success can contribute to the perception that the excep-
tional coercive measures of the nondemocratic regime are no longer necessary and may possibly erode the soundness of the new economic prosperity";
at times, moreover, sustained growth "may also contribute to social changes
that raise the cost of repression and thus indirectly facilitate a transition to
democracy." Indeed, the active promotion of economic development—even
when it is motivated entirely by a regime's desire to improve performance
legitimacy—generally reaches a point where growth can only be sustained
through the creation of a more knowledgeable, skilled workforce, thereby
requiring educational reforms that open the door to the diffusion of values
that cause ordinary people increasingly to question the legitimacy of current
arrangements of power. And while inclusive political systems have historically also been threatened by the diffusion of authoritarian ideologies appro-
priated by local "anti-system" forces, it is in the nature of pluralism to permit
the coexistence of radically different ideas. The same cannot be said about
authoritarian regimes, whose survival is threatened by the influx of values
and preferences at odds with the ideas based on which a political order justifies its existence.

Another criterion adopted by Linz and Stepan (1996) to distinguish
between nondemocratic political orders is the extent to which the groups
that dominate the regimes in question rely on *ideology* to justify their superordinate status as well as their actions in government. Of course, the tendency of nondemocratic regimes around the world to rely on "an elaborate
and guiding ideology" has declined over the past several decades. With the
exception of the Democratic People's Republic of Korea, each of the *totalitarian* regimes inaugurated over the course of the twentieth century eventually
either collapsed or reformed itself into a "post-totalitarian" regime, in which
ideology, to the extent that it still matters, no longer meaningfully orients
the actions of rulers and ruled. Still, the "mentalities" of *authoritarian* and
post-totalitarian regimes are often grounded in nondemocratic worldviews
typically claimed to form integral parts of their societies' cultural heritage.

In turn, insofar as the protection of "traditional" values, beliefs, and customs against the encroachments of corrupting foreign influences becomes the stated raison d'être of non-Western, nondemocratic regimes, their defense is commonly elevated to a matter of cultural pride and patriotic duty. To a varying degree, similar arguments—including the much-debated "Asian Values" thesis (Thompson 2001)—have helped authoritarian and post-totalitarian regimes in East and Southeast Asia deal with challenges arising from their reliance on economic performance in order to maintain their legitimacy. Anecdotally, they have proved especially effective in preventing the defection of relatively privileged constituencies, characteristically inclined to think of themselves as the guardians of their nations' culture and traditions. It helps that the values and ideas said to define many such non-Western cultures generally serve to emphasize the justice/sanctity of "natural hierarchies" and the virtues of "staying in one's place," thereby identifying the interests of an entire people with the privilege of its ruling class.

The final among the defining characteristics of modern nondemocracies that are of interest in this analysis is the issue of *leadership*. The main distinction drawn by Linz and Stepan (1996: 44–45) on this dimension is between (i) *authoritarian* regimes, where "a leader or occasionally a small group exercises power within formally ill-defined but actually quite predictable norms"; (ii) *totalitarian* regimes, whose frequently "charismatic" leadership "rules with undefined limits and great unpredictability"; and (iii) *sultanistic* regimes, whose leadership, which often exhibits dynastic tendencies, is "highly personalized and arbitrary," with "no rational legal constraints" to hold it in check. Meanwhile, compared with their *totalitarian* precursors, *post-totalitarian* regimes tend to select less charismatic, more technocratic leaders as well as place them under a more stringent set of checks. Certainly, while the concentration of broad, unchecked powers into the hands of a small number of officials makes it easy to enact institutional reforms supported by superordinate groups, regimes of this kind conceivably render those with the power to change the rules less likely to experience the requisite change of heart, given their psychological investment in the status quo and the personal stakes typically involved in its preservation. As Svolik (2012: 75–78) points out, the emergence of "established" forms of personal autocracy entails the complete disempowerment of the elite actors who may once have been able to check the autocrat's power, which explains why these dictators' exit from office is very rarely the result of conflicts with former regime allies and insiders. Indeed, it is for this very reason that the leaders of personalized dictatorships, when faced with the inevitability of their regime's demise, often find it impossible to negotiate their way off the sinking ship. And if the leaders of authoritarian and (post-)totalitarian regimes have at times also met dramatic, violent ends, the options available to them in a crisis often include the possibility of reaching a better deal for themselves, their associates, and their supporters.

All in all, the vulnerability of nondemocratic regimes to mechanisms of gradual institutional change driven by the logics of power and legitimation—indeed, the likelihood that such mechanisms are set in motion, endogenously, by the regime's own workings—may be hypothesized systematically to vary across regime "type." By their very nature, personalized, *sultanistic* regimes provide the least likely setting for the development of inclusive institutions through processes of gradual change. Having stripped friend and foe alike of their powers, *sultanistic* leaders generally do not spontaneously relinquish their prerogatives away through institutional reforms designed to usher in a more "just" or "appropriate" political order. As the historical record seems to suggest, such systems are decidedly more likely to change in rather abrupt, dramatic fashion (e.g., see Huntington 1991: chap. 3). Conversely, given the aggressive enforcement of limitations against all forms of pluralism characteristic of *totalitarian* societies, transitions from *totalitarian* to *post-totalitarian* or *authoritarian* rule are most likely to be initiated by regime insiders. Gradual shifts in the distribution of power and prevailing standards of appropriateness are most likely to drive the incremental transformation of nondemocratic regimes under *authoritarian* and, to a lesser extent, *post-totalitarian* institutional arrangements. As noted, higher degrees of pluralism help regime opponents mobilize followers and disseminate information designed to delegitimize the status quo. Moreover, the fact that such regimes generally rely on broader, more diverse coalitions makes it more likely that reformist preferences, including those stemming from the workings of education systems sensitive to the needs of capitalist growth, will spread to the members of constituencies whose support is crucial to the regime's survival. In these circumstances, whether or not the process ushers in transformative, game-changing reforms depends on what agents of change actually do to exploit available opportunities, on how the status quo's defenders choose to respond, and on the outcome of their strategic interactions.

In practice, an authoritarian regime's transition to a fully inclusive political system often hinges on the capacity exhibited by agents of change to make use of the support they enjoy in the population and among regime "insiders" in order to pressure a regime into lifting or loosening some of the restrictions that have hitherto been responsible for enforcing a "limited" version of political pluralism and then to exploit the opportunities such concessions afford them to disseminate their ideas, mobilize followers, and pressure the regime into enacting further reforms. In this effort, agents of change can benefit from the fact that, as Przeworski (1991: 58) has pointed out, "liberalization is inherently unstable." Invariably conceived as a "controlled opening of the political space" to be managed from above and made "continually contingent on the compatibility of its outcomes with the interests or values of the authoritarian bloc" (57–58), an authoritarian regime's liberalization tends to unleash forces that may prove impossible to control, as the "outburst of autonomous organizing" likely to follow any discernible reduction in levels of repression threatens to cause "a melting in the iceberg of civil society that overflows the dams of the authoritarian regime." Far from serving, as intended, to bolster a regime's stability, liberalization is therefore most commonly responsible for hastening its replacement. Once the process has been set in motion, elites unwilling to accept the system's gradual democratization may be left with few options other than to crack down violently and establish a new dictatorship, which can be "broader" or "narrower" than the original depending on whether it entails an expansion of the ruling coalition or, conversely, is achieved through the violent suppression of regime "reformers" and civil society "moderates."

Crucially, the reason why an authoritarian regime's "liberalization" is an "inherently unstable" process has as much to do with the logic of legitimation as it does with the logic of power. Przeworski (1991: 54–55) describes the threat presented by the emergence of "autonomous" political organizations in these terms:

> What is threatening to authoritarian regimes is not the breakdown of legitimacy but the organization of counterhegemony: collective projects for an alternative future. Only when collective alternatives are available does political choice become available to isolated individuals. This is why authoritarian regimes abhor independent organizations; they either incorporate them under centralized command or repress them by force.

More broadly, the logic of legitimation also helps explain why it is so difficult for authoritarian regimes to reverse the system's partial liberalization once the process has been set in motion—indeed, why it becomes more difficult to do so the further a political system has already traveled down the road to democratization. Aside from the fact that "organized" groups are, by definition, better equipped to fight back than a collection of isolated individuals, the reason why liberalization increases the levels of repression required to neutralize the threat presented by the same constituencies is that their partial, temporary inclusion likely renders opposition actors/groups more acceptable as legitimate political forces and correspondingly harder to ignore or demonize. What is more, insofar as such groups made effective use of the chance temporarily afforded to them to mobilize support more openly and more widely, through appeals that effectively combine an affirmative vision of a society's future with an incisive critique of its past, their increased popularity makes them all the more formidable. Indeed, the more successful such groups are in their efforts to extract concessions from the old regime, the more their popularity should grow—and the old regime should decline— purely as a result of the public's tendency to rate particular eventualities more positively as they become more familiar and/or prospectively more likely to come to pass.

Certainly, imposing after a period of liberalization the levels of repression required to restore a narrower version of the old regime carries costs and risks grave enough to give hard-liners second thoughts about the wisdom of attempting it. A major set of risks is generally thought to arise from the regime's increased reliance on its repressive apparatus. When a country's security forces are hierarchical and cohesive, the most serious danger is that its leadership will exploit the situation to secure more powers and prerogatives for itself; when the repressive apparatus is less hierarchical and/or more internally divided, conversely, different factions may be moved to consider their options, including the prospect of defying unlawful or unpopular orders. Another major set of risks derives from the potential that repression might cause the ruling coalition to break down. Indeed, insofar as a narrower dictatorship can only be established through the repression of "reformist" insiders, the effort's prospects of success should vary depending on how widely and how deeply reformist preferences have penetrated the ruling coalition. When such preferences are shared rather widely inside the ruling class, the problem is not only the commitment of resources and political capital required but also the possibility that the repression of regime insiders may counsel even broader segments of the ruling class that change is warranted—or, at a minimum, that alternatives to the establishment of an even more repressive dictatorship must be considered. One such alternative is to co-opt some of the constituencies currently excluded from power, who may be integrated in the ruling coalition in exchange for moderating some of their demands. Another is to let the process of democratization continue, in the hope of retaining some control over the transition's pace and direction. Having chosen to do so, elites may themselves evolve into genuinely committed democrats (Fukuyama 2014: 423–25), whether by adjusting their preferences to match their behavior or through their exposure to a process of cultural transmission increasingly dominated by inclusive, egalitarian ideas.

Of course, elite actors frequently do *not* respond to their nations' democratization by becoming "committed democrats." Members of superordinate groups may continue to hold preferences for more exclusive, more extractive arrangements and/or to perceive inclusive, democratic regimes as a threat to their wealth, power, and status. The failure on the part of a society's elites to reconcile themselves to the procedures or the outcomes of democratic competition has been cited throughout this book as a major obstacle to the completion of democratic transitions and the consolidation of newly established democratic regimes. Likewise, the weakness of preexisting opposition forces and other civil society organizations is a major part of the reason why Linz and Stepan (1996) consider the failure to develop a consolidated democracy to be, in Snyder and Mahoney's words (1999: 116), "almost overdetermined" in countries transitioning from *totalitarian* or *sultanistic* rule. The previous, nondemocratic regime's "defining characteristics" are not as dispositive in transitions from authoritarianism and mature forms of post-totalitarianism, where the prospects faced by new democracies are more uncertain and "context-dependent" (Linz and Stepan 1996: 65). In reference to "context," it may be hypothesized that the obstacles arising from the presence of "unreformed elites" should be all the more difficult to surmount in conditions of underdevelopment, extreme levels of inequality, and intense identity-based conflict or competition, especially when the categorical inequalities produced by the workings of the economy largely overlap with—and quite possibly reinforce—hierarchies of citizenship status that originate in racial, ethnic, or regional cleavages. As noted above, however, a "long tradition of robust, organized, and pragmatic conservative parties" may ultimately prove to be the most important contextual determinant of whether or not a society's elites ever provide "their reluctant acquiescence to a political order they had initially resisted" (Ziblatt 2017: xii).

Power and Legitimation: From Inclusive to Extractive Regimes

Situations where "unreformed" elites make use of their superior wealth and power in order gradually to replace inclusive with extractive political institutions, exploiting the rights and freedoms afforded to them by inclusive institutions in their effort to turn crucial constituencies against inclusive regimes, constitute one of the main modern routes from democratic to nondemocratic rule. When successful, these efforts may be expected to usher in something of a plutocracy—an oligarchic system of government dominated by society's wealthiest actors and groups—the dangers of which are typically highlighted in the works of progressive writers. Over the last one hundred years or so, leftist critiques of democratic regimes have ranged from relatively sympathetic accounts aiming to sound the alarm on the ease with which elites may capture democratic institutions and effectively deprive "the people" of their sovereign status (Schattschneider [1960] 1988) to more hostile treatments that dismiss democratic rules and procedures as a mere facade for oligarchic, plutocratic arrangements of power claimed to be already in place. Recent developments have lent some credence to the notion that "consolidated," mature democracies such as the United States have traveled far enough down this route as to no longer qualify as a democracy in any meaningful sense of the word (Gilens and Page 2014). These developments have not gone unnoticed by the organizations responsible for publishing yearly comparative ratings of "freedom" and "democracy," which have cited increasing levels of inequality and decreasing levels of trust in government as the reason why the United States' "democratic institutions have suffered some erosion" (Freedom House 2017) or as the justification for downgrading the United States from a "full" to a "flawed" democracy (EIU 2017).

An entirely different set of threats to the viability of democracy is the subject of writings inspired by teachings originally articulated in Book V of Aristotle's *Politics* and, especially, in Book VIII of Plato's *Republic*. For both philosophers, it is precisely what makes a system of government "democratic"—namely, its expansive array of rights and freedoms, to be enjoyed by every citizen in equal measures, and its celebration of the attendant diversity of lifestyles and beliefs—that most threatens its viability. More specifically, democracy's empowerment of the masses at the expense of elites tends to engender demands for even greater equality and freedom, while making any restrictions thereto increasingly unpalatable for growing swathes of the voting population. In turn, insofar as wealthy elites come to be seen as an obstacle to the achievement of full equality, democracy makes it all too easy for aspiring autocrats to exploit the masses' resentment of the rich, or otherwise to exploit conflicts pitting "the few" against "the many," in order to establish a tyrannical regime. Unsurprisingly, the idea that democracy is threatened most severely by the same properties that make it so attractive to so many has often been featured in the works of conservative writers (for a recent example, see Sullivan 2016).

Another major route from democracy to nondemocracy features the rise of right-wing "populist" leaders as a prelude to the emergence of an autocratic, kleptocratic regime that enjoys the support of the country's elites. It bears reiterating that while fascist and other "right populist" leaders have typically founded their appeal on the argument that the institutions of open, liberal-democratic societies cannot adequately protect ordinary people from rapacious elites, their rise to positions of power has generally been followed by the establishment of a system of government whose workings are in practice even more favorable to the interests of elites. In these cases, as the regime entrenches its power and cultivates the support of elites eager to profit from their association with the new government, economic populism is almost invariably jettisoned in favor of the demonization and repression of minorities still widely regarded as unworthy of an equal political role. Frum (2017) illustrates the point by comparing Donald Trump's rise to the experience of right-wing populists elsewhere, whose success was rooted in the capacity to keep "culturally conservative" citizens "feeling misunderstood and victimized by liberals, foreigners, and Jews."

Once again, it is reasonable to expect that a democratic regime's vulnerability to each of these routes to nondemocratic rule should in part be determined by its own institutional structure. Linz and Stepan (1996) go even further back in the transition sequence, identifying in the "defining characteristics" of the old, nondemocratic regime's institutions the source of a series of "consolidation tasks" that a new democracy must complete before it can become "the only game in town," requiring the achievement and entrenchment of (i) civil society autonomy; (ii) political society autonomy; (iii) constitutionalism and the rule of law; (iv) professional norms and autonomy of state bureaucracy; and (v) economic society with a degree of market autonomy and plurality of ownership forms. Consistent with the reasoning above, democracies established in countries previously governed by *sultanistic* and *totalitarian* regimes are expected to face the greatest difficulties, owing to the fact that they must complete each of the required tasks from scratch or thereabouts. By contrast, *authoritarian* and *post-totalitarian* regimes may develop, depending on the specifics of their regimes, some of the features conducive to the success of democracy—indeed, perhaps all except the emergence of an autonomous political society—before the transition even starts.

Of course, what requirements are not met under nondemocratic rule must be fulfilled in accordance with the rules that take shape during the transition. For these cases, Linz and Stepan (1996) list two "actor-centered" variables and three "contextual" variables hypothesized to affect the outcome of the transition. With regard to *actors*, what matters is the "institutional composition and leadership of the preceding non-democratic regime" and the identity of the actors who "start" and "control" the transition. In brief, "civilian-led regimes" are expected to "have greater institutional, symbolic, and absorptive capacities than either military or sultanistic leaders to initiate, direct, and manage a democratic transition" (1996: 68), especially when they are constituted in interim governments determined rapidly to cede power to an elected administration. Conversely, transitions managed by the old regime, or by the leadership of a country's armed forces, are thought likely to delay holding elections on the pretext that the country needs "reforms" that typically amount, in practice, to the establishment of "reserve domains" for unelected institutions and the imposition of a series of constraints, restrictions, and limitations circumscribing the autonomy and authority of elected officials (66–72). With regard to *context*, Linz and Stepan (1996: 72–83) emphasize the contributions made by (i) international influence, including the foreign policies of regional and global powers, the attractiveness of alternatives to democracy in the prevailing zeitgeist, and the potential demonstration effects exerted by events and trends observed in other countries; (ii) economic trends and conditions, including episodes of prolonged growth and "severe economic problems," the effects of which are said to hinge on the perceived viability of alternatives to the status quo; and (iii) "constitution-making environments," which refer to the consequences exerted by the institutional setting in which the transition takes place, as well as the formal procedures governing the process by which the new, democratic rules of the game are deliberated, drafted, and ratified.

On the last point, it is noteworthy that Linz and Stepan (1996) do not appear to place a great deal of faith in the possibility that the main obstacles to democratization can be overcome through the purposive, skillful design of democratic institutions—the promise of which is a major part of the reason behind the field's latest institutional turn. A more extensive, systematic treatment of the subject is reserved for the next chapter, which reflects on how this book's theoretical innovations might inform efforts to "engineer" outcomes conducive to the entrenchment of democratic regimes and to the neutralization of threats thereto. For the moment, it may suffice to observe that the three routes to "de-democratization" identified above further illustrate the idea that democratic regimes can suffer from the presence of overly rapacious, powerful elites as well as from the absence, the weakness, or the thorough delegitimation of elites who may otherwise be capable of protecting democracy by tempering some of its most destabilizing excesses. It follows from this consideration that democratic institutions should neither favor elites to the point of allowing them to change the system at will or hijack its institutions in a way that discredits both nor damage elites to the point of forcing them to choose between renouncing all of their power, wealth, and status or overthrowing the system in an attempt to avert their utter disempowerment.

Institutional Change and the "Regime Volatility Trap"

The theory assembled in this chapter has notable implications for a phenomenon the literature has referred to as the "institutional instability trap" (Helmke 2010; Levitsky and Murillo 2009). The label in question refers to situations in which the chronic volatility exhibited by a set of institutions itself becomes self-reinforcing, as each instance of "breakdown and replacement" makes it less likely that the institutions concerned will develop the requisite staying power and thereby increases the likelihood that periodic discontinuities will continue to plague the institutions' development. As Levitsky and Murillo (2009: 123; see also Helmke 2007: 28) have pointed out, "An initial period of institutional failure or instability, which may be the product of historically contingent circumstances (including sheer bad luck), may effectively lock in a polity into a path of institutional weakness." In these circumstances, "actors develop expectations that institutions will not endure and, consequently, do not invest in them." In turn, "the costs of institutional replacement will remain low, which increases the likelihood of further rounds of change—and reinforces expectations of institutional weakness."

As noted, something akin to the institutional instability trap is known to have historically ensnared the political regimes of nations that experimented with democracy "early," relative to levels of development, in the likely event that their nascent democratic institutions succumbed to authoritarian reversals (Przeworski 2009). Indeed, the logic of the institutional instability trap helps to clarify the workings of the so-called military legacy identified in Przeworski (2009) as the main reason why authoritarian reversals tend to make *future* regimes less durable. Aside from generating a certain habituation to military interventions, and besides making elites so accustomed to getting their way through extra-constitutional means that they never develop the capacity effectively to compete on the strength of their programmatic appeals, it stands to reason that repeated military coups would decrease the willingness of political actors more generally to "invest" valuable resources in what is known to make democratic regimes stronger and more durable— above all, in those activities that may give rise to a system of "national" and potentially governing political parties (Sartori 1968).

How, then, does the theory of institutional change specified in this chapter help inform efforts to explain self-reinforcing cycles of regime volatility? Consistent with the findings presented in Przeworski (2009), this book is replete with references to the reasons why conditions of low development and high economic inequality are inimical to the stabilization and eventual consolidation of democratic regimes. The reasons in question are similar to those frequently mentioned throughout the literature, with one major exception. Specifically, while it is quite well established that democracy in poor, unequal societies is most commonly threatened by the unwillingness of elites to play by the rules, as well as by the insecure, flighty disposition that almost invariably distinguishes middle-class citizens in countries that have yet to achieve levels of development high enough to qualify as "middle class societies" (Fukuyama 2014), what these constituencies abhor and fear about the workings of inclusive, democratic institutions goes beyond wealth redistribution or the inability of such regimes to prevent the disorder and upheaval resulting from the mobilization of forces and movements representing a variety of subordinate, marginalized groups. Indeed, the empirical record shows that democracies rarely produce, on their own, levels of redistribution radical enough to threaten the interests of elites, who commonly retain a variety of means to protect their wealth and status from the whims of democratic electorates (Gleditsch and Ward 2006: 920–21). By some accounts, even the moderate reduction in inequality achieved by Western democracies in the wake of World War II cannot be ascribed primarily—much less entirely—to majority rule (Scheidel 2017).

More than the loss of wealth or privilege, then, what relatively affluent constituencies often find hardest to accept is the tendency of democracy to produce governments that, regardless of what they actually stand for, are perceived to have been chosen by segments of the population still regarded as morally inferior. As Fukuyama (1992: 182) pointed out long ago, the continued "recognition" of their superior worth and status (*megalothymia*) can motivate members of superordinate groups as powerfully as their desire to be recognized as equal (*isothymia*). It almost goes without saying that the levels of resentment generated by the empowerment of subordinate groups should be all the greater in societies where cleavages rooted in race, ethnicity, language, religion, and other largely ascriptive, unchanging sources of identity overlap with class divisions, likely reinforcing the intensity with which the members of high-status constituencies practice in-group favoritism and out-group discrimination.

Then again, while the presence of shared, higher-level identities can remove an important obstacle to democratization, underdeveloped societies may be presented with a challenge no less insidious by the "traditional" values and beliefs forming the *content* of their national identities, especially those designed to rationalize existing social hierarchies with reference to principles that are antithetical to ideals of universal equality, popular sovereignty, and individual autonomy. Though the extent to which subordinates actually believe in official narratives that sanction their own inferiority, and/or sincerely acknowledge the morality of the obligation imposed on them not to challenge the status quo, remains contested (for a skeptical view, see Scott 1985, 1990), at a minimum it may be hypothesized that "traditional" and otherwise official ideologies—especially inasmuch as they were successfully elevated to the status of a developing nation's "culture"—can work as "permission structures" that enable the opponents of inclusive, democratic institutions to act on their prejudices and illusions of superiority in the name of preserving local customs and worldviews, the threats to which the leaders of Third World dictatorships rarely fail to overhype with reference to shadowy international conspiracies.

Much like the relationship found to exist between levels of development and the viability of democratic institutions, the "military legacy" said to account for the tendency of failed experiments with democracy to generate ever-increasing levels of regime instability is also a matter of ideas at least as much as it is about the effects that military interventions have on the distribution of power and material resources. This is not to dismiss the importance of the latter, for the tendency of military coups to tilt the playing field against the forces generally responsible for leading democratization efforts can be profound. To the extent that the coup makers are willing to return to the barracks upon having killed or otherwise rendered inoffensive the requisite number of actors (Przeworski 2009), the neutralization of some of the most prominent members of a nation's political class, as well as the destruction of major civil society organizations, can do lasting damage to a country's democratic prospects, depriving the actors who are likely to succeed the coup leaders in office of the resources to govern effectively. Having caused the loss of any investment made in the political and social organizations targeted for repression, moreover, military coups will also discourage political entrepreneurs from making any future investment of the sort, particularly in view of the heightened potential for further military interventions. What is worse, returns to civilian rule may be preceded by the introduction of rules that guarantee the armed forces continued access to the funds required for their leaders to live in luxury, maintain vast networks of patronage, and exercise functions far beyond those associated with a country's external defense. Even when the generals came to power with "the transitional mission of re-establishing order" (2009: 28), their formal withdrawal may follow the establishment of new institutions designed to restrict the authority of civilian governments, weaken civil society, and otherwise prevent elected officials from ever developing the strength to encroach upon the military's "reserve domains."

As consequential as military coups can be for a society's distribution of power and material resources, however, their effects on the values, preferences, and beliefs of relevant political actors can be just as far-reaching. Most prominently, the dysfunction likely to characterize democracies with a history of coups can end up justifying, in the eyes of a sizable portion of the electorate, the military's continuing tutelage, up to and including the periodic dismantlement of regimes that fail to guarantee the requisite degree of "order." Worse still, the iterated breakdown of inclusive, democratic institutions may affect the expectations of political actors in such a way as to render the failure of elected governments to manage conflicts and meet acceptable standards of performance effectively self-fulfilling, just as prophesized by the elite actors responsible for undermining democracy in the first place.

In turn, the imbalance of power and stature likely to develop between unelected officials and elected politicians—compounded by the reluctance likely shown by these societies' most talented, resourceful individuals to join the electoral fray—makes it all too easy for constituencies that otherwise stand to gain from their country's democratization to lose sight of the fact that democracy's chronic dysfunction is the consequence, not the cause, of its periodic suspension at the hands of unelected officials. The latter's routine interference may therefore continue to be perceived as necessary and/or legitimate, even as it continues to deny elected governments the cooperation of elites, the compliance of officials staffing the military and civilian bureaucracies, and the full exercise of the constitutional authority formally vested in civilian authorities. Meanwhile, the members of relatively privileged groups are likely to cite democracy's travails in support of their suspicion that electoral majorities cannot be entrusted with the responsibility to select the nation's governments, on the pretext that average voters remain unprepared judiciously to make use of the rights deriving from their inclusion. As long as these perceptions endure, military officers and other unelected officials not only will be placed in a position to exercise, legitimately, a variously broad set of constitutional and extra-constitutional prerogatives but may even be credited for their "stabilizing" influence on the nation's politics. Of course, the truth is that no real stability will ever be achieved as long as these officials are exempt from the control of civilian, elected institutions—the more expansive their "reserve domains," the more "unsettled" the road to developing a viable democratic regime.

CHAPTER FIVE

Institutional Engineering

The Purposive Design of Political Institutions

The promise held by institutions to structure human interactions in ways that might help societies achieve a host of desirable ends has been debated since the beginning of the history of political thought (Peters 1999). For different reasons, political science as it is practiced today has done *relatively* little to realize that promise. Broadly speaking, the "paradoxical" mismatch that Sartori (1968: 261–72) once lamented between the "pure" and the "applied" knowledge produced by a discipline whose "increasing power of comprehension" was said to have coincided with "increasing political impotence" has assured the continuing relegation of political scientists to the role of "spectators" to processes of political development. The "explanatory turn" the discipline has undergone in the intervening time did not meaningfully change this state of affairs. Indeed, its practitioners' growing mastery of a vastly expanded technical repertoire and technological arsenal has coincided not only with the intensified pursuit of the "unimaginative" quantitative analyses that Sartori (267) had already blamed for the discipline's practical irrelevance half a century ago but also with the growing popularity of theoretical models in which, by all appearances, the "desire to explain or predict the behavior of actual individuals" takes a back seat to "aesthetic" pretensions (Elster 2007: 461).

Meanwhile, though a great many institutionalists have remained adamant that explanatory theories of political development must treat "ideas as fundamental causes" (Fukuyama 2011: 442), research programs that emphasize individual self-interest or group-level struggles over material resources as the engine of the process have all too often dismissed preoccupations with ideas, culture, and identity as the stuff of the "soft" social sciences. Theorizing the nonmaterial dimensions of human behavior, therefore, has all too often remained the preserve of scholars who are skeptical of the viability of "polity-building" projects involving the manipulation of institutions qua "incentive-based structures" (Sartori 1997: ix), not to mention deeply suspicious of the notion that political scientists should aspire to "perform qua specialist" (Sartori 1968: 263) to assist in that endeavor. In point of fact, the study of ideas, culture, and identity has increasingly been dominated by theoretical approaches whose proponents have sworn off all pretensions to "explaining" anything in the first place.

Notwithstanding the limitations confronting any actor seeking to "engineer" desired outcomes through the purposeful design of institutions, there are also reasons to believe that the modern world does offer opportunities for effective polity building. Indeed, no less an advocate of the importance of human nature, historical legacies, and shared cultural values than Fukuyama (2011: 18) insists that "human societies are not trapped by their pasts," particularly given the "new dynamics" introduced over the past two centuries by developments related to the Industrial Revolution. Of course, the work of political scientists can only inform polity building to the extent that it provides sound causal explanations for key aspects of the process of political development. Before turning to the applied, normative implications of the theory assembled in these pages, therefore, this concluding chapter reviews the book's most notable contributions to the formulation of a general explanation of processes of institutional reproduction, institutional decay, and institutional change.

Contributions to the Theory of Institutional Development

With regard to each of the three dimensions of the process of institutional development under consideration, the explanation assembled in this book set out to accomplish the following objectives:

(i) *The specification of temporal sequences governed by the dynamics of "legitimation," whose workings are grounded in individual microfoundations derived from realistic assumptions regarding human motivation, cognition, and behavior.*

The emphasis placed throughout this book on the proper specification of sequences driven by the "dynamics (de)legitimation" served above all to render explanations of institutional development attuned to the role of *motiva-*

tions that are at least as important in guiding individual behavior as those undergirding the "logic of instrumentality," as well as the role of *beliefs* that human beings acquire as a result of cognitive processes that bear little resemblance to the dispassionate, unbiased way they *ought* to go about forming the expectations involved in an instrumental calculus.

The theory of institutional development set forth in this book rests on the fundamental claim that institutions have "normative force." Institutions, that is, orient human beings to act in particular ways, not exclusively in the pursuit of material self-interest or in an effort to avoid incurring the penalties attached to noncompliance but out of a sense of moral obligation, the satisfaction of which is measured in the currency of self-esteem and social approval. In other words, to the extent that human beings, at least some of the time, are committed to "doing the right thing" in a moral, normative sense, institutions help them determine what is, and is not, "the right thing to do." The theory developed in previous chapters identified a major driving force behind the self-reinforcing, "increasing legitimation" processes said to account for the stabilization and *reproduction* of institutions in the tendency of human beings retroactively to adopt values, preferences, and beliefs that serve to justify their conformist behavior or to rationalize the workings of "systems" they feel powerless to change. Similarly, the inquiry conducted into the phenomenon of institutional *decay* pointed to the declining capacity of institutions to produce high levels of "quasi-voluntary compliance"—in other words, the deterioration in their "normative force"—as a crucial driving force behind the self-undermining, "increasing delegitimation" processes by which institutions were hypothesized to forfeit their "value and stability." The considerations made in those contexts also informed the effort made in the last chapter to theorize processes of gradual institutional *change*, whose workings were hypothesized to combine the logics that govern sequences of institutional reproduction and institutional decay. In brief, major transformations were said to rest on the capacity of agents of change to secure incremental reforms that trigger processes of increasing legitimation boosting the diffusion of the desired institutions as well as processes of increasing delegitimation promoting the destabilization and devaluation of status quo institutions.

(ii) *The formulation of an integrated approach centered on the interaction between the dynamics of "power" and the dynamics of "legitimation," with primary reference to the development of "inclusive" and "extractive" regimes.*

The efforts made to specify temporal sequences governed by the "dynamics of (de)legitimation" were not meant to provide an "ideas-based" alternative to the "power-distributional" explanations that dominate the historical institutionalist literature. On the contrary, the formulation of an integrated explanation accounting for the interactions between the "dynamics of power" and the "dynamics of legitimation" ranks as this book's second main objective.

The manner in which the interaction drives processes of institutional reproduction and institutional decay—in other words, how it affects variations in the value and stability of institutions—may be summarized as follows. Just as the logic of "increasing returns to power" essentially boils down to the notion that "power begets power"—in other words, that a shift in the distribution of power and material resources provides its beneficiaries with the means further to widen existing asymmetries of power—the logic of processes of increasing legitimation is founded on the notion that "legitimation begets legitimation." More prosaically, when shifts in a society's distribution of values, preferences, and beliefs cause levels of quasi-voluntary compliance with an institution or a set of institutions to increase, the increased effectiveness with which the institutions concerned structure the behavior of relevant actors provides an additional boost to the diffusion of ideas consistent with the institutions' appropriateness.

In turn, it is not difficult to envision scenarios in which the two logics end up working in conjunction with one another, whether in a mutually reinforcing or a mutually exhausting fashion. On the one hand, while it is reasonable to expect that "power begets legitimation"—that is, that power comes with the resources required to bolster an institution's legitimacy—it is also to be expected that "legitimation begets power" insofar as an increase in an institution's legitimacy makes the exercise of power more efficient, freeing up resources that might otherwise be spent on monitoring and enforcing compliance. On the other hand, a decrease in a superordinate group's power may very well cause an erosion in the legitimacy of the institutions that govern a relation of power, and vice versa, in the event that the resulting decline in levels of compliance forces the status quo's defenders to take measures that further antagonize the members of subordinate groups and/or deplete the "resource stocks" upon which asymmetries of power are built. The same, interactive dynamics conceivably help to drive processes of gradual institutional change, which are shown in this book to combine the logics of institutional reproduction and institutional decay.

(iii) The identification of conditions, or variables, affecting whether sequences of institutional development are triggered, as well as the "rapidity and decisiveness" with which they contribute to institutional reproduction, institutional decay, and institutional change.

The inquiry conducted into the conditions or variables affecting the activation as well as the "rapidity and decisiveness" of sequences of institutional development governed by the dynamics of "power" and "legitimation" emphasized the role of structural factors as well as contingencies expected to recur frequently enough—and with significant enough consequences—to warrant consideration. Each of the preceding three chapters took care to acknowledge that the complexity of the phenomena involved makes it impossible to assemble a comprehensive causal explanation of the development of political institutions. Instead, the goal was to reduce the indeterminacy surrounding the most important explanatory variables at play, as well as the effect of variables that might conceivably affect the outcomes of interest in different directions. Perhaps the most recurrent among the structural variables invoked to explain aspects of the process of institutional development may be subsumed under the headings of "social structure" and "social change"—the former including the composition of society as well as levels of socioeconomic development and inequality and the latter comprising processes of modernization as well as demographic/cultural transformations. Among the "contingent" factors considered, the main ones relate to (i) the manner in which a society's institutions are introduced, interpreted, and enforced; (ii) the prevalence of certain values, identities, and beliefs among the members of major social constituencies; and (iii) the main groups' socialization and mobilization into politics, including their internal cohesiveness, their historical rivalries and alliances, the effectiveness of their political and civil society organizations, the quality of their leadership, and the outcomes of their strategic interactions.

Implications for the Practice of Institutional Engineering

The contributions made in this book to the literature on political development have implications for each of the major issues involved in the practice of "political engineering" or "institutional engineering"—namely, its overall feasibility and effectiveness, the objectives it should pursue and their order of priority, and the sorts of interventions or manipulations offering the best chance to bring about the desired outcomes. This section examines these issues in turn.

On the Efficacy of Institutional Engineering

Thousands of years since political philosophers first entertained the possibility that suitably designed rules and procedures might structure human behavior effectively and predictably enough to aid in the creation of a "good" polity, the notion that anything of value can be achieved in the real world through the purposive design of political institutions remains controversial. While this book was dedicated to assembling an explanatory theory featuring political institutions as the explanandum, the importance of the development of political institutions stems in part from the assumption, or the expectation, that institutions are a crucial determinant (or explanans) of a society's prospects of peace and prosperity, among the many states of the world potentially arising from the human interactions that political institutions help structure. Indeed, a vast literature is dedicated to the study of the most disparate outcomes believed to be affected by the workings of institutions functioning as *independent* variables.

Certainly, the study of institutions no longer *defines* political science to the extent that it did when the discipline was more or less coterminous with "old institutionalism" (Peters 1999: 3–11), whose principal concern was to "analyze the successes and failures of constitutions" and other formal institutions (Ginsburg 2012: 1). The so-called behavioral revolution caused a shift in emphasis from formal to informal aspects of politics—in retrospect, a much-needed shift, especially after the initial excesses of the "revolution" were later tempered as a result of the revival of "new institutionalism." What is more, the field's rediscovery of institutions took place at a time when an equally profound shift in the discipline's prevailing ontology and methodology had revolutionized the purpose, the style, the instruments, and the language of political science research, prompting many of its practitioners to abandon mere description in exchange for tackling questions calling for a causal explanation (Hall 2003: 375–81; Peters 1999: 11–15).

In the time since—and especially in the wake of the collapse of scores of dictatorial regimes across Africa, Asia, Eastern Europe, and Latin America—a great deal of work has focused on how institutions affect the longevity, stability, and quality of democratic regimes, whether directly or indirectly, through their effect on variables such as political polarization or legislative fragmentation. By any reasonable standard, this literature has produced *relatively* few "actionable" findings capable of informing the design or choice of the "right" institutions at a particular point in time and space. On the contrary, while decades of theoretical inquiry and empirical analysis have created limited amounts of applicable knowledge, "our predictions of how institutions will operate are, at best, probabilistic guesses" (Ginsburg 2012: 1). In some instances, the reason why institutions do not produce consistent effects across time and/or space is that the variation in the "strength" of the institutions concerned, as well as in their enforcement, causes relevant actors to respond differently to their provisions (Levitsky and Murillo 2009). It is worth pointing out that it may not be enough to "control" for contingencies of the sort in order to produce more robust, credible findings, given the influence many ascribe to "unobservable deep structures of society" (Ginsburg 2012: 5); the resilience of ingrained, habitual patterns of thought and behavior (e.g., Norris 2004: 21–22); and what Offe (1996: 212) has referred to as "unreconstructed mental or moral dispositions." Certainly, the problem is not unique to, or unusually pronounced in, "new institutionalism" or for that matter the discipline of political science. The unrealistic assumptions often undergirding predictions and post-dictions about the effects of institutions have come under attack in other scientific disciplines as well, as exemplified by the literature dedicated to debunking the entire construct of *homo oeconomicus* (as popularized in Thaler and Sunstein 2008; Kahneman 2011; and Thaler 2015). Indeed, Elster (1999: 1–10) faults the "social sciences" *as a whole* for the failure to produce a single, empirically established "lawlike generalization."

Either way, given the paucity of research seeking to derive predictions of institutional effects from more realistic models of human motivation, cognition, and behavior, one cannot but concur with Elster (1988: 309) that the social sciences are "light years away" from being capable of making precise and accurate predictions about the consequences of "major institutional changes" in the real world. And, in the continuing absence of clear evidence of the effectiveness of institutional engineering, there appears to be a growing consensus regarding its limitations. Aside from generally recognizing that the opportunity rarely presents itself comprehensively to overhaul a nation's institutions autonomously enough from the influence of the past to enact major change (e.g., see Elster 1988; Offe 1996; Pierson 2004: chap. 4; Vermeule 2007; Renwick 2010), the literature has recently witnessed a backlash against the "institutional turn" of comparative political research writ large, as some writers have called into question the power of institutions to *shape* outcomes of interest as opposed to simply *mediate* the effect of structural, background conditions, as well as the availability of research designs capable of distinguishing "the effects of institutions on outcomes from the effects of structural variables or elite preferences that shape both" (Pepinsky 2014: 631–32).

How does the theory of institutional development assembled in these pages speak to the feasibility and the potential effectiveness of attempts to "engineer" desirable outcomes through the purposive design of political institutions? On the one hand, some of the book's main insights and findings have implications that are consistent with the scholarship that emphasizes the limitations inherent to projects of institutional engineering. Aside from underscoring the inadequacy of models built on the assumptions of the rational choice research program, the analysis featured in some of the book's chapters reiterates that it is only rarely the case that a set of actors operate with the autonomy and freedom of choice required to enact reforms designed to produce major change, especially because of the difficulties involved in dislodging institutions whose entrenchment benefits from the mutual reinforcement between the dynamics of power and legitimation. Indeed, the synthesis of "power-based" and "ideas-based" explanations emerging from this book suggests that the societies most in need of reforms capable of improving the efficiency of their political system, among other desirable outcomes, are also the least likely to benefit from institutional engineering, as conditions of underdevelopment and extreme inequality were repeatedly shown to hinder the stabilization of inclusive, egalitarian institutions, however well designed. On the other hand, the emphasis placed throughout this study on the "normative force" of institutions—that is, their capacity to define, for the individuals involved, what "the right thing to do" is—potentially renders the design of institutions even more consequential than it is in theories that treat institutions exclusively as "incentive-based structures" (Sartori 1997: ix).

On the Objectives of Institutional Engineering

Before an attempt can be made to describe in greater detail how the model of individual behavior adopted in this book might inform expectations about the effects of institutions, it is worth addressing what the main goals of institutional engineering should be, especially in light of the findings presented in this book. Ginsburg (2012: 2) points out that while "the field of compara-tive constitutional studies" has "a long and distinguished lineage" dating back to Aristotle and "his counterparts in ancient China, India, and elsewhere," "constitutional design in its contemporary sense is associated with the rise and spread of the written constitutional form, conventionally understood to have emerged in full flower in the late eighteenth century." Indeed, it is only in the last two centuries that scholars have placed "a discrete emphasis on constitution-making as an act of purposive institutional design." What is more, while political thinkers have long seen it worthwhile to theorize the effects of "the machinery of the governmental system" (Peters 1999: 4), it was only in the late twentieth century that "the revival of various institutional-isms in the social sciences," combined with the effects of the so-called third wave of democratization (Huntington 1991), "brought new attention to con-stitutions as instruments of democratization" and "prompted a new round of efforts to theorize and analyze institutional design" (Ginsburg 2012: 3–4). Having converged on the study of how institutions affect the longevity, stabil-ity, and quality of democracy, however, disagreements have persisted over the indicators that best capture the variables of interest, as well as on the specific outcomes to be promoted to strengthen democratic regimes indirectly.

Up until recently, prominent scholars still found it necessary (and polit-ically correct) to speculate about the ideal timing with which universal suf-frage should be granted in a country's political development. In his initial plea to political scientists to become involved in political engineering, Sartori (1968: 277) proposed that "the massive enfranchisement of largely illiterate and deprived masses will not do any good to whatever embryonic democ-racy may exist in the countries that are starting from scratch"—on the con-trary, universal suffrage "makes rulership demagogic, and demagogic ruler-ship easy." On this point, Sartori's argument echoes Huntington's (1968) fear that a breakdown in political order might be in the cards in countries where elected governments with uncertain roots in civil society are placed in charge of weak states that cannot handle the surge in popular demands resulting from fast-paced modernization. Both scholars also agreed about the funda-mental importance of political parties. For Sartori (1968), the first priority of political engineering was the development of a "structured" party system—a system of nationwide party organizations with a meaningful enough "brand" to become more important than the personalities involved—capable of pre-senting a country's voters with a choice between a limited, stable set of aggre-gated, programmatic governing alternatives.

The view Sartori (1968) had articulated before an unprecedentedly broad and sustained "wave" of democratization ushered in the diffusion of democratic regimes to some of the world's least developed regions remained popular years after the wave had run its course. By the turn of the century, Schmitter (2001: 67) pointed out, mainstream political scientists overwhelmingly still held the position that the main imperative for countries undergoing democratic transitions was to "get the parties right!" Certainly, Schmitter (2001) was not the first to urge colleagues to look beyond political parties to understand how best to promote the consolidation of functioning democratic regimes. Even before it became apparent that political parties throughout the world had undergone transformations undermining their capacity to play "consolidation functions," such as integrating diverse electorates, leading scholars had attempted to broaden the range of outcomes to be accomplished through the purposive design of institutions on the way to building democratic regimes presiding over peaceful and prosperous societies.

By far the best known among such attempts remains Arend Lijphart's vision of a "consensus" (1984, 1999) or "power-sharing" (1997, 2004) democracy, articulated over several decades beginning with the author's own work (1968, 1969, 1977) on the virtues of "consociationalism" and "consociational democracy" in "divided societies"—societies, that is, that are "both ethnically diverse and where ethnicity is a politically salient cleavage around which interests are organized for political purposes" (Reilly 2001: 4; see also Rabushka and Shepsle 1972: 21). Thirty-five years into the research agenda's prosecution, Lijphart (2004: 96–97) cited as "a point of broad, if not absolute, agreement" among "experts of divided societies and constitutional engineering" the notion that "the successful establishment of democracy in divided societies requires two key elements: power sharing and group autonomy." In a footnote, Lijphart (107, fn. 1) added that a power-sharing democracy's "secondary characteristics are proportionality, especially in legislative elections . . . and a minority veto on the most vital issues that affect the rights and autonomy of minorities." Lijphart's (1999: 3–5) broader concept of "consensus democracy" also requires a rough balance of power between executive and legislative power, a "corporatist interest-group system aimed at compromise and concertation," relatively "rigid" constitutions, a system of courts endowed with the power of judicial review, and central bank independence.

In one of his more recent contributions to the subject's literature, Lijphart's (2004: 97–99) specific recommendations to those tasked with designing institutions in divided societies are preceded by an attempt to rebut the "critics of power sharing"—in the abstract as well as in reference to cases, like Lebanon in the 1970s, that have long been cited by those seeking to discredit the model. In this connection, Lijphart argues that "the relative success of a power-sharing system is contingent upon the specific mechanisms devised to yield the broad representation that constitutes its core" (99). Alas, Lijphart (2004) fails to entertain, much less rebuts, the fundamental criticism of power sharing featured in Sartori's (1997) own book-length treatment of "comparative constitutional engineering." While conceding that "Lijphart was absolutely right in holding that a democracy could work even under adverse conditions (especially a fragmented political culture) by having recourse to non-majoritarian, consociational practices," Sartori (70–71) faults Lijphart for having "blown up these premises into a 'grand theory' of a superior form of democracy" disconnected from the circumstances in which consociational arrangements had originally proven effective—namely, a "segmented social structure" where politicized social cleavages are "cumulative and self-reinforcing," as opposed to "crosscutting."

After listing some of the specific downsides of "grand coalitions," the "dispersal of power among executive and legislature," "proportional representation," and ".minority veto," Sartori points out that "Lijphart's argument can be turned around all the way":

> By facilitating something you make it happen. The more you give in, the more you are asked to give. And what is not discouraged becomes in fact encouraged. If you reward divisions and divisiveness (and that is precisely what *proporz* and veto power do), you increase and eventually heighten divisions and divisiveness. In the end, then, Lijphart's machinery may well engender more consensus-breaking than consensus-making. (1997: 71–72)

In this sense, power-sharing arrangements may offer the only real hope for those wishing to "neutraliz[e] the centrifugal pulls of their societies" (72) in the presence of the segmented social structures for which consociationalism was originally devised, where deep divisions are based on a single cleavage or a set of overlapping, mutually reinforcing cleavages. In other divided societies, however, Sartori appears justified in his fear that power-sharing arrangements will end up encouraging the same divisive rhetoric and behavior that earned a group's representatives a share of real political power. Worse, given the tendency of human beings to internalize attitudes that are consistent with their public statements or behavior, the group's membership may come genuinely to believe the extremist positions their leaders took for purely strategic reasons. In societies where cleavages are crosscutting and social identities are multidimensional, power-sharing arrangements might actually undermine the efforts made to defuse conflict through the politicization and "institutionalization" of multiple dimensions of a person's social identity, originally undertaken in the hope of preventing any of them from fueling the rise of chauvinists and extremists (Chandra 2005).

The same goes for Lijphart's (2004) preference for group autonomy. Consistent with the theory of gradual institutional change developed in this book, it may prove unwise to reward the groups responsible for threatening secession or civil war with the control of a sizable portion of the national territory. Far from being successfully appeased, major concessions of this nature may very well embolden the groups in question to press forward, in a quest to parlay into additional concessions the power and legitimacy accruing from the implicit recognition of their claims to a particular territory. Just as in the case of power-sharing arrangements, an earnest attempt to meet the demands for autonomy of relevant minorities could end up placing a fledgling democracy on "a one-way slope that leads to a self-reinforcing system of minority appetites" (Sartori 1997: 72).

On the Instruments of Institutional Engineering

Having described the implications that the explanation of institutional development articulated in this book has for the viability and potential effectiveness of political/institutional engineering, as well as for the outcomes worth pursuing through the manipulation of political institutions, what remains to be done is draw some conclusions about the choice of institutions best suited to bolster the stability and quality of "inclusive," democratic regimes, which includes the peaceful coexistence of groups potentially in conflict with one another.

It is worth stipulating up front, as implied by the theory of institutional development assembled in these pages, that the *process* by which a democratic regime's institutions are designed, deliberated, enacted, and enforced can be just as crucial to the regime's prospects as the institutions' *contents*. As shown earlier in this study, the reproduction and eventual entrenchment of a set of institutions hinges in part on their capacity to harness what has been referred to as the "dynamics of legitimation," which were said to be driven by the tendency of "legitimation to beget legitimation." In turn, an institution's legitimacy is partially a function of the legitimacy accorded to the *process* that brought the institution into existence—as determined, above all, by the process's inclusiveness and its fulfillment of shared standards of procedural and distributive justice. The inclusiveness of the process also benefits a democratic regime by preventing any one group from designing rules and procedures conferring upon it an early advantage in terms of power and material resources, which might otherwise allow the group in question eventually to parlay the "dynamics of power" into the assertion of a position dominant enough for it to "capture" or overthrow the regime itself.

As for the *contents* of institutions, the vast literature dedicated to studying their effects on the resilience and the effectiveness of democratic regimes has identified a variety of potential "levers of political intervention" (Sartori 1968: 272). Among them, the institutions that have received the most attention are the form of government (presidential, semi-presidential, or parliamentary), the electoral systems that govern the election of presidents and assemblies, the territorial concentration or dispersion of governmental authority, the configuration and relative inclusiveness of policy-making procedures, the rules structuring the competition between special interest groups and their relationship with the state, the availability and openness of "direct democracy" access channels, and the structure and/or independence of the judiciary, the bureaucracy, and the central bank. The remainder of this chapter focuses most intently on the first three sets of institutions on this list, though the discussion will occasionally touch upon some of the remaining instruments of institutional engineering.

The work by Lijphart (2004) discussed above in reference to the *objectives* of institutional engineering also provides a good representation of the conventional wisdom that has emerged concerning some of the major levers of political intervention, which may be credited to previous writings by Lijphart himself as well as a host of other scholars. Once again, Lijphart's (96) recommendations are corollaries of the claim—described as enjoying "broad agreement" among scholars and practitioners—that "the successful establishment of democratic government in divided societies requires . . . power sharing and group autonomy." If that is the case, it should follow logically that "power sharing" is best achieved in the context of a parliamentary system with a largely ceremonial, indirectly elected head of state and a highly proportional electoral system that ensures the representativeness of legislative assemblies. Conversely, group autonomy is presumably best achieved through a federal (or an otherwise highly decentralized) system if the main groups are concentrated geographically or through the concession of non-territorial forms of autonomy to territorially dispersed groups, which should as much as possible be allowed to live by "their" own rules. That is the case of some of India's main religious minorities, especially on matters of civil law (marriage, adoption, etc.).

The comparative literature studying the effects of political institutions has produced a modicum of empirical support for Lijphart's (2004) recommendations. Perhaps best known is the debate over the dangers of presidential systems in "divided," underdeveloped, and/or transitional societies. Most influentially, Linz (1994: 70) argued that "presidentialism seems to involve greater risk for stable democratic politics," largely because of the unrepresentativeness characteristic of "winner-take-all" systems, the divisiveness/polarization promoted by the excessive stakes attached to presidential elections, and the likelihood that presidents will end up abusing their extensive powers whenever faced with significant opposition. Around the same time, Sartori (1997: 93) noted that "the problem" with presidentialism may ultimately have less to do with the presence of overly powerful presidents than "the separation of power principle; a separation that keeps Latin American presidentialisms in a perennial, unsteady oscillation between power abuse and power deficiency." The plausibility of these arguments notwithstanding, the task of establishing empirical support for Linz's argument is complicated by the fact that while there is a clear association between presidentialism and the breakdown of democratic regimes, presidential and semi-presidential systems have historically been most prevalent in the postcolonial regimes of Latin America and Africa, while parliamentary systems are dominant in Western Europe and in the Commonwealth nations of the Caribbean, North America, Asia, and Oceania. Confusing matters further, presidential and semi-presidential systems were adopted in many of the formal democracies that replaced communist and military regimes during the most recent "wave" of democratization (Francisco 2000: 141–56).

Do these systematic differences between presidential and parliamentary democracies qualify the conventional wisdom regarding presidentialism? Do they negate it altogether? Interpretations vary. According to Boix (2003: 150–55), who focuses on the distribution of economic resources, presidential and parliamentary democracies become equally stable as a country's economy grows less unequal and/or more developed, more industrialized, and more urban. Still, Boix (155) argues that "adopting presidentialism is probably a bad idea in sub-Saharan Africa and a substantial part of Latin America" as well as in "postsocialist economies rich in natural resources"—for conditions of inequality, underdevelopment, and low asset mobility heighten the potential for the abuse of presidential powers. Conversely, Cheibub (2007: 140) found the adoption of presidential or parliamentary institutions to have no effect on a country's democratic prospects when important aspects of a country's political development are taken into account—"what kills democracies," he argues, "is not presidentialism but rather their military legacy." Almost contemporarily, Svolik's (2008: 155) statistical analysis concluded that "both a military past and presidential executive have a large, negative, and independent effect on a democracy's *susceptibility* to reversals"—that is, these variables *indirectly* make democracies more "susceptible to other factors that will eventually lead to a democratic breakdown," the most important being an economic downturn—but neither is found to "have any direct effect on the hazard of authoritarian reversals faced by transitional democracies."

None of these caveats appear anywhere in Lijphart's (2004: 101–3) recommendations, which simply reiterate the need for power sharing based on Linz's argument against presidentialism, supplemented by a short passage purporting to justify the claim that "semi-presidential systems represent only a slight improvement over pure presidentialism." In previous works, however, Lijphart had shown himself to be rather more attuned to the importance of the specific characteristics of each system. Among presidential and semi-presidential systems, for instance, a crucial distinction must be drawn between those where presidents are extremely powerful and those where presidents are constitutionally weak and/or constrained by powerful legislatures. Both types may well be unstable—albeit, as Sartori (1997) has shown, for reasons that stand diametrically opposed to one another. Internal differences are equally if not more consequential among parliamentary systems. In the highly majoritarian forms of parliamentarism typical of the "Westminster model of democracy," the powers wielded by the prime minister can, in practice, be more extensive than those presidential systems typically reserved for elected presidents, especially in situations where the prime minister also leads the largest party in a two-party system. More compatible with Lijphart's (1999) "consensus model of democracy" are those parliamentary systems where political power is more dispersed and the authority of the prime minister is subject to far more stringent limitations, deriving from the presence of a highly fragmented legislature that makes it necessary for the chief executive to build and manage a coalition featuring multiple political parties, some of them potentially quite small. In turn, securing this outcome typically requires the manipulation of another "lever" of institutional engineering—namely, the electoral system, or the set of rules that govern the casting of votes and the translation of votes into seats in legislative elections.

A highly proportional electoral system governing the election of national legislative assemblies is another key feature of power sharing or consensus democracies. Of course, the downsides of proportional representation are well known. Above all, high levels of legislative fragmentation entail the presence of a number of small and mid-sized political parties, which often play a vital role in the coalitions supporting a national executive (e.g., see Olson and Zeckhauser 1966), potentially undermining its effectiveness. Coalition governments also have a tendency to be rather unstable, especially in light of the fact that highly proportional systems can encourage party leaders to take more extreme positions to stand out from the competition (Downs 1957: 125–27)—in Sartori's (1976: 127) famous typology of "party systems," "(ideologically) *polarized* pluralism" can only develop in the context of high fragmentation (five or more relevant parties). As Sartori (1997: 60) himself put it, "Proportional representation does not *necessarily* lead . . . to quarrelsome and stalemated coalition government"; the "ungovernability charge" often leveled against it, however, does apply "when P.R. [proportional representation] brings about heterogeneous coalitions between partners or, indeed, non-partners that play a veto game against each other," as is typically the case of divided societies. Lijphart (2004), to be sure, does not deny the downsides of proportional representation but appears to treat them as the price to pay to ensure that minorities are represented and power is shared. Lijphart (103–4) also proposes a remedy specifically designed to reduce government instability—namely, the adoption of the "constructive vote of no confidence." As noted, however, his work does not address the divisiveness likely to characterize institutional arrangements where divisiveness is rewarded with a seat at the "power sharing" table (Sartori 1997: 72).

Once again, a very similar charge can be leveled against the proposition that ethnic and ethno-regional minorities should, whenever possible, be granted the autonomy required to govern "their" own affairs and live under laws of "their" own choosing. In practice, Lijpart (2004: 104–5) argues that "a federal system is undoubtedly an excellent way to provide autonomy" for "geographically concentrated communal groups," especially if the main territorial units to which governmental authority is devolved are kept "relatively small—both to increase the prospects that each unit will be relatively homogenous and to avoid dominance of large states on the federal level." But though Lijphart (105) acknowledges that there are "a great many decisions to be made regarding details that will vary from country to country," he does not address a major, fundamental problem with federalism—namely, the potential for decentralization to "fan," as opposed to "dampen," the "flames of extremism" (Brancati 2006, 2008). Aside from fueling the rise of ethno-regional parties—and, in the process, hardening the "lower-level identities" to which they appeal—decentralization makes it possible for such forces to introduce illiberal and/or discriminatory laws, policies, and practices in the territories they administer or, worse, to appropriate the resources made available by their control of local governments in order to pursue an extremist, secessionist agenda. In these contexts, even relatively "moderate" forces may be compelled to take similar positions or measures to fend off the challenges leveled by more extremist competitors, in accordance with the logic of "ethnic outbidding" (Rabushka and Shepsle 1972). The same goes for the potential abuse of non-territorial forms of autonomy, which must not afford any group an exemption from respecting the rights and freedoms to which every citizen is entitled in a genuine democracy.

As it happens, the discussion of the conventional wisdom articulated by Lijphart (2004) and others with regard to the practice of institutional engineering points to a conclusion that is entirely consistent with one of this book's main recurring themes—that is, at the end of the day, whether it makes sense to adopt institutions designed to instantiate power sharing and group autonomy depends on the context in which the arrangements in questions are meant to operate. Having said that, the question addressed in this book's final pages is how the theory formulated in this study—which features the development of political institutions as the explanandum or dependent variable—can help devise expectations about the *consequences* that the manipulation of the main levers of political intervention is likely to have in different contexts, as defined by particular combinations of structural and contingent factors or variables. For each of several, stylized scenarios, the following discussion seeks to identify, in accordance with the theory assembled in this book, the political institutions with the best chance to bolster, or the smallest chance to compromise, a democratic regime's prospects of success. Once again, the discussion assumes that the goal is to help maximize the longevity of "inclusive" regimes that guarantee the peaceful coexistence of major social groups, passably "good" quality of government, and acceptable levels of economic performance, in addition to protecting the rights that all citizens should enjoy on an equal basis or encouraging the participation of all eligible persons in the decisions that shape their nations' present and future.

In relatively wealthy, "middle-class societies," the main threat to the value and stability of "inclusive," democratic regimes is represented by the potential that elites will take advantage of the public's disillusionment with decaying pluralist institutions in order to "capture" the system and take measures that heighten levels of economic inequality, starve the government of resources for the benefit of themselves and their peers, dismantle welfare protections to finance the upward redistribution of wealth, and hence render even more widespread the perception that the system is "rigged" and indifferent to the needs and aspirations of ordinary people, all of which helps to fuel the disillusionment that made it possible for elites to "capture" the system and hijack democratic institutions in the first place. It follows from this consideration that the choice of institutions in relatively wealthy societies should aim primarily to bolster levels of political participation, as well as to maximize the political system's efficiency and responsiveness to the public's demands.

Beyond this, the empirical record tends to support the idea that democracy in affluent societies can thrive in the presence of very different configurations of institutions. Then again, the literature also suggests that levels of political participation are bolstered by the relevance and by the competitiveness of national elections as well as by the representativeness of the legislative bodies they produce (e.g., see Franklin 1996; Lijphart 1997)—outcomes that are conceivably favored by the workings of a moderately proportional electoral system in the context of parliamentarism or a presidential system with a strong legislative branch. Moreover, while the establishment of a federal system may have the downside of detracting from the policy significance of national elections, this may be an acceptable price to pay in exchange for the improvements that decentralization brings to the system's accessibility and responsiveness. In countries where a limited number of national parties are set to dominate competition, it also may be worth electing at least part of the national legislature through nominal voting (open-list proportional representation or a mixed-member proportional system with a single-member district component) to incentivize constituency service and make the system more accessible to ordinary citizens.

Nothing approximating such an embarrassment of riches characterizes the design of democratic institutions in underdeveloped and highly unequal societies. Perhaps most importantly, conditions of underdevelopment and extreme inequality make "inclusive," democratic regimes potentially most threatening to the interests of economic elites, while also increasing the likelihood that elites will command sufficient resources to undermine or reverse their societies' democratization. The situation may be complicated further because underdeveloped nations have often embarked on their transitions to democracy before their populations have come strongly to identify as the members of a single national community. Indeed, underdevelopment is among the principal reasons why these societies tend to be deeply divided along communal lines. As Barkan, Densham, and Rushton (2006: 929) have observed, "considerations of place, ethnicity, and language" are crucial sources of social identities in pre-industrial societies where "voters are rooted to the land and the local communities to which they belong." And, when winning elections requires above all the efficient distribution of patronage goods and services, the traits that define ethnicity often allow politicians to distinguish in-groups from out-groups more effectively, while providing voters with an easier way to form expectations about the likely beneficiaries of patronage services (Fearon 1999; Chandra 2004). Alas, the danger is that the competition for scarce patronage resources and coveted "goods of modernity" (Bates 1983) could generate enough fear and loathing, especially in contexts of underdevelopment, that the groups concerned end up ensnared in a no-holds-barred fight for control of the state. Alternatively, minorities may threaten to secede in response to the efforts made by the state to integrate or assimilate them into a single nation—policies whose prosecution has long been known all too frequently to feature the use of repressive, illiberal measures (Linz and Stepan 1996: 25).

As noted, then, the politics of divided societies can be a formidable impediment to the reproduction and eventual consolidation of "inclusive," democratic institutions. Worse, while the politicization of communal identities may aggravate the challenges presented by underdevelopment and inequality—among other things, the added potential for conflict, disorder, and unrest could end up strengthening the argument made by "unreformed" elites as justification for intervening in the democratic process—conditions of underdevelopment may in turn heighten the potential for social divisions to derail a country's democratization, raising the stakes of intergroup competition as well as increasing the costs of a group's exclusion from government. In these circumstances, political institutions should ideally be designed in such a way as to (i) reassure minorities (including the country's elites) that they will fare well enough under "inclusive" institutions to make it worth their while to play by the rules of the democratic game, instead of turning to alternative, extra-constitutional means to protect their interests and status; and (ii) strengthen political parties in an effort to promote responsible government, discourage unelected officials from interfering in the country's political process, and provide all major constituencies with an organizational vehicle dedicated to a group's representation and the defense of its interests and status.

In most divided societies, the likelihood that the mobilization of communal, ethnic identities will take on its most extreme form in a context of weak and unstructured parties militates against the adoption of presidential or semi-presidential systems. Beyond the old debate about the downsides of presidentialism, the mere fact that presidential elections tend to make politics about personalities—as opposed to promoting the aggregation and crystallization of a limited, stable set of programmatically meaningful, national parties capable of offering voters a real choice between plausible governing alternatives—renders these systems of government inappropriate for most underdeveloped, divided societies.

As suggested above, the power-sharing arrangements championed by Lijphart (2004) are arguably best suited for so-called segmented societies—as Sartori (1976: 180–81) defined them, based on Lorwin (1971: 141), these are countries where "cultural heterogeneity" results in the "segmentation" or "compartmentalization" of society, complete with the duplication of the educational system, the mass media, and civil society organizations on each side of the communal cleavages that divide the population. Certainly, the adoption of power sharing (i.e., consociationalism) in ethnically diverse or "plural" societies—segmented and otherwise—is not without potential complication or downside. For while, as Sartori (1997: 70) pointed out, "the necessary condition for the successful working of consociational democracy is an 'elite cooperation' that intentfully counters the disintegrative tendencies of their societies," the logic of "ethnic outbidding" (Rabushka and Shepsle 1972) exposes the ease with which political elites may lose the wherewithal to cooperate across communal lines upon being outflanked by the extreme, ethno-centrist appeals issued by rivals within their communal groups. Having said that, the overlapping, mutually reinforcing cleavage structure and the relatively pronounced separation between communal groups characteristic of segmented societies render the principal alternatives to power sharing—for example, the adoption of an electoral system that incentivizes politicians to campaign for second- and third-preference votes in other groups (Horowitz 2003; Reilly 2001) or the introduction of rules that leverage the multidimensionality of most people's social identities to undermine the resonance of extremist appeals—even more impracticable. All in all, therefore, the com-

bination of a parliamentary system of government and a moderately proportional electoral system arguably remains the best choice for segmented
societies, especially at low levels of development. As Diamond (1999: 104)
has written, "Where cleavage groups are sharply defined and group identities
deeply felt, the overriding imperative is to avoid broad and indefinite exclusion from power of any significant group."

In other varieties of culturally heterogeneous, divided societies, the discussion above has highlighted the possibility that power-sharing arrangements might actually incentivize extremism across communal lines. To para-
phrase Sartori's (1997) criticism, not only do these arrangements encourage
the leaders of the groups that were granted a more or less permanent share of
political power to engage in the same divisive behavior that won them a seat
at the "power sharing" table while incentivizing the groups excluded from
power to adopt even more divisive rhetoric and behavior. What is more, the
arrangements in question tend to increase the availability of voters to support
divisive political forces by boosting the primacy of the source of social identification recognized as the basis for the apportionment of cabinet posts, government agencies, committee chairmanships, state-owned utilities and cor-
porations, public employment quotas, and formal roles in the policy-making
process. This reasoning is rather consistent with the logic employed in this
study—above all, the "normative force" of institutions as well as the tendency
for self- and system justification to cause relevant actors to adjust their beliefs
about what is, and is not, "the right thing to do" in accordance with behavior
undertaken in compliance with existing rules and procedures.

In culturally and/or ethnically diverse societies that are not segmented,
to the extent that the relevant cleavages are crosscutting—or that multiple
sources of most people's social identities are politicized—it makes sense to
attempt to design institutions that give party elites an incentive to coordinate across communal lines, form multiethnic organizations or alliances, or
appeal to the members of multiple groups in the run-up to election day, while
forcing voters to think beyond a single dimension of their identities prior to
casting their ballots. Where most of the politically salient, mobilized groups
are dispersed throughout the national territory, this may be accomplished
through an electoral system that combines low district magnitude (just how
low might hinge on the degree of ethnic diversity; in highly fragmented societies, larger districts with more seats in play prevent the systematic exclusion
of smaller groups) with rules that grant voters the capacity to rank-order candidates (the Alternative Vote for single-member districts; the Single Trans-

ferable Vote, or STV, for multimember districts) or force candidates who did not clear a certain threshold to submit to a runoff.

Alternatively, a proportional, closed-list system where voters choose from among party lists in large (potentially national) districts—combined with a relatively high legal threshold—might better serve the goal of promoting the aggregation of meaningful political parties. On the one hand, larger electoral districts water down the support of local notables, making it more difficult for any of them to win seats by going it alone, while rewarding electoral forces capable of putting together support coalitions spanning multiple regions. On the other hand, closed lists confer greater primacy to party organizations, inducing voters to think of elections as competitions between *parties*, as opposed to individual candidates. The confluence of these two factors should in turn lay the groundwork for the existing parties to penetrate peripheral constituencies. For if the rules reward electoral forces capable of garnering support throughout the entirety of the national territory, the reduction in the number of wasted votes offers budding national parties an incentive to campaign in places where they do not enjoy anywhere close to plurality support. The establishment of a relatively prohibitive legal threshold can serve to prevent excessive fragmentation in the distribution of votes and seats, while further compromising the electoral prospects of unaffiliated, local big men.

Potentially more problematic are those divided societies where the relevant communal groups are geographically concentrated in territorial enclaves where each constitutes a plurality or a majority of the population. The impact that the groups' geographic concentration has on the viability of democracy has been the subject of contradictory theoretical expectations. On the one hand, some research suggests that groups living in ethnically diverse communities face a particularly extreme version of the "security dilemma" and are hence more prone to outbidding and violence (Posen 1993). Kaufmann (1996) went so far as to advocate the physical separation of rival groups to defuse any such potential escalation. On the other hand, Fearon and Laitin (2003) find that groups with a regional, rural base are far more likely to rebel and engage in violence on a large scale. They explain this finding by noting that (i) secessionist wars are by far the most common form of violent ethnic conflict; and (ii) widely dispersed or mainly urban groups typically have no particular claim to make about a separate territory deserving of self-determination, independence, or some measure of autonomy. All things considered, the evidence seems to point to the conclusion that divided societies where internally homogenous groups live in territorially segregated enclaves are most prone to outbidding and extremism, as the opportunities to press for the dismemberment of a developing polity are greatest when ethnic and territorial cleavages overlap (Weidmann 2009).

In these cases, whether a majoritarian or a proportional electoral system is in place makes little difference to a communal group's chances to win seats in national elections. Indeed, whereas proportional representation is typically advocated to permit even small groups to earn representation in national legislatures, in these cases the adoption of a proportional electoral system might serve a different purpose—namely, to prevent a single ethnoregional party from dominating elections in each group's territorial enclaves, thereby providing other, perhaps more moderate parties a chance to remain competitive in peripheral districts. This consideration, however, comes with the obvious caveat that the workings of a highly proportional system might result in excessive legislative fragmentation, especially in the presence of high levels of ethnic diversity. In addition, the effect in question may conceivably be stronger—or, at any rate, carry more serious implications for the stability of democracy—at low levels of development, where governments hampered by their coalitions' excessive fragmentation risk providing the opening required for the country's armed forces, characteristically acting at the behest of wealthy elites, to suspend electoral democracy.

Of course, the primary institutional means that much of the literature advocates implementing to reduce the potential for intergroup conflict in societies where communal groups are concentrated geographically are those arrangements that guarantee group autonomy to govern their own affairs. Group autonomy generally entails the establishment of a "federal," as opposed to a "unitary," state—that is, a state where subnational, regional governments exercise independent, constitutionally sanctioned authority over the passage, the enforcement, and the adjudication of laws governing one or more issue areas, as well as the power to raise tax revenue. Beyond this, a great deal of variation characterizes real-world federal systems, on dimensions that include the structure/organization of subnational governments, the extensiveness and symmetry of the powers exercised by local authorities, and the role played by regional representatives in the legislative and the policymaking processes at the national level (Stepan 1999). Group autonomy can also exist—usually in a more limited form—in "unitary" states. In these cases, however, decentralization may *not* be constitutionally ordained.

As Stepan (1999: 20) pointed out two decades ago, while few of the world's so-called multinational polities are democracies, what "multinational democracies" do exist "are *all* federal." As previewed above, however, a case can be made that group autonomy can exacerbate intergroup conflict and help derail the democratization of divided societies. For if, as this book's analysis of institutional change has shown, recognizing a group's sovereignty over a particular territory may embolden its leaders further to increase their regions' autonomy from the central government, the situation is all the more likely to degenerate into violent conflict when the state lacks the capacity required to prevent or rectify potential abuses of group autonomy. Incidentally, such abuses may feature the discrimination of groups constituting a minority of the region's population as well as the redirection of government resources toward activities designed to undermine the country's territorial integrity. At the very minimum, then, decentralization should only be considered in the presence of a "high-capacity" state that has already effectively asserted sufficient control over peripheral territories to curb potential abuses of the authority entrusted to the subnational level. Especially at low levels of development, it may be preferable to experiment with alternatives aiming to incentivize ethno-regional minorities to pursue their objectives through the democratic process. A potential solution might be to combine limited forms of devolution with the establishment of a bicameral legislature at the national level—one whose upper chamber, elected on a regional basis, is granted extensive legislative powers as well as an important role in the process of making and breaking governments. Conversely, in situations where granting group autonomy is virtually unavoidable, care should be taken to design a system whose ancillary institutions might help to weaken or moderate extremist forces. Brancati (2006, 2008) has identified a number of ways to reduce the strength of ethno-regional parties as well as the intensity of intercommunal conflict.

It goes without saying that this brief discussion could barely scratch the surface of a topic as complex as institutional engineering—after all, the main purpose of this study has been to theorize the *development* of political institutions, as opposed to their consequences. Admittedly, a great deal more remains to be done on both fronts—even with regard to the development of institutions, this book has only begun to "bridge the gap" currently separating explanations based on the logic of "power," which revolve around intergroup battles over scarce material resources, and explanations based on the logic of "legitimation," where matters of dignity, morality, and conviction supplement considerations of historical necessity and material self-interest. At a minimum, however, this study set out to showcase the promise held by the pursuit of a synthesis of power-based and ideas-based theories of political development—and, more broadly, by the adoption of a model of individual behavior where human beings are not constrained by the unrealistic assumptions imposed by the logic of "instrumental rationality." Ultimately, the hope is that the approach in question will prove equally valuable to the specification of theories where processes of institutional reproduction, institutional decay, and institutional change feature as the dependent variables as to the formulation of explanations where political institutions function as independent variables. In the meantime, it is clear that the quest for an improved understanding of the ways in which power and legitimacy affect the stability of political order and the quality of governance—the study of which may be traced back to the dawn of the history of political thought—remains a key part of the way forward.

REFERENCES

Abercrombie, Nicholas, and Bryan S. Turner. 1978. "The Dominant Ideology Thesis." *British Journal of Sociology* 29:149–70.

Acemoglu, Daron, and James A. Robinson. 2006. *Economic Origins of Dictatorship and Democracy*. Cambridge: Cambridge University Press.

Acemoglu, Daron, and James A. Robinson. 2012. *Why Nations Fail: The Origins of Power, Prosperity, and Poverty*. New York: Crown Business.

Agamben, Giorgio. 2005. *State of Exception*. Chicago: University of Chicago Press.

Albarracin, Dolores, Harry M. Wallace, William Hart, and Rick D. Brown. 2012. "How Judgments Change Following Comparison of Current and Prior Information." *Basic Applied Social Psychology* 34:44–55.

Alinsky, Saul D. 1972. *Rules for Radicals: A Pragmatic Primer for Realistic Radicals*. New York: Vintage.

Anderson, Benedict. [1983] 1991. *Imagined Communities: Reflections on the Origin and Spread of Nationalism*. London: Verso.

Anderson, Perry. 1976. "The Antinomies of Antonio Gramsci." *New Left Review* 100:5–78.

Antonucci, Lorenza, Laszlo Horvath, Yordan Kutiyski, and André Krouwel. 2017. "The Malaise of the Squeezed Middle: Challenging the Narrative of the 'Left Behind' Brexiter." *Competition & Change* 21:211–29.

Aphichat Sathitniramai. 2010. "Suea daeng khue khrai: Mob tem ngoen rue chon chan klang mai kap thang phraeng sangkhom" [Who are the Red Shirts? Rent-a-mob or new middle class and social alternative?] In various authors (eds.), *Red Why, Daeng . . . thammai*. Bangkok: Open Books.

Ariely, Dan. 2008. *Predictably Irrational: The Hidden Forces That Shape Our Decisions*. New York: HarperCollins.

Armingeon, Klaus, and Kai Guthmann. 2014. "Democracy in Crisis? The Declining Support for National Democracy in European Countries, 2007–2011." *European Journal of Political Research* 53:423–42.

Aronson, Elliot. 1973. "The Rationalizing Animal." *Psychology Today* 6:46–52.

Arthur, W. Brian. 1994. *Increasing Returns and Path Dependence in the Economy*. Ann Arbor: University of Michigan Press.

Asch, Solomon E. 2012. "Opinions and Social Pressure." In Joshua Aronson and Elliot Aronson (eds.), *Readings about the Social Animal*. New York: Worth.

Barkan, Joel D., Paul J. Densham, and Gerard Rushton. 2006. "Space Matters: Designing Better Electoral Systems for Emerging Democracies." *American Journal of Political Science* 50:926–39.

Bates, Robert H. 1983. "Modernization, Ethnic Competition, and the Rationality of Politics in Contemporary Africa." In Donald Rothchild and Victor A. Olunsorola (eds.), *State Versus Ethnic Claims: African Policy Dilemmas*. Boulder: Westview Press.

Baumeister, Roy F. 1996. *Evil: Inside Human Cruelty and Violence*. San Francisco: W. H. Freeman.

Baumeister, Roy F. 2005. *The Cultural Animal: Human Nature, Meaning, and Social Life*. Oxford: Oxford University Press.

Beetham, David. 1991. *The Legitimation of Power*. Basingstoke: Palgrave.

Béland, Daniel. 2005. "Ideas and Social Policy: An Institutionalist Perspective." *Social Policy and Administration* 39:1–18.

Béland, Daniel. 2009. "Ideas, Institutions, and Policy Change." *Journal of European Public Policy* 16:701–18.

Bell, Stephen. 2011. "Do We Really Need a New 'Constructivist Institutionalism' to Explain Institutional Change?" *British Journal of Political Science* 41:883–906.

Bennett, Andrew, and Colin Elman. 2006. "Complex Causal Relations and Case Study Methods: The Example of Path Dependence." *Political Analysis* 14:250–67.

Berger, Peter L., and Thomas Luckmann. 1966. *The Social Construction of Reality: A Treatise in the Sociology of Knowledge*. New York: Penguin Books.

Berman, Sheri. 1998. *The Social Democratic Moment: Ideas and Politics in the Making of Interwar Europe*. Cambridge, MA: Harvard University Press.

Beyer, Jürgen. 2010. "The Same or Not the Same—On the Variety of Mechanisms of Path Dependence." *International Journal of Social Sciences* 5 (1): 1–11.

Blyth, Mark. 2016. "The New Ideas Scholarship in the Mirror of Historical Institutionalism: A Case of Old Whines in New Bottles?" *Journal of European Public Policy* 23:464–71.

Blyth, Mark, Oddny Helgadottir, and William Kring. 2016. "Ideas and Historical Institutionalism." In Orfeo Fioretos, Tulia G. Falleti, and Adam Sheingate (eds.), *The Oxford Handbook of Historical Institutionalism*. Oxford: Oxford University Press.

Boix, Carles. 2003. *Democracy and Redistribution*. Cambridge: Cambridge University Press.

Bond, Michael. 2015. *The Power of Others: Peer Pressure, Groupthink, and How the People Around Us Shape Everything We Do*. London: Oneworld.

Bowles, Samuel. 1998. "Endogenous Preferences: The Cultural Consequences of Markets and Other Economic Institutions." *Journal of Economic Literature* 36:75–111.

Brancati, Dawn. 2006. "Decentralization: Fueling the Fire or Dampening the Flames of Ethnic Conflict and Secessionism?" *International Organization* 60:651–85.

Brancati, Dawn. 2008. "The Origins and Strengths of Regional Parties." *British Journal of Political Science* 38:135–59.

Brehm, Sharon S., and Jack W. Brehm. 1981. *Psychological Reactance: A Theory of Freedom and Control*. New York: Academic Press.

Brinks, Daniel, and Michael Coppedge. 2006. "Diffusion Is No Illusion: Neighbor Emulation in the Third Wave of Democracy." *Comparative Political Studies* 39:463–89.

Campbell, John L. 2010. "Institutional Reproduction and Change." In Glenn Morgan, John L. Campbell, Colin Crouch, Ove Kaj Pedersen, and Richard Whitley (eds.), *The Oxford Handbook of Comparative Institutional Analysis*. Oxford: Oxford University Press.

Capoccia, Giovanni. 2015. "Critical Junctures and Institutional Change." In James Mahoney and Kathleen Thelen (eds.), *Advances in Comparative-Historical Analysis*. Cambridge: Cambridge University Press.

Capoccia, Giovanni, and R. Daniel Kelemen. 2007. "The Study of Critical Junctures: Theory, Narrative, and Counterfactuals in Historical Institutionalism." *World Politics* 59:341–69.

Capoccia, Giovanni, and Daniel Ziblatt. 2010. "The Historical Turn in Democratization Studies: A New Research Agenda for Europe and Beyond." *Comparative Political Studies* 43:931–68.

Carey, John M. 2000. "Parchment, Equilibria, and Institutions." *Comparative Political Studies* 33:735–61.

Centola, Damon. 2018. *How Behavior Spreads: The Science of Complex Contagions*. Princeton: Princeton University Press.

Chandra, Kanchan. 2004. *Why Ethnic Parties Succeed: Patronage and Ethnic Head Counts in India*. Cambridge: Cambridge University Press.

Chandra, Kanchan. 2005. "Ethnic Parties and Democratic Stability." *Perspectives on Politics* 3:235–52.

Cheibub, José Antonio. 2007. *Presidentialism, Parliamentarism, and Democracy*. Cambridge: Cambridge University Press.

Choi Jung-Kyoo, and Samuel Bowles. 2007. "The Co-Evolution of Parochial Altruism and War." *Science* 318:636–40.

Cialdini, Robert B. 2009. *Influence: Science and Practice*. Boston: Pearson.

Cialdini, Robert B. 2016. *Pre-Suasion: A Revolutionary Way to Influence and Persuade*. New York: Random House.

Conran, James, and Kathleen Thelen. 2016. "Institutional Change." In Orfeo Fioretos, Tulia G. Falleti, and Adam Sheingate (eds.), *The Oxford Handbook of Historical Institutionalism*. Oxford: Oxford University Press.

Cooper, Joel. 2007. *Cognitive Dissonance: Fifty Years of a Classic Theory*. London: Sage.

Diamond, Jared. 2005. *Collapse: How Societies Choose to Fail or Succeed*. New York: Penguin Books.

Diamond, Larry. 1999. *Developing Democracy: Toward Consolidation*. Baltimore: Johns Hopkins University Press.

DiMaggio, Paul J., and Walter W. Powell. 1983. "The Iron Cage Revisited: Institutional Isomorphism and Collective Rationality in Organizational Fields." *American Sociological Review* 48:147–60.

Downs, Anthony. 1957. *An Economic Theory of Democracy*. New York: Harper & Row.

Easton, David. 1965. *A Framework for Political Analysis*. Englewood Cliffs, NJ: Prentice-Hall.

Economist Intelligence Unit (EIU). 2017. *Democracy Index 2016—Revenge of the "Deplorables."* London: Economist Group.

Ehrenreich, Barbara. 1990. *Fear of Falling: The Inner Life of the Middle Class*. New York: Harper.

Eidelman, Scott, and Christian S. Crandall. 2009. "A Psychological Advantage for the Status Quo." In John T. Jost, Aaron C. Kay, and Hulda Thorisdottir (eds.), *Social and Psychological Bases of Ideology and System Justification*. Oxford: Oxford University Press.

Elster, Jon. 1988. "Consequences of Constitutional Choice: Reflections on Tocqueville." In Jon Elster and Rune Slagstad (eds.), *Constitutionalism and Democracy*. Cambridge: Cambridge University Press.

Elster, Jon. 1998. "A Plea for Mechanisms." In Peter Hedström and Richard Swedberg (eds.), *Social Mechanisms: An Analytical Approach to Social Theory*. Cambridge: Cambridge University Press.

Elster, Jon. 1999. *Alchemies of the Mind: Rationality and the Emotions*. Cambridge: Cambridge University Press.

Elster, Jon. 2007. *Explaining Social Behavior: More Nuts and Bolts for the Social Sciences*. Cambridge: Cambridge University Press.

Engel, David M., and Jaruwan S. Engel. 2010. *Tort, Custom, and Karma: Globalization and Legal Consciousness in Thailand*. Stanford: Stanford University Press.

Fearon, James D. 1999. "Why Ethnic Politics and 'Pork' Tend to Go Together." Unpublished paper, Stanford University.

Fearon, James D., and David D. Laitin. 2003. "Ethnicity, Insurgency, and Civil War." *American Political Science Review* 97:75–90.

Ferrara, Federico. 2015. *The Political Development of Modern Thailand*. Cambridge: Cambridge University Press.

Feygina, Irina, and Tom R. Tyler. 2009. "Procedural Justice and System-Justifying Motivations." In John T. Jost, Aaron C. Kay, and Hulda Thorisdottir (eds.), *Social and Psychological Bases of Ideology and System Justification*. Oxford: Oxford University Press.

Fioretos, Orfeo. 2011. *Creative Reconstructions: Multilateralism and European Varieties of Capitalism after 1950*. Ithaca: Cornell University Press.

Fioretos, Orfeo, Tulia G. Falleti, and Adam Sheingate. 2016. "Historical Institutionalism in Political Science." In Orfeo Fioretos, Tulia G. Falleti, and Adam Sheingate (eds.), *The Oxford Handbook of Historical Institutionalism*. Oxford: Oxford University Press.

Foa, Roberto Stefan, and Yascha Mounk. 2016. "The Danger of Deconsolidation: The Democratic Disconnect." *Journal of Democracy* 27:5–17.

Francisco, Ronald A. 2000. *The Politics of Regime Transitions*. Boulder: Westview Press.

Franklin, Mark N. 1996. "Electoral Participation." In Lawrence LeDuc, Richard G. Niemi, and Pippa Norris (eds.), *Comparing Democracies: Elections and Voting in Comparative Perspective*. Thousand Oaks, CA: Sage.

Freedom House. 2017. "Freedom in the World 2017—United States Country Report." https://www.refworld.org/docid/58ff3e167.html

Fromm, Erich, and Michael Maccoby. 1970. *Social Character in a Mexican Village: A Sociopsychoanalytic Study*. Englewood Cliffs, NJ: Prentice-Hall.

Frum, David. 2017. "How to Build an Autocracy." *The Atlantic*, March.

Fukuyama, Francis. 1992. *The End of History and the Last Man*. New York: Free Press.

Fukuyama, Francis. 2011. *The Origins of Political Order: From Prehuman Times to the French Revolution*. New York: Farrar, Straus and Giroux.

Fukuyama, Francis. 2014. *Political Order and Political Decay: From the Industrial Revolution to the Globalization of Democracy*. New York: Farrar, Straus and Giroux.

Galanter, Marc. 1999. *Cults: Faith, Healing, and Coercion*. Oxford: Oxford University Press.

Gandhi, Jennifer. 2008. *Political Institutions under Dictatorship*. Cambridge: Cambridge University Press.

Garud, Raghu, Cynthia Hardy, and Steve McGuire. 2007. "Institutional Entrepreneurship as Embedded Agency: An Introduction to the Special Issue." *Organization Studies* 28:957–69.

Gerring, John. 2012. *Social Science Methodology: A Unified Framework*. 2nd ed. Cambridge: Cambridge University Press.

Gidron, Noam, and Peter A. Hall. 2020. "Populism as a Problem of Social Integration." *Comparative Political Studies* 53:1027–59.

Gilens, Martin, and Benjamin I. Page. 2014. "Testing Theories of American Politics: Elites, Interest Groups, and Average Citizens." *Perspectives on Politics* 12:564–81.

Ginsburg, Tom. 2012. "Introduction." In Tom Ginsburg (ed.), *Comparative Constitutional Design*. Cambridge: Cambridge University Press.

Gleditsch, Kristian Skrede, and Michael D. Ward. 2006. "Diffusion and the International Context of Democratization." *International Organization* 60:911–33.

Goldstone, Jack A. 1991. *Revolution and Rebellion in the Early Modern World*. Berkeley: University of California Press.

Goldstone, Jack A. 1998. "Initial Conditions, General Laws, Path Dependence, and Explanation in Historical Sociology." *American Journal of Sociology* 104:829–45.

Goodin, Robert E. 1996. "Institutions and their Design." In Robert E. Goodin (ed.), *The Theory of Institutional Design*. Cambridge: Cambridge University Press.

Gramsci, Antonio. 1977. *Quaderni del carcere*. Torino: Einaudi.

Granovetter, Mark. 1973. "The Strength of Weak Ties." *American Journal of Sociology* 78:1360–80.

Granovetter, Mark. 1978. "Threshold Models of Collective Behavior." *American Journal of Sociology* 83:1420–43.

Greene, Joshua. 2013. *Moral Tribes: Emotion, Reason, and the Gap between Us and Them*. New York: Penguin Press.

Greenwald, Anthony. 1980. "The Totalitarian Ego: Fabrication and Revision of Personal History." *American Psychologist* 35:603–18.

Greif, Avner, and David D. Laitin. 2004. "A Theory of Endogenous Institutional Change." *American Political Science Review* 98:633–52.

Haidt, Jonathan. 2012. *The Righteous Mind: Why Good People Are Divided by Politics and Religion*. New York: Vintage Books.

Hall, Peter A. 2003. "Aligning Ontology and Methodology in Comparative Politics." In J. Mahoney and D. Rueschemeyer (eds.), *Comparative Historical Analysis in the Social Sciences*. Cambridge: Cambridge University Press.

Hall, Peter A. 2016. "Politics as a Process Structured in Space and Time." In Orfeo Fioretos, Tulia G. Falleti, and Adam Sheingate (eds.), *The Oxford Handbook of Historical Institutionalism*. Oxford: Oxford University Press.

Hall, Peter A., and Rosemary C. R. Taylor. 1996. "Political Science and the Three New Institutionalisms." *Political Studies* 44 (5): 936–57.

Harmon-Jones, Eddie. 2000. "A Cognitive Dissonance Theory Perspective on the Role of Emotion in the Maintenance and Change of Beliefs and Attitudes." In Nico H. Frijda,

Antony S. R. Manstead, and Sacha Bem (eds.), *Emotions and Beliefs: How Feelings Influence Thoughts*. Cambridge: Cambridge University Press.

Hatemi, Peter K., and Rose McDermott. 2011. "Introduction." In Peter K. Hatemi and Rose McDermott (eds.), *Man Is by Nature a Political Animal: Evolution, Biology, and Politics*. Chicago: University of Chicago Press.

Hay, Colin. 2011. "Ideas and the Construction of Interests." In Daniel Béland and Robert H. Cox (eds.), *Ideas and Politics of Social Science Research*. Oxford: Oxford University Press.

Hay, Colin, and Daniel Wincott. 1998. "Structure, Agency and Historical Institutionalism." *Political Studies* 46:951–57.

Helmke Gretchen. 2007. "The Origins of Institutional Crises in Latin America: A Unified Strategic Model and Test." Presented at the Annual Meeting of the Midwest Political Science Association, Chicago.

Helmke, Gretchen. 2010. "The Origins of Institutional Crises in Latin America: A Unified Strategic Model and Test." *American Journal of Political Science* 54:737–50.

Hetherington, Marc J., and Jonathan D. Weiler. 2009. *Authoritarianism and Polarization in American Politics*. Cambridge: Cambridge University Press.

Horowitz, Donald L. 2003. "Electoral Systems: A Primer for Decision Makers." *Journal of Democracy* 14:122–23.

Huntington, Samuel P. 1965. "Political Development and Political Decay." *World Politics* 17 (3): 386–430.

Huntington, Samuel P. 1968. *Political Order in Changing Societies*. New Haven: Yale University Press.

Huntington, Samuel P. 1991. *The Third Wave: Democratization in the Late Twentieth Century*. Norman: University of Oklahoma Press.

Inglehart, Ronald, and Christian Welzel. 2005. *Modernization, Cultural Change, and Democracy: The Human Development Sequence*. Cambridge: Cambridge University Press.

Issenberg, Sasha. 2012. *The Victory Lab: The Secret Science of Winning Campaigns*. New York: Crown.

Izuma, Keise. 2013. "The Neural Basis of Social Influence and Attitude Change." *Current Opinion in Neurobiology* 23:1–7.

Joslyn, Mark R. 2003. "The Determinants and Consequences of Recall Error about Gulf War Preferences." *American Journal of Political Science* 47:440–52.

Jost, John T., and Mahzarin R. Banaji. 1994. "The Role of Stereotyping in System Justification and the Production of False Consciousness." *British Journal of Social Psychology* 33:1–27.

Jost, John T., Mahzarin R. Banaji, and Brian A. Nosek. 2004. "A Decade of System Justification Theory: Accumulated Evidence of Conscious and Unconscious Bolstering of the Status Quo." *Political Psychology* 25:881–919.

Kahneman, Daniel. 2011. *Thinking, Fast and Slow*. New York: Farrar, Strauss and Giroux.

Kahneman, Daniel, and Amos Tversky. 1979. "Prospect Theory: An Analysis of Decision under Risk." *Econometrica* 47:263–92.

Karklins, Rasma, and Roger Petersen. 1993. "Decision Calculus of Protesters and Regimes: Eastern Europe 1989." *Journal of Politics* 55:588–614.

Katznelson, Ira, and Barry R. Weingast. 2005. "Intersections between Historical and Rational Choice Institutionalism." In Ira Katznelson and Barry R. Weingast (eds.), *Preferences and Situations: Points of Intersection between Historical and Rational Choice Institutionalism*. New York: Russell Sage Foundation.

Kaufmann, Chaim. 1996. "Possible and Impossible Solutions to Ethnic Civil Wars." *International Security* 20:136–75.

Kay, Aaron C., Danielle Gaucher, Jennifer M. Peach, Kristin Laurin, Justin Friesen, Mark P. Zanna, and Steven J. Spencer. 2009. "Inequality, Discrimination, and the Power of the Status Quo: Direct Evidence for a Motivation to See the Way Things Are as the Way They Should Be." *Journal of Personality and Social Psychology* 97:421–34.

Kelman, Herbert C. 2001. "Reflections on Social and Psychological Processes of Legitimation and Delegitimation." In John T. Jost and Brenda Major (eds.), *The Psychology of Legitimacy: Emerging Perspectives on Ideology, Justice, and Intergroup Relations*. Cambridge: Cambridge University Press.

Krasner, Stephen D. 1988. "Sovereignty: An Institutional Perspective." *Comparative Political Studies* 21:66–94.

Kunda, Ziva. 1990. "The Case for Motivated Reasoning." *Psychological Bulletin* 108:480–98.

Kuntz, Philipp, and Mark R. Thompson. 2009. "More Than Just the Final Straw: Stolen Elections as Revolutionary Triggers." *Comparative Politics* 41:253–72.

Kurer, Thomas. 2020. "The Declining Middle: Occupational Change, Social Status, and the Populist Right." *Comparative Political Studies* 53:1798–1835.

Lakatos, Imre. 1978. *The Methodology of Scientific Research Programmes: Philosophical Papers*. Vol. 1. Cambridge: Cambridge University Press.

Lakner, Christoph, and Branko Milanovic. 2013. "Global Income Distribution: From the Fall of the Berlin Wall to the Great Recession." World Bank Policy Research Working Paper 6719.

Lakoff, George. 2009. *The Political Mind: A Cognitive Scientist's Guide to Your Brain and Its Politics*. New York: Penguin.

Laurin, Kristin, Aaron C. Kay, and Gavan J. Fitzsimons. 2012. "Reactance versus Rationalization: Divergent Responses to Policies That Constrain Freedom." *Psychological Science* 23:205–9.

Lenski, Gerhard E. 1966. *Power and Privilege: A Theory of Social Stratification*. New York: McGraw-Hill.

Lenz, Tobias, and Lora Anne Viola. 2017. "Legitimacy and Institutional Change in International Organizations: A Cognitive Approach." *Review of International Studies* 43:939–61.

Levi, Margaret. 1988. *Of Rule and Revenue*. Berkeley: University of California Press.

Levi, Margaret. 1997. *Consent, Dissent, and Patriotism*. Cambridge: Cambridge University Press.

Levitsky, Steven, and María Victoria Murillo. 2009. "Variation in Institutional Strength." *Annual Review of Political Science* 12:115–33.

Levitsky, Steven, and Daniel Ziblatt. 2018. *How Democracies Die*. New York: Crown.

Lewis, Orion A., and Sven Steinmo. 2012. "How Institutions Evolve: Evolutionary Theory and Institutional Change." *Polity* 44 (3): 314–39.

Lichbach, Mark I., and Alan S. Zuckerman (eds.). 1997. *Comparative Politics: Rationality, Culture, and Structure*. Cambridge: Cambridge University Press.

Lieberman, Robert C. 2002. "Ideas, Institutions, and Political Order: Explaining Political Change." *American Political Science Review* 96:697–712.

Lijphart, Arend. 1968. *The Politics of Accommodation: Pluralism and Democracy in the Netherlands*. Berkeley: University of California Press.

Lijphart, Arend. 1969. "Consociational Democracy." *World Politics* 21:207–25.

Lijphart, Arend. 1977. *Democracy in Plural Societies: A Comparative Exploration*. New Haven: Yale University Press.

Lijphart, Arend. 1984. *Democracies: Patterns of Majoritarian and Consensus Government in Twenty-One Countries*. New Haven: Yale University Press.

Lijphart, Arend. 1997. "Unequal Participation: Democracy's Unresolved Dilemma." *American Political Science Review* 91:1–14.

Lijphart, Arend. 1999. *Patterns of Democracy: Government Forms and Performance in Thirty-Six Countries*. New Haven: Yale University Press.

Lijphart, Arend. 2004. "Constitutional Design for Divided Societies." *Journal of Democracy* 15:96–109.

Linz, Juan J. 1994. "Presidential or Parliamentary Democracy: Does It Make a Difference?" In Juan J. Linz and Arturo Valenzuela (eds.), *The Failure of Presidential Democracy*. Baltimore: Johns Hopkins University Press.

Linz, Juan J., and Alfred Stepan. 1996. *Problems of Democratic Transition and Consolidation*. Baltimore: Johns Hopkins University Press.

Lipset, Seymour Martin. 1959. "Some Social Requisites of Democracy: Economic Development and Political Legitimacy." *American Political Science Review* 53:69–105.

Lorwin, Val R. 1971. "Segmented Pluralism: Ideological Cleavages and Political Cohesion in the Smaller European Democracies." *Comparative Politics* 3:141–75.

Machiavelli, Niccolò. [1517] 1971. *Discorsi sopra la prima Deca di Tito Livio*. In Mario Martelli (ed.), *Niccolò Machiavelli: tutte le opere*. Firenze: Sansoni Editore.

Machiavelli, Niccolò. [1532] 1971. *Il principe*. In Mario Martelli (ed.), *Niccolò Machiavelli: tutte le opere*. Firenze: Sansoni Editore.

Mahoney, James. 2000. "Path Dependence in Historical Sociology." *Theory and Society* 29 (4): 507–48.

Mahoney, James, and Richard Snyder. 1999. "Rethinking Agency and Structure in the Study of Regime Change." *Studies in Comparative International Development* 34:3–32.

Mahoney, James, and Kathleen Thelen. 2010. "A Theory of Gradual Institutional Change." In James Mahoney and Kathleen Thelen (eds.), *Explaining Institutional Change: Ambiguity, Agency, and Power*. Cambridge: Cambridge University Press.

Mahoney, James, and Kathleen Thelen. 2015. "Comparative-Historical Analysis in Contemporary Political Science." In James Mahoney and Kathleen Thelen (eds.), *Advances in Comparative-Historical Analysis*. Cambridge: Cambridge University Press.

Major, Brenda, and Toni Schmader. 2001. "Legitimacy and the Construal of Social Disadvantage." In John T. Jost and Brenda Major (eds.), *The Psychology of Legitimacy: Emerging Perspectives on Ideology, Justice, and Intergroup Relations*. Cambridge: Cambridge University Press.

March, James G., and Johan P. Olsen. 1989. *Rediscovering Institutions.* New York: Free Press.

March, James G., and Johan P. Olsen. 1996. "Institutional Perspectives on Political Institutions." *Governance* 9:247–67.

March, James G., and Johan P. Olsen. 2009. "The Logic of Appropriateness." ARENA Working Papers WP 04/09, University of Oslo.

McRaney, David. 2011. *You Are Not So Smart: Why You Have Too Many Friends on Facebook, Why Your Memory Is Mostly Fiction, and 46 Other Ways You're Deluding Yourself.* New York: Gotham.

Meyer, John W., and Brian Rowan. 1977. "Institutionalized Organizations: Formal Structure as Myth and Ceremony." *American Journal of Sociology* 83:340–63.

Milgram, Stanley. 1963. "Behavioral Study of Obedience." *Journal of Abnormal and Social Psychology* 67:371–78.

Miron, Anca M., and Jack W. Brehm. 2006. "Reactance Theory—40 Years Later." *Zeitschrift für Sozialpsychologie* 37:3–12.

Montesano, Michael J. 2010. "Four Thai Pathologies, Late 2009." In Marc Askew (ed.), *Legitimacy Crisis in Thailand.* Chiang Mai: Silkworm Books.

Moore, Barrington. 1978. *Injustice: The Social Bases of Obedience and Revolt.* London: Macmillan.

Mussweiler, Thomas. 2003. "Comparison Processes in Social Judgment: Mechanisms and Consequences." *Psychological Review* 110:472–89.

Nidhi Eoseewong. 2010. *Kan mueang khong suea daeng* [The politics of the Red Shirts]. Bangkok: Open Books.

Noelle-Neumann, Elisabeth. 1974. "The Spiral of Silence: A Theory of Public Opinion." *Journal of Communication* 24:43–51.

Norris, Pippa. 2004. *Electoral Engineering: Voting Rules and Political Behavior.* Cambridge: Cambridge University Press.

North, Douglass C. 1990. *Institutions, Institutional Change, and Economic Performance.* Cambridge: Cambridge University Press.

North, Douglass C., John Joseph Wallis, and Barry R. Weingast. 2009. *Violence and Social Orders: A Conceptual Framework for Interpreting Recorded Human History.* Cambridge: Cambridge University Press.

Offe, Claus. 1996. "Designing Institutions in East European Transitions." In Robert E. Goodin (ed.), *The Theory of Institutional Design.* Cambridge: Cambridge University Press.

Offe, Claus. 2006. "Political Institutions and Social Power: Conceptual Explorations." In Ian Shapiro, Stephen Skowronek, and Daniel Galvin (eds.), *Rethinking Political Institutions: The Art of the State.* New York: New York University Press.

Olson, James M., and Carolyn L. Hafer. 2001. "Tolerance of Personal Deprivation." In John T. Jost and Brenda Major (eds.), *The Psychology of Legitimacy: Emerging Perspectives on Ideology, Justice, and Intergroup Relations.* Cambridge: Cambridge University Press.

Olson, Mancur. 1993. "Dictatorship, Democracy, and Development." *American Political Science Review* 87:567–76.

Olson, Mancur, and Richard Zeckhauser. 1966. "An Economic Theory of Alliances." *Review of Economics and Statistics* 48:266–79.

Orren, Karen. 1991. *Belated Feudalism: Labor, the Law, and Liberal Development in the United States*. Cambridge: Cambridge University Press.

Orren, Karen, and Stephen Skowronek. 2004. *The Search for American Political Development*. Cambridge: Cambridge University Press.

Ostrom, Elinor. 1986. "An Agenda for the Study of Institutions." *Public Choice* 48:3–25.

Page, Scott E. 2006. "Path Dependence." *Quarterly Journal of Political Science* 1:87–115.

Parsons, Talcott. 1951. *The Social System*. New York: Free Press.

Pepinsky, Thomas. 2014. "The Institutional Turn in Comparative Authoritarianism." *British Journal of Political Science* 44:631–53.

Peters, B. Guy. 1999. *Institutional Theory in Political Science: The "New Institutionalism."* London and New York: Pinter.

Peters, B. Guy, Jon Pierre, and Desmond S. King. 2005. "The Politics of Path Dependency: Political Conflict in Historical Institutionalism." *Journal of Politics* 67:1275–1300.

Petty, Richard E., and Pablo Briñol. 2010. "Attitude Change." In Roy F. Baumeister and Eli J. Finkel (eds.), *Advanced Social Psychology: The State of the Science*. Oxford: Oxford University Press.

Pierson, Paul. 2000. "Increasing Returns, Path Dependence, and the Study of Politics." *American Political Science Review* 94 (2): 251–67.

Pierson, Paul. 2004. *Politics in Time: History, Institutions, and Social Analysis*. Princeton: Princeton University Press.

Pierson, Paul. 2015. "Power and Path Dependence." In James Mahoney and Kathleen Thelen (eds.), *Advances in Comparative-Historical Analysis*. Cambridge: Cambridge University Press.

Pierson, Paul, and Theda Skocpol. 2002. "Historical Institutionalism in Contemporary Political Science." In Ira Katznelson and Helen V. Milner (eds.), *Political Science: The State of the Discipline*. New York: W. W. Norton.

Pinker, Steven. 1999. *How the Mind Works*. New York: W. W. Norton.

Posen, Barry. 1993. "The Security Dilemma and Ethnic Conflict." *Survival* 35:27–47.

Przeworski, Adam. 1988. "Democracy as a Contingent Outcome of Conflict." In Jon Elster and Rune Slagstad (eds.), *Constitutionalism and Democracy*. Cambridge: Cambridge University Press.

Przeworski, Adam. 1991. *Democracy and the Market*. Cambridge: Cambridge University Press.

Przeworski, Adam. 2006. "Self-Enforcing Democracy." In Donald Wittman and Barry Weingast (eds.), *Oxford Handbook of Political Economy*. Oxford: Oxford University Press.

Przeworski, Adam. 2009. "The Mechanics of Regime Instability in Latin America." *Journal of Politics in Latin America* 1:5–36.

Przeworski, Adam, Michael E. Alvarez, Jose Antonio Cheibub, and Fernando Limongi. 2000. *Democracy and Development: Political Institutions and Well-Being in the World, 1950–1990*. Cambridge: Cambridge University Press.

Przeworski, Adam, and Fernando Limongi. 1997. "Modernization: Theories and Facts." *World Politics* 49:155–83.

Rabushka, Alvin, and Kenneth Shepsle. 1972. *Politics in Plural Societies: A Theory in Democratic Instability*. Columbus, OH: Charles E. Merrill.

Reilly, Benjamin. 2001. *Democracy in Divided Societies: Electoral Engineering for Conflict Management*. Cambridge: Cambridge University Press.

Renwick, Alan. 2010. *The Politics of Electoral Reform: Changing the Rules of Democracy*. Cambridge: Cambridge University Press.

Ridgeway, Cecilia L. 2001. "The Emergence of Status Beliefs: From Structural Inequality to Legitimizing Ideology." In John T. Jost and Brenda Major (eds.), *The Psychology of Legitimacy: Emerging Perspectives on Ideology, Justice, and Intergroup Relations*. Cambridge: Cambridge University Press.

Ridgeway, Cecilia L. 2014. "Why Status Matters for Inequality." *American Sociological Review* 79:1–16.

Rixen, Tomas, and Lora Anne Viola. 2014. "Putting Path Dependence in Its Place: Toward a Taxonomy of Institutional Change." *Journal of Theoretical Politics* 26:1–23.

Rixen, Thomas, and Lora Anne Viola. 2016. "Historical Institutionalism and International Relations: Towards Explaining Change and Stability in International Institutions." In Thomas Rixen, Lora Anne Viola, and Michael Zürn (eds.), *Historical Institutionalism and International Relations: Explaining Institutional Development in World Politics*. Oxford: Oxford University Press.

Ross, Lee D., Teresa M. Amabile, and Julia L. Steinmetz. 1977. "Social Roles, Social Control, and Biases in Social-Perception Processes." *Journal of Personality and Social Psychology* 35:485–94.

Ross, Marc H. 1997. "Culture and Identity in Comparative Politics." In Mark I. Lichbach and Alan S. Zuckerman (eds.), *Comparative Politics: Rationality, Culture, and Structure*. Cambridge: Cambridge University Press.

Ross, Marc H. 2009. "Culture in Comparative Political Analysis." In Mark I. Lichbach and Alan S. Zuckerman (eds.), *Comparative Politics: Rationality, Culture, and Structure*, 2nd ed. Cambridge: Cambridge University Press.

Rueschemeyer, Dietrich, Evelyne Huber Stephens, and John D. Stephens. 1992. *Capitalist Development and Democracy*. Chicago: University of Chicago Press.

Sanders, Elizabeth. 2006. "Historical Institutionalism." In R. A. W. Rhodes, Sarah A. Binder, and Bert A. Rockman (eds.), *The Oxford Handbook of Political Institutions*. Oxford: Oxford University Press.

Sapolsky, Robert M. 2017. *Behave: The Biology of Humans at Our Best and Worst*. New York: Penguin.

Sartori, Giovanni. 1968. "Political Development and Political Engineering." In J. D. Montgomery and A. O. Hirschman (eds.), *Public Policy*, vol. 17. Cambridge, MA: Harvard University Press.

Sartori, Giovanni. 1970. "Concept Misformation in Comparative Politics." *American Political Science Review* 64:1033–53.

Sartori, Giovanni. 1976. *Parties and Party Systems, Volume I: A Framework for Analysis*. Cambridge: Cambridge University Press.

Sartori, Giovanni. 1997. *Comparative Constitutional Engineering: An Inquiry into Structures, Incentives, and Outcomes*. 2nd ed. New York: New York University Press.

Schattschneider, Elmer E. [1960] 1988. *The Semisovereign People: A Realist's View of Democracy in America*. Boston: Wadsworth.

Scheidel, Walter. 2017. *The Great Leveler: Violence and the History of Inequality from the Stone Age to the Twenty-First Century.* Princeton: Princeton University Press.

Schmidt, Vivien A. 2010. "Taking Ideas and Discourse Seriously: Explaining Change through Discursive Institutionalism as the Fourth 'New Institutionalism.'" *European Political Science Review* 2:1–25.

Schmidt, Vivien A. 2011. "Reconciling Ideas and Institutions through Discursive Institutionalism." In Daniel Béland and Robert H. Cox (eds.), *Ideas and Politics of Social Science Research.* Oxford: Oxford University Press.

Schmitter, Philippe C. 2001. "Parties Are Not What They Once Were." In Larry Diamond and Richard Gunther (eds.), *Political Parties and Democracy.* Baltimore: Johns Hopkins University Press.

Scott, James C. 1976. *The Moral Economy of the Peasant: Rebellion and Subsistence in Southeast Asia.* New Haven: Yale University Press.

Scott, James C. 1985. *Weapons of the Weak: Everyday Forms of Peasant Resistance.* New Haven: Yale University Press.

Scott, James C. 1990. *Domination and the Arts of Resistance: Hidden Transcripts.* New Haven: Yale University Press.

Sen, Amartya. 1997. "Human Rights and Asian Values: What Kee Kuan Yew and Le Peng Don't Understand about Asia." *New Republic,* July 14.

Sherif, Muzafer. 1937. "An Experimental Approach to the Study of Attitudes." *Sociometry* 1:90–98.

Simon, Bernd, and Penelope Oakes. 2006. "Beyond Dependence: An Identity Approach to Social Power and Domination." *Human Relations* 59:105–39.

Skaaning, Svend-Erik. 2006. "Political Regimes and Their Changes: A Conceptual Framework." CDDRL Working Papers Number 55, Stanford University.

Skocpol, Theda. 1979. *States and Social Revolutions.* Cambridge: Cambridge University Press.

Slater, Dan. 2010. *Ordering Power: Contentious Politics and Authoritarian Leviathans in Southeast Asia.* Cambridge: Cambridge University Press.

Smith, Tom W. 1984. "Recalling Attitudes: An Analysis of Retrospective Questions on the 1982 GSS." *Public Opinion Quarterly* 48:639–49.

Snyder, Richard, and James Mahoney. 1999. "The Missing Variable: Institutions and the Study of Regime Change." *Comparative Politics* 32:103–22.

Stepan, Alfred C. 1999. "Federalism and Democracy: Beyond the U.S. Model." *Journal of Democracy* 10:19–34.

Stinchcombe, Arthur L. 1968. *Constructing Social Theories.* New York: Harcourt, Brace & World.

Streeck, Wolfgang, and Kathleen Thelen. 2005. "Introduction: Institutional Change in Advanced Political Economies." In Wolfgang Streeck and Kathleen Thelen (eds.), *Beyond Continuity: Institutional Change in Advanced Political Economics.* Oxford: Oxford University Press.

Suchman, Mark C. 1995. "Managing Legitimacy: Strategic and Institutional Approaches." *Academy of Management Review* 20:571–610.

Sullivan, Andrew. 2016. "America Has Never Been So Ripe for Tyranny." *New York Magazine,* May 1.

Sunstein, Cass R. 2011. *Going to Extremes: How Like Minds Unite and Divide*. Oxford: Oxford University Press.

Svolik, Milan. 2008. "Authoritarian Reversals and Democratic Consolidation." *American Political Science Review* 102:153–68.

Svolik, Milan W. 2012. *The Politics of Authoritarian Rule*. Cambridge: Cambridge University Press.

Tainter, Joseph A. 1988. *The Collapse of Complex Societies*. Cambridge: Cambridge University Press.

Tajfel, Henri, and John C. Turner. 1986. "The Social Identity Theory of Inter-Group Behavior." In S. Worchel and L. W. Austin (eds.), *Psychology of Intergroup Relations*. Chicago: Nelson-Hall.

Tang Shiping. 2011. *A General Theory of Institutional Change*. New York: Routledge.

Tavris, Carol, and Elliot Aronson. 2007. *Mistakes Were Made (but Not by Me): Why We Justify Foolish Beliefs, Bad Decisions, and Hurtful Acts*. Orlando: Harcourt.

Taylor, Kathleen. 2006. *Brainwashing: The Science of Thought Control*. Oxford: Oxford University Press.

Thaler, Richard H. 2015. *Misbehaving: The Making of Behavioral Economics*. New York: Norton.

Thaler, Richard H., and Cass R. Sunstein. 2008. *Nudge: Improving Decisions about Health, Wealth, and Happiness*. New Haven: Yale University Press.

Thelen, Kathleen. 1999. "Historical Institutionalism in Comparative Politics." *Annual Review of Political Science* 2 (1): 369–404.

Thelen, Kathleen. 2004. *How Institutions Evolve: The Political Economy of Skills in Germany, Britain, the United States, and Japan*. Cambridge: Cambridge University Press.

Thelen, Kathleen. 2006. "Institutions and Social Change: The Evolution of Vocational Training in Germany." In Ian Shapiro, Stephen Skowronek, and Daniel Galvin (eds.), *Rethinking Political Institutions: The Art of the State*. New York: New York University Press.

Thelen, Kathleen, and Sven Steinmo. 1992. "Historical Institutionalism in Comparative Politics." In Sven Steinmo, Kathleen Thelen, and Frank Longstreth (eds.), *Structuring Politics: Historical Institutionalism in Comparative Analysis*. Cambridge: Cambridge University Press.

Thompson, Mark R. 2001. "Whatever Happened to 'Asian Values'?" *Journal of Democracy* 12:154–65.

Thorisdottir, Hulda, John T. Jost, and Aaron C. Kay. 2009. "On the Social and Psychological Bases of Ideology and System Justification." In John T. Jost, Aaron C. Kay, and Hulda Thorisdottir (eds.), *Social and Psychological Bases of Ideology and System Justification*. Oxford: Oxford University Press.

Tilly, Charles. 1985. "War Making and State Making as Organized Crime." In Peter Evans, Dietrich Rueschemeyer, and Theda Skocpol (eds.), *Bringing the State Back In*. Cambridge: Cambridge University Press.

Tilly, Charles. 2007. *Democracy*. Cambridge: Cambridge University Press.

Tooby, John, and Leda Cosmides. 1992. "The Psychological Foundations of Culture." In Jerome H. Barkow, Leda Cosmides, and John Tooby (eds.), *The Adapted Mind: Evolutionary Psychology and the Generation of Culture*. Oxford: Oxford University Press.

Trivers, Robert L. 2011. *Deceit and Self-Deception: Fooling Yourself the Better to Fool Others*. London: Allen Lane.

Tuchman, Barbara W. 1984. *The March of Folly: From Troy to Vietnam*. New York: Ballantine Books.

Turner, John C. 1991. *Social Influence*. Milton Keynes: Open University Press.

Tyler, Tom R. 1990. *Why People Obey the Law*. New Haven: Yale University Press.

Tyler, Tom R. 2006. "Psychological Perspectives on Legitimacy and Legitimation." *Annual Review of Psychology* 57:375–400.

Tyler, Tom R. 2010. *Why People Cooperate: The Role of Social Motivations*. New Haven: Yale University Press.

Vermeule, Adrian. 2007. *Mechanisms of Democracy: Institutional Design Writ Small*. Cambridge: Cambridge University Press.

Walzer, Michael. 1982. *The Revolution of the Saints: A Study in the Origins of Radical Politics*. Cambridge, MA: Harvard University Press.

Weber, Max. [1919] 1946. "Politics as Vocation." In Hans H. Gerth and C. Wright Mills (eds.), *From Max Weber: Essays in Sociology*. Oxford: Oxford University Press.

Weber, Max. [1922] 1978. *Economy and Society: An Outline of Interpretive Sociology*. Berkeley: University of California Press.

Weidmann, Nils B. 2009. "Geography as Motivation and Opportunity: Group Concentration and Ethic Conflict." *Journal of Conflict Resolution* 53:526–43.

Weyland, Kurt. 2008. "Toward a New Theory of Institutional Change." *World Politics* 60:281–314.

Wright, Robert. 1995. *The Moral Animal: Evolutionary Psychology and Everyday Life*. New York: Vintage Books.

Yzerbyt, Vincent, and Anouk Rogier. 2001. "Blame It on the Group: Entitativity, Subjective Essentialism, and Social Attribution." In John T. Jost and Brenda Major (eds.), *The Psychology of Legitimacy: Emerging Perspectives on Ideology, Justice, and Intergroup Relations*. Cambridge: Cambridge University Press.

Zaki, Jamil, Jessica Schirmer, and Jason P. Mitchell. 2011. "Social Influence Modulates the Neural Computation of Value." *Psychological Science* 22:894–900.

Zelditch, Morris, Jr. 2001. "Theories of Legitimacy." In John T. Jost and Brenda Major (eds.), *The Psychology of Legitimacy: Emerging Perspectives on Ideology, Justice, and Intergroup Relations*. Cambridge: Cambridge University Press.

Ziblatt, Daniel. 2006. "How Did Europe Democratize?" *World Politics* 58:311–38.

Ziblatt, Daniel. 2017. *Conservative Parties and the Birth of Democracy*. Cambridge: Cambridge University Press.

Zucker, Lynne G. 1977. "The Role of Institutionalization in Cultural Persistence." *American Sociological Review* 42:726–43.

INDEX

Acemoglu, Daron, 11, 19, 56, 61, 82, 86–88, 96, 115–18, 122–23, 126–27, 133–34

Agamben, Giorgio, 43

agency, human (its role in theories of institutional development), 5–6, 12–14, 53–54. *See also* methodological individualism; microfoundations

Alinsky, Saul, 67, 79

Anderson, Benedict, 35, 85

Anderson, Perry, 2, 35

appropriateness. *See* logic of [social] appropriateness

Ariely, Dan, 5

Aristotle, 1, 149–50, 165

armed forces. *See* military

Aronson, Elliot, 26–27

Arthur, W. Brian, 31

Asch, Solomon E., 27, 37

Asian Values (thesis), 144

authoritarianism. *See* regimes, authoritarian; regimes, non-democratic/extractive

authority crisis/state crisis, 66–68, 74–75, 80–107, 111–12, 146–47. *See also* breakdown in political order/state breakdown

autocracy, *See* regimes, autocratic. *See also* regimes, non-democratic/extractive

automation, industrial, 82, 127

Bates, Robert H., 81, 175

Baumeister, Roy F., 6, 22, 34, 84, 136

Beetham, David, 3, 21, 23–25, 28–29, 57, 66–67, 72–73, 77–80, 82–83, 85–88, 95, 99, 104–5, 107, 131

behavioral economics, 5, 13, 25–26, 33–34, 78–79, 83, 106, 128, 163

Black Death, the, 116–18

Blyth, Mark, 3, 5, 112

Bowles, Samuel, 28, 39, 99, 114, 129, 137, 139, 141

breakdown in political order/state breakdown, 66–68, 75, 80–86, 95–96, 103–7, 111–12. *See also* authority crisis

Brehm, Jack W., 31, 34

Capoccia, Giovanni, 11, 12, 19, 32, 115, 119, 123

Chandra, Kanchan, 38, 81, 168, 175

Cialdini, Robert B., 34, 70, 71

cleavages, social. *See* social/socioeconomic structure or conditions

cognitive dissonance, 25–28, 34–36, 70, 129–30, 167. *See also* self-justification

comparative politics (and approaches to), 2–3, 65–66, 157–58. *See also* political science

compliance. *See* institutions, compliance and non-compliance with

conformism. *See* institutions, compliance and non-compliance with; *see also* social influence

consociationalism. *See* institutional engineering, objectives of, power-sharing

consolidation, democratic. *See* regimes, democratic/inclusive, consolidation of